MARGARET ATWOOD

CORNELSEN SENIOR ENGLISH LIBRARY

The Handmaid's Tale

Cornelsen

Herausgegeben von:
Gunthild Porteous-Schwier
Ingrid Ross

Verlagsredaktion: Neil Porter

Technische Umsetzung: Ingo Ostermaier

Umschlaggestaltung: Cornelsen Schulverlage Design;
Bildrecherche: Josephine Wolff

Umschlagillustration:
© Jane Leon/Photonica/Getty Images

The author would like to thank the D.A.A.D. in West
Berlin and the English department at the University of
Alabama, Tuscaloosa for providing time and space.

www.cornelsen.de

1. Auflage, 11. Druck 2021

Alle Drucke dieser Auflage sind inhaltlich unverändert
und können im Unterricht nebeneinander verwendet werden.

Druck: AZ Druck und Datentechnik GmbH, Kempten

ISBN 978-3-06-031177-4

PEFC
PEFC/04-31-2260

PEFC zertifiziert
Dieses Produkt stammt aus nachhaltig
bewirtschafteten Wäldern und kontrollierten
Quellen.

www.pefc.de

And when Rachel saw that she bare Jacob no children, Rachel envied her sister; and said unto Jacob, Give me children, or else I die.
And Jacob's anger was kindled against Rachel; and he said, Am I in God's stead, who hath withheld from thee the fruit of the womb?
And she said, Behold my maid Bilhah, go in unto her; and she shall bear upon my knees, that I may also have children by her.

– Genesis, 30:1–3

But as to myself, having been wearied out for many years with offering vain, idle, visionary thoughts, and at length utterly despairing of success, I fortunately fell upon this proposal . . .

– Jonathan Swift, *A Modest Proposal*

In the desert there is no sign that says, Thou shalt not eat stones.

– Sufi proverb

ANNOTATIONS

Books of the Bible

There are many references to the Bible in the novel. For this reason you will find references to the books of the Bible in the annotations, e.g. Genesis 5:3; in this case the reference is to chapter 5, verse 3 of the Book of Genesis. As the names of the books of the Bible differ in English and German, here is a list of the books referred to in the annotations.

Genesis	1. Buch Moses (Genesis)
Deuteronomy	5. Buch Moses (Deutoronomium)
I Kings	1 Könige
II Kings	2 Könige
II Chronicles	2. Buch der Chronik
Isaiah	Das Buch Jesaja
Jeremiah	das Buch Jeremia
Matthew	das Matthäus-Evangelium
Luke	das Lukas-Evangelium
Acts	die Apostelgeschichte
1 Corinthians	der 1. Brief an die Korinther
I Timothy	der 1. Brief an Timotheus
1 Peter	der 1. Brief des Petrus
Revelation	die Offenbarung des Johannes

Abbreviations

adj	adjective	infml	informal
adv	adverb	jdm./jdn.	jemandem/en
AE	American English	n	noun
cf.	confer; see	p., pp.	page, pages
derog	derogatory	pl	plural
e.g.	exempli gratia; for example	sb.	somebody
esp.	especially	sl	slang
etc.	et cetera; and so on	sth.	something
fml	formal	usu.	usually
i.e.	id est; in other words	v	verb

The annotations are arranged chronologically: the first time a word is used is where you will find it explained. All pronunciations given are American English.

CONTENTS

I

Night

CHAPTER 1

We slept in what had once been the gymnasium. The floor was of varnished wood, with stripes and circles painted on it, for the games that were formerly played there; the hoops for the basketball nets were still in place, though the nets were gone. A balcony ran around the room, for the spectators, and I thought I could smell, faintly like an afterimage, the pungent scent of sweat, shot through with the sweet taint of chewing gum and perfume from the watching girls, felt-skirted as I knew from pictures, later in mini-skirts, then pants, then in one earring, spiky green-streaked hair. Dances would have been held there; the music lingered, a palimpsest of unheard sound, style upon style, an undercurrent of drums, a forlorn wail, garlands made of tissue-paper flowers, cardboard devils, a revolving ball of mirrors, powdering the dancers with a snow of light.

There was old sex in the room and loneliness, and expectation, of something without a shape or name. I remember that yearning, for something that was always about to happen and was never the same as the hands that were on us there and then, in the small of the back, or out back, in the parking lot, or in the television room with the sound turned down and only the pictures flickering over lifting flesh.

We yearned for the future. How did we learn it, that talent for insatiability? It was in the air; and it was still in the air, an afterthought, as we tried to sleep, in the army cots that had been set up in rows, with spaces between so we could not talk. We had flannelette sheets, like children's, and army-issue blankets, old ones that still said U.S. We folded our clothes neatly and laid them on the stools at the ends of the beds. The lights were turned down but not out. Aunt Sara and Aunt Elizabeth patrolled; they had electric cattle prods slung on thongs from their leather belts.

▷ **2** *varnished:* versiegelt, lackiert **6** *pungent* ['pʌndʒənt]: (of a smell) unpleasantly strong **7** *taint:* faint aroma **8** *felt:* Filz **10** *linger* ['lɪŋgər]: stay around • *palimpsest* (fml): sth. that has many different layers of meaning **11** *wail:* sad cry **15** *yearning:* strong wish **17** *small of the back:* Kreuz **21** *insatiability* [ɪnˌseɪʃə'bɪləti]: condition of never having enough **22** *army cot:* Feldbett **24** *army-issue:* handed out by the army to be used by army personnel **27** *cattle prod:* stick with which animals are pushed to make them go in a certain direction

No guns though, even they could not be trusted with guns. Guns were for the guards, specially picked from the Angels. The guards weren't allowed inside the building except when called, and we weren't allowed out, except for our walks, twice daily, two by two around the football field which was enclosed now by a chain-link fence topped with barbed wire. The Angels stood outside it with their backs to us. They were objects of fear to us, but of something else as well. If only they would look. If only we could talk to them. Something could be exchanged, we thought, some deal made, some trade-off, we still had our bodies. That was our fantasy. We learned to whisper almost without sound. In the semidarkness we could stretch out our arms, when the Aunts weren't looking, and touch each other's hands across space. We learned to lip-read, our heads flat on the beds, turned sideways, watching each other's mouths. In this way we exchanged names, from bed to bed:

Alma. Janine. Dolores. Moira. June.

▷ **6** *barbed wire:* Stacheldraht

II

Shopping

CHAPTER 2

A chair, a table, a lamp. Above, on the white ceiling, a relief ornament in the shape of a wreath, and in the center of it a blank space, plastered over, like the place in a face where the eye has been taken out. There must have been a chandelier, once. They've removed anything you could tie a rope to.

A window, two white curtains. Under the window, a window seat with a little cushion. When the window is partly open – it only opens partly – the air can come in and make the curtains move. I can sit in the chair, or on the window seat, hands folded, and watch this. Sunlight comes in through the window too, and falls on the floor, which is made of wood, in narrow strips, highly polished. I can smell the polish. There's a rug on the floor, oval, of braided rags. This is the kind of touch they like: folk art, archaic, made by women, in their spare time, from things that have no further use. A return to traditional values. Waste not want not. I am not being wasted. Why do I want?

On the wall above the chair, a picture, framed but with no glass: a print of flowers, blue irises, watercolor. Flowers are still allowed. Does each of us have the same print, the same chair, the same white curtains, I wonder? Government issue?

Think of it as being in the army, said Aunt Lydia.

A bed. Single, mattress medium-hard, covered with a flocked white spread. Nothing takes place in the bed but sleep; or no sleep. I try not to think too much. Like other things now, thought must be rationed. There's a lot that doesn't bear thinking about. Thinking can hurt your chances, and I intend to last. I know why there is no glass, in front of the watercolor picture of blue irises, and why the window only opens partly and why the glass in it is shatterproof. It isn't running away they're afraid of. We wouldn't get far. It's those other escapes, the ones you can open in yourself, given a cutting edge.

▷ **2** *wreath* [ri:θ]: Kranz **3** *plaster sth. over:* etwas zugipsen **4** *chandelier* [ˌʃændəlˈɪər]: Kronleuchter **12** *braid sth.:* etwas flechten **15** *Waste not want not* (proverb): if you are careful with things when you have them, you will not have to do without them later **26** *I intend to last:* I aim to live for a long time

So. Apart from these details, this could be a college guest room, for the less distinguished visitors; or a room in a rooming house, of former times, for ladies in reduced circumstances. That is what we are now. The circumstances have been reduced; for those of us who still have circumstances.

But a chair, sunlight, flowers: these are not to be dismissed. I am alive, I live, I breathe, I put my hand out, unfolded, into the sunlight. Where I am is not a prison but a privilege, as Aunt Lydia said, who was in love with either/or.

The bell that measures time is ringing. Time here is measured by bells, as once in nunneries. As in a nunnery too, there are few mirrors.

I get up out of the chair, advance my feet into the sunlight, in their red shoes, flat-heeled to save the spine and not for dancing. The red gloves are lying on the bed. I pick them up, pull them onto my hands, finger by finger. Everything except the wings around my face is red: the color of blood, which defines us. The skirt is ankle-length, full, gathered to a flat yoke that extends over the breasts, the sleeves are full. The white wings too are prescribed issue; they are to keep us from seeing, but also from being seen. I never looked good in red, it's not my color. I pick up the shopping basket, put it over my arm.

The door of the room – not *my* room, I refuse to say *my* – is not locked. In fact it doesn't shut properly. I go out into the polished hallway, which has a runner down the center, dusty pink. Like a path through the forest, like a carpet for royalty, it shows me the way.

The carpet bends and goes down the front staircase and I go with it, one hand on the banister, once a tree, turned in another century, rubbed to a warm gloss. Late Victorian, the house is, a family house, built for a large rich family. There's a grandfather clock in the hallway, which doles out time, and then the door to the motherly front sitting room, with its fleshtones and hints. A sitting room in which I never sit, but stand or kneel only. At the end of the hallway, above the front door, is a fanlight of colored glass: flowers, red and blue.

There remains a mirror, on the hall wall. If I turn my head so that the white wings framing my face direct my vision towards it, I can see it as I go down the stairs, round, convex, a pier-glass, like the eye of a fish, and myself in it like a distorted shadow, a parody of something, some fairytale figure in a red cloak, descending towards a moment of carelessness that is the same as danger. A Sister, dipped in blood.

At the bottom of the stairs there's a hat-and-umbrella stand, the bentwood kind, long rounded rungs of wood curving gently up into hooks shaped like the opening fronds of a fern. There are several umbrellas in it: black, for the Commander, blue, for the Commander's Wife, and the one assigned to me, which is red. I leave the red umbrella where it is, because I know from the window that the day is sunny. I wonder whether or not the Commander's Wife is in the sitting room. She doesn't always sit. Sometimes I can hear her pacing back and forth, a heavy step and then a light one, and the soft tap of her cane on the dusty-rose carpet.

I walk along the hallway, past the sitting-room door and the door that leads into the dining room, and open the door at the end of the hall and go through into the kitchen. Here the smell is no longer of furniture polish. Rita is in here, standing at the kitchen table, which has a top of chipped white enamel. She's in her usual Martha's dress, which is dull green, like a surgeon's gown of the time before. The dress is much like mine in shape, long and concealing, but with a bib apron over it and without the white wings and the veil. She puts the veil on to go outside, but nobody much cares who sees the face of a Martha. Her sleeves are rolled to the elbow, showing her brown arms. She's making bread, throwing the loaves for the final brief kneading and then the shaping.

Rita sees me and nods, whether in greeting or in simple acknowledgement of my presence it's hard to say, and wipes her floury hands on her apron and rummages in the kitchen drawer for the token book. Frowning, she tears out three tokens and hands them to me. Her face might be kindly if she would smile. But the frown isn't

▷ **3** *in reduced circumstances:* not having a lot of money **11** *nunnery:* Nonnenkloster **17** *yoke:* (here) the top part of a dress from which the rest hangs down loosely **23** *runner:* long rug **26** *banister* ['bænɪstər]: hand-rail along a set of stairs **28** *grandfather clock:* Standuhr **29** *dole sth. out:* give out sth. in portions **35** *pier-glass:* convex round mirror that distorts the reflection **40** *bentwood:* wood that has been steamed and bent into shape to make furniture • *rung:* Sprosse **41** *frond of a fern:* Farnwedel **48** *cane:* walking stick **53** *chipped:* having a slightly damaged surface • *enamel:* shiny finish for worktop surfaces, etc. **55** *bib apron:* Latzschürze **59** *knead sth.* [niːd]: etwas kneten **61–62** *acknowledgement:* act of recognizing that sb./sth. is there **63–64** *token book:* Bezugsscheinbuch

personal: it's the red dress she disapproves of, and what it stands for. She thinks I may be catching, like a disease or any form of bad luck.

Sometimes I listen outside closed doors, a thing I never would have done in the time before. I don't listen long, because I don't want to be caught doing it. Once, though, I heard Rita say to Cora that she wouldn't debase herself like that.

Nobody asking you, Cora said. Anyways, what could you do, supposing?

Go to the Colonies, Rita said. They have the choice.

With the Unwomen, and starve to death and Lord knows what all? said Cora. Catch you.

They were shelling peas; even through the almost-closed door I could hear the light clink of the hard peas falling into the metal bowl. I heard Rita, a grunt or a sigh, of protest or agreement.

Anyways, they're doing it for us all, said Cora, or so they say. If I hadn't of got my tubes tied, it could of been me, say I was ten years younger. It's not that bad. It's not what you'd call hard work.

Better her than me, Rita said, and I opened the door. Their faces were the way women's faces are when they've been talking about you behind your back and they think you've heard: embarrassed, but also a little defiant, as if it were their right. That day, Cora was more pleasant to me than usual, Rita more surly.

Today, despite Rita's closed face and pressed lips, I would like to stay here, in the kitchen. Cora might come in, from somewhere else in the house, carrying her bottle of lemon oil and her duster, and Rita would make coffee – in the houses of the Commanders there is still real coffee – and we would sit at Rita's kitchen table, which is not Rita's any more than my table is mine, and we would talk, about aches and pains, illnesses, our feet, our backs, all the different kinds of mischief that our bodies, like unruly children, can get up to. We would nod our heads as punctuation to each other's voices, signalling that yes, we know all about it. We would exchange remedies and try to outdo each other in the recital of our physical miseries; gently we would complain, our voices soft and minor key and mournful as pigeons in the eaves troughs. *I know what you mean*, we'd say. Or, a quaint expression you sometimes hear, still, from older people: *I hear where you're coming from*, as if the voice itself were a traveller, arriving from a distant place. Which it would be, which it is.

How I used to despise such talk. Now I long for it. At least it was talk. An exchange, of sorts.

Or we would gossip. The Marthas know things, they talk among themselves, passing the unofficial news from house to house. Like me, they listen at doors, no doubt, and see things even with their eyes averted. I've heard them at it sometimes, caught whiffs of their private conversations. *Stillborn, it was.* Or, *Stabbed her with a knitting needle, right in the belly. Jealousy, it must have been, eating her up.* Or, tantalizingly, *It was toilet cleaner she used. Worked like a charm, though you'd think he'd of tasted it. Must've been that drunk; but they found her out all right.*

Or I would help Rita to make the bread, sinking my hands into that soft resistant warmth which is so much like flesh. I hunger to touch something, other than cloth or wood. I hunger to commit the act of touch.

But even if I were to ask, even if I were to violate decorum to that extent, Rita would not allow it. She would be too afraid. The Marthas are not supposed to fraternize with us.

Fraternize means to behave like a brother. Luke told me that. He said there was no corresponding word that meant *to behave like a sister. Sororize*, it would have to be, he said. From the Latin. He liked knowing about such details. The derivations of words, curious usages. I used to tease him about being pedantic.

I take the tokens from Rita's outstretched hand. They have pictures on them, of the things they can be exchanged for: twelve eggs, a piece of cheese, a brown thing that's supposed to be a steak. I place them in the zippered pocket in my sleeve, where I keep my pass.

"Tell them fresh, for the eggs," she says. "Not like the last time. And a chicken, tell them, not a hen. Tell them who it's for and then they won't mess around."

"All right," I say. I don't smile. Why tempt her to friendship?

▷ **2** *catching* (adj): ansteckend **6** *debase yourself:* do sth. that is below your dignity **11** *Catch you* (non-standard): I doubt if I'd catch you doing that **16** *hadn't of got* (non-standard) = *hadn't have got* (non-standard): hadn't got • *have your tubes tied* (infml): sich sterilisieren lassen • *could of been* (non-standard): could have been **21** *defiant* [dəˈfaɪənt]: trotzig **22** *surly* [ˈsɜːrli] (adj): unpleasant, unkind **34** *minor key:* (here) low **35** *eaves trough* [ˈiːvz ˌtrɔːf]: Dachrinne **36** *quaint:* pleasantly old-fashioned **41** *gossip:* talk about other people's private lives **45** *stillborn:* dead at birth **54** *decorum:* the standards of moral behavior or good manners

CHAPTER 3

I go out by the back door, into the garden, which is large and tidy: a lawn in the middle, a willow, weeping catkins; around the edges, the flower borders, in which the daffodils are now fading and the tulips are opening their cups, spilling out color. The tulips are red, a darker crimson towards the stem; as if they had been cut and are beginning to heal there.

This garden is the domain of the Commander's Wife. Looking out through my shatterproof window I've often seen her in it, her knees on a cushion, a light blue veil thrown over her wide gardening hat, a basket at her side with shears in it and pieces of string for tying the flowers into place. A Guardian detailed to the Commander does the heavy digging; the Commander's Wife directs, pointing with her stick. Many of the Wives have such gardens, it's something for them to order and maintain and care for.

I once had a garden. I can remember the smell of the turned earth, the plump shapes of bulbs held in the hands, fullness, the dry rustle of seeds through the fingers. Time could pass more swiftly that way. Sometimes the Commander's Wife has a chair brought out, and just sits in it, in her garden. From a distance it looks like peace.

She isn't here now, and I start to wonder where she is: I don't like to come upon the Commander's Wife unexpectedly. Perhaps she's sewing, in the sitting room, with her left foot on the footstool, because of her arthritis. Or knitting scarves, for the Angels at the front lines. I can hardly believe the Angels have a need for such scarves; anyway, the ones made by the Commander's Wife are too elaborate. She doesn't bother with the cross-and-star pattern used by many of the other Wives, it's not a challenge. Fir trees march along the ends of her scarves, or eagles, or stiff humanoid figures, boy and girl, boy and girl. They aren't scarves for grown men but for children.

Sometimes I think these scarves aren't sent to the Angels at all, but unravelled and turned back into balls of yarn, to be knitted again in their turn. Maybe it's just something to keep the Wives busy, to give them a sense of purpose. But I envy the Commander's Wife her knitting. It's good to have small goals that can be easily attained.

What does she envy me?

She doesn't speak to me, unless she can't avoid it. I am a reproach to her; and a necessity.

We stood face to face for the first time five weeks ago, when I arrived at this posting. The Guardian from the previous posting brought me to the front door. On first days we are permitted front doors, but after that we're supposed to use the back. Things haven't settled down, it's too soon, everyone is unsure about our exact status. After a while it will be either all front doors or all back.

Aunt Lydia said she was lobbying for the front. Yours is a position of honour, she said.

The Guardian rang the doorbell for me, but before there was time for someone to hear and walk quickly to answer, the door opened inwards. She must have been waiting behind it. I was expecting a Martha, but it was her instead, in her long powderblue robe, unmistakeable.

So, you're the new one, she said. She didn't step aside to let me in, she just stood there in the doorway, blocking the entrance.

She wanted me to feel that I could not come into the house unless she said so. There is push and shove, these days, over such toeholds.

Yes, I said.

Leave it on the porch. She said this to the Guardian, who was carrying my bag. The bag was red vinyl and not large. There was another bag, with the winter cloak and heavier dresses, but that would be coming later.

The Guardian set down the bag and saluted her. Then I could hear his footsteps behind me, going back down the walk, and the click of the front gate, and I felt as if a protective arm were being withdrawn. The threshold of a new house is a lonely place.

She waited until the car started up and pulled away. I wasn't looking at her face, but at the part of her I could see with my head lowered: her blue waist, thickened, her left hand on the ivory head of her cane, the large diamonds on the ring finger, which must once have been fine and was still finely kept, the fingernail at the end of the

▷ **2** *catkin:* hanging spikey branch with soft buds **3** *border:* Rabatte **10** *shears:* a garden tool like scissors for cutting **11** *be detailed to sb.:* be appointed to do jobs for sb. **16** *rustle:* noise made by leaves, etc. **36** *reproach:* Vorwurf **54** *toehold:* position which you hope will give you an advantage **63** *threshold:* Schwelle

knuckly finger filed to a gentle curving point. It was like an ironic smile, on that finger; like something mocking her.

You might as well come in, she said. She turned her back on me and limped down the hall. Shut the door behind you.

I lifted the red bag inside, as she'd no doubt intended, then closed the door. I didn't say anything to her. Aunt Lydia said it was best not to speak unless they asked you a direct question. Try to think of it from their point of view, she said, her hands clasped and wrung together, her nervous pleading smile. It isn't easy for them.

In here, said the Commander's Wife. When I went into the sitting room she was already in her chair, her left foot on the footstool, with its petit-point cushion, roses in a basket. Her knitting was on the floor beside the chair, the needles stuck through it.

I stood in front of her, hands folded. So, she said. She had a cigarette, and she put it between her lips and gripped it there while she lit it. Her lips were thin, held that way, with the small vertical lines around them you used to see in advertisements for lip cosmetics. The lighter was ivory-colored.

The cigarettes must have come from the black market, I thought, and this gave me hope. Even now that there is no real money any more, there's still a black market. There's always a black market, there's always something that can be exchanged. She then was a woman who might bend the rules. But what did I have, to trade?

I looked at the cigarette with longing. For me, like liquor and coffee, cigarettes are forbidden.

So old what's-his-face didn't work out, she said.

No, ma'am, I said.

She gave what might have been a laugh, then coughed. Tough luck on him, she said. This is your second, isn't it?

Third, Ma'am, I said.

Not so good for you either, she said. There was another coughing laugh. You can sit down. I don't make a practice of it, but just this time.

I did sit, on the edge of one of the stiff-backed chairs. I didn't want to stare around the room, I didn't want to appear inattentive to her; so the marble mantelpiece to my right and the mirror over it and the bunches of flowers were just shadows, then, at the edges of my eyes. Later I would have more than enough time to take them in.

Now her face was on a level with mine. I thought I recognized her; or at least there was something familiar about her. A little of her hair was showing, from under her veil. It was still blonde. I thought then that maybe she bleached it, that hair dye was something else she could get through the black market, but I know now that it really is blonde. Her eyebrows were plucked into thin arched lines, which gave her a permanent look of surprise, or outrage, or inquisitiveness, such as you might see on a startled child, but below them her eyelids were tired-looking. Not so her eyes, which were the flat hostile blue of a midsummer sky in bright sunlight, a blue that shuts you out. Her nose must once have been what was called cute but now was too small for her face. Her face was not fat but it was large. Two lines led downwards from the corners of her mouth; between them was her chin, clenched like a fist.

I want to see as little of you as possible, she said. I expect you feel the same way about me.

I didn't answer, as a yes would have been insulting, a no contradictory.

I know you aren't stupid, she went on. She inhaled, blew out the smoke. I've read your file. As far as I'm concerned, this is like a business transaction. But if I get trouble, I'll give trouble back. You understand?

Yes, ma'am, I said.

Don't call me ma'am, she said irritably. You're not a Martha.

I didn't ask what I was supposed to call her, because I could see that she hoped I would never have the occasion to call her anything at all. I was disappointed. I wanted, then, to turn her into an older sister, a motherly figure, someone who would understand and protect me. The Wife in my posting before this had spent most of her time in her bedroom; the Marthas said she drank. I wanted this one to be different. I wanted to think I would have liked her, in another time and place, another life. But I could see already that I wouldn't have liked her, nor she me.

▷ **24** *liquor* ['lɪkər]: strong alcoholic drink **45** *outrage:* shocked anger **46** *startled:* frightened (by sth.)

She put her cigarette out, half-smoked, in a little scrolled ashtray on the lamp table beside her. She did this decisively, one jab and one grind, not the series of genteel taps favored by many of the Wives.

As for my husband, she said, he's just that. My husband. I want that to be perfectly clear. Till death do us part. It's final.

Yes, Ma'am, I said again, forgetting. They used to have dolls, for little girls, that would talk if you pulled a string at the back; I thought I was sounding like that, voice of a monotone, voice of a doll. She probably longed to slap my face. They can hit us, there's Scriptural precedent. But not with any implement. Only with their hands.

It's one of the things we fought for, said the Commander's Wife, and suddenly she wasn't looking at me, she was looking down at her knuckled, diamond-studded hands, and I knew where I'd seen her before.

The first time was on television, when I was eight or nine. It was when my mother was sleeping in, on Sunday mornings, and I would get up early and go to the television set in my mother's study and flip through the channels, looking for cartoons. Sometimes when I couldn't find any I would watch the Growing Souls Gospel Hour, where they would tell Bible stories for children and sing hymns. One of the women was called Serena Joy. She was the lead soprano. She was ashblonde, petite, with a snub nose and huge blue eyes which she'd turn upwards during hymns. She could smile and cry at the same time, one tear or two sliding gracefully down her cheek, as if on cue, as her voice lifted through its highest notes, tremulous, effortless. It was after that she went on to other things.

The woman sitting in front of me was Serena Joy. Or had been, once. So it was worse than I thought.

CHAPTER 4

I walk along the gravel path that divides the back lawn, neatly, like a hair parting. It has rained during the night; the grass to either side is damp, the air humid. Here and there are worms, evidence of the fertility of the soil, caught by the sun, half dead; flexible and pink, like lips.

I open the white picket gate and continue, past the front lawn and towards the front gate. In the driveway, one of the Guardians assigned to our household is washing the car. That must mean the Commander is in the house, in his own quarters, past the dining room and beyond, where he seems to stay most of the time.

The car is a very expensive one, a Whirlwind; better than the Chariot, much better than the chunky, practical Behemoth. It's black, of course, the color of prestige or a hearse, and long and sleek. The driver is going over it with a chamois, lovingly. This at least hasn't changed, the way men caress good cars.

He's wearing the uniform of the Guardians, but his cap is tilted at a jaunty angle and his sleeves are rolled to the elbow, showing his forearms, tanned but with a stipple of dark hairs. He has a cigarette stuck in the corner of his mouth, which shows that he too has something he can trade on the black market.

I know this man's name: *Nick*. I know this because I've heard Rita and Cora talking about him, and once I heard the Commander speaking to him: Nick, I won't be needing the car.

He lives here, in the household, over the garage. Low status: he hasn't been issued a woman, not even one. He doesn't rate: some defect, lack of connections. But he acts as if he doesn't know this, or

▷ **3** *grind* [graɪnd]: mahlende Drehbewegung • *genteel:* elegant, ladylike **5** *till death do us part:* phrase from the marriage ceremony in the *Book of Common Prayer* **9** *Scriptural:* referring to the Bible; in the Bible **10** *precedent* ['presɪdənt]: example of sth. that has happened before and therefore can happen again • *implement:* tool **21** *lead* (n): first, main **24–25** *on cue:* exactly at the right moment **30** *parting* (n): Scheitel **34** *picket:* Palisade **42** *chamois* ['ʃæmi]: leather cloth used for polishing **44–45** *at a jaunty angle:* not quite straight (so that he appears self-confident) **53** *rate:* be important enough to be treated in a particular way

care. He's too casual, he's not servile enough. It may be stupidity, but I don't think so. Smells fishy, they used to say; or, I smell a rat. Misfit as odor. Despite myself, I think of how he might smell. Not fish or decaying rat: tanned skin, moist in the sun, filmed with smoke. I sigh, inhaling.

He looks at me, and sees me looking. He has a French face, lean, whimsical, all planes and angles, with creases around the mouth where he smiles. He takes a final puff of the cigarette, lets it drop to the driveway, and steps on it. He begins to whistle. Then he winks.

I drop my head and turn so that the white wings hide my face, and keep walking. He's just taken a risk, but for what? What if I were to report him?

Perhaps he was merely being friendly. Perhaps he saw the look on my face and mistook it for something else. Really what I wanted was the cigarette.

Perhaps it was a test, to see what I would do.

Perhaps he is an Eye.

I open the front gate and close it behind me, looking down but not back. The sidewalk is red brick. That is the landscape I focus on, a field of oblongs, gently undulating where the earth beneath has buckled, from decade after decade of winter frost. The color of the bricks is old, yet fresh and clear. Sidewalks are kept much cleaner than they used to be.

I walk to the corner and wait. I used to be bad at waiting. They also serve who only stand and wait, said Aunt Lydia. She made us memorize it. She also said, Not all of you will make it through. Some of you will fall on dry ground or thorns. Some of you are shallow-rooted. She had a mole on her chin that went up and down while she talked. She said, Think of yourselves as seeds, and right then her voice was wheedling, conspiratorial, like the voices of those women who used to teach ballet classes to children, and who would say, Arms up in the air now; let's pretend we're trees.

I stand on the corner, pretending I am a tree.

A shape, red with white wings around the face, a shape like mine, a nondescript woman in red carrying a basket, comes along the brick sidewalk towards me. She reaches me and we peer at each other's faces, looking down the white tunnels of cloth that enclose us. She is the right one.

"Blessed be the fruit," she says to me, the accepted greeting among us.

"May the Lord open," I answer, the accepted response. We turn and walk together past the large houses, towards the central part of town. We aren't allowed to go there except in twos. This is supposed to be for our protection, though the notion is absurd: we are well protected already. The truth is that she is my spy, as I am hers. If either of us slips through the net because of something that happens on one of our daily walks, the other will be accountable.

This woman has been my partner for two weeks. I don't know what happened to the one before. On a certain day she simply wasn't there any more, and this one was there in her place. It isn't the sort of thing you ask questions about, because the answers are not usually answers you want to know. Anyway there wouldn't be an answer.

This one is a little plumper than I am. Her eyes are brown. Her name is Ofglen, and that's about all I know about her. She walks demurely, head down, red-gloved hands clasped in front, with short little steps like a trained pig's on its hind legs. During these walks she has never said anything that was not strictly orthodox, but then, neither have I. She may be a real believer, a Handmaid in more than name. I can't take the risk.

"The war is going well, I hear," she says.

"Praise be," I reply.

"We've been sent good weather."

"Which I receive with joy."

"They've defeated more of the rebels, since yesterday."

"Praise be," I say. I don't ask her how she knows. "What were they?"

▷ **2** *smells fishy / I smell a rat* (infml): sth. is not quite as it seems; sth. is not to be trusted **7** *whimsical:* unusual • *plane:* flat surface • *crease:* Falte **9** *wink:* give sb. a signal by quickly closing and opening one eye **20** *undulate:* have a surface that goes up and down **21** *buckle* (v): move upwards to create a small bump **24–25** *They also serve who only stand and wait:* last line of a religious sonnet by the English poet John Milton (1608–1674) **27–29** *fall on dry ground or thorns / shallow-rooted / seeds:* reference to the Parable of the Sower (cf. Matthew 13:3–8) **28** *mole:* black spot, birthmark **35** *nondescript:* with no special features **44** *notion:* idea **47** *accountable:* made responsible **55** *demure* [dɪˈmjʊər]: humble, without showing pride

"Baptists. They had a stronghold in the Blue Hills. They smoked them out."

"Praise be."

Sometimes I wish she would just shut up and let me walk in peace. But I'm ravenous for news, any kind of news; even if it's false news, it must mean something.

We reach the first barrier, which is like the barriers blocking off roadworks, or dug-up sewers: a wooden crisscross painted in yellow and black stripes, a red hexagon which means Stop. Near the gateway there are some lanterns, not lit because it isn't night. Above us, I know, there are floodlights, attached to the telephone poles, for use in emergencies, and there are men with machine guns in the pillboxes on either side of the road. I don't see the floodlights and the pillboxes, because of the wings around my face. I just know they are there.

Behind the barrier, waiting for us at the narrow gateway, there are two men, in the green uniforms of the Guardians of the Faith, with the crests on their shoulders and berets: two swords, crossed, above a white triangle. The Guardians aren't real soldiers. They're used for routine policing and other menial functions, digging up the Commander's Wife's garden for instance, and they're either stupid or older or disabled or very young, apart from the ones that are Eyes incognito.

These two are very young: one moustache is still sparse, one face is still blotchy. Their youth is touching, but I know I can't be deceived by it. The young ones are often the most dangerous, the most fanatical, the jumpiest with their guns. They haven't yet learned about existence through time. You have to go slowly with them.

Last week they shot a woman, right about here. She was a Martha. She was fumbling in her robe, for her pass, and they thought she was hunting for a bomb. They thought she was a man in disguise. There have been such incidents.

Rita and Cora knew the woman. I heard them talking about it, in the kitchen.

Doing their job, said Cora. Keeping us safe.

Nothing safer than dead, said Rita, angrily. She was minding her own business. No call to shoot her.

It was an accident, said Cora.

No such thing, said Rita. Everything is meant.

I could hear her thumping the pots around, in the sink.

Well, someone'll think twice before blowing up this house, anyways, said Cora.

All the same, said Rita. She worked hard. That was a bad death.

I can think of worse, said Cora. At least it was quick.

You can say that, said Rita. I'd choose to have some time, before, like. To set things right.

The two young Guardians salute us, raising three fingers to the rims of their berets. Such tokens are accorded to us. They are supposed to show respect, because of the nature of our service.

We produce our passes, from the zippered pockets in our wide sleeves, and they are inspected and stamped. One man goes into the right-hand pillbox, to punch our numbers into the Compuchek.

In returning my pass, the one with the peach-colored moustache bends his head to try to get a look at my face. I raise my head a little, to help him, and he sees my eyes and I see his, and he blushes. His face is long and mournful, like a sheep's, but with the large full eyes of a dog, spaniel not terrier. His skin is pale and looks unwholesomely tender, like the skin under a scab. Nevertheless, I think of placing my hand on it, this exposed face. He is the one who turns away.

It's an event, a small defiance of rule, so small as to be undetectable, but such moments are the rewards I hold out for myself, like the candy I hoarded, as a child, at the back of a drawer. Such moments are possibilities, tiny peepholes.

What if I were to come at night, when he's on duty alone – though he would never be allowed such solitude – and permit him beyond my white wings? What if I were to peel off my red shroud and show myself to him, to them, by the uncertain light of the lanterns? This is what they must think about sometimes, as they stand endlessly beside this barrier, past which nobody ever comes except the Commanders of the Faithful in their long black murmurous cars, or their blue Wives and white-veiled daughters on their dutiful way to

▷ **5** *ravenous:* extremely hungry **12** *pillbox:* small shelter for soldiers made of concrete **19** *menial* ['miːnɪəl]: unimportant **24** *blotchy:* full of spots **36** *call* (n): reason **45** *like* (adv; infml): (here) for example **47** *token:* (here) sign **57** *scab:* crust of dried blood that forms over a wound **59** *defiance:* (here) disobedience **61** *hoard sth.:* save large amounts of sth. **65** *shroud:* cloth that (usually) covers a dead body

Salvagings or Prayvaganzas, or their dumpy green Marthas, or the occasional Birthmobile, or their red Handmaids, on foot. Or sometimes a black-painted van, with the winged eye in white on the side. The windows of the vans are dark-tinted, and the men in the front seats wear dark glasses: a double obscurity.

The vans are surely more silent than the other cars. When they pass, we avert our eyes. If there are sounds coming from inside, we try not to hear them. Nobody's heart is perfect.

When the black vans reach a checkpoint, they're waved through without a pause. The Guardians would not want to take the risk of looking inside, searching, doubting their authority. Whatever they think.

If they do think; you can't tell by looking at them.

But more likely they don't think in terms of clothing discarded on the lawn. If they think of a kiss, they must then think immediately of the floodlights going on, the rifle shots. They think instead of doing their duty and of promotion to the Angels, and of being allowed possibly to marry, and then, if they are able to gain enough power and live to be old enough, of being allotted a Handmaid of their own.

The one with the moustache opens the small pedestrian gate for us and stands back, well out of the way, and we pass through. As we walk away I know they're watching, these two men who aren't yet permitted to touch women. They touch with their eyes instead and I move my hips a little, feeling the full red skirt sway around me. It's like thumbing your nose from behind a fence or teasing a dog with a bone held out of reach, and I'm ashamed of myself for doing it, because none of this is the fault of these men, they're too young.

Then I find I'm not ashamed after all. I enjoy the power; power of a dog bone, passive but there. I hope they get hard at the sight of us and have to rub themselves against the painted barriers, surreptitiously. They will suffer, later, at night, in their regimented beds. They have no outlets now except themselves, and that's a sacrilege. There are no more magazines, no more films, no more substitutes; only me and my shadow, walking away from the two men, who stand at attention, stiffly, by a roadblock, watching our retreating shapes.

CHAPTER 5

Doubled, I walk the street. Though we are no longer in the Commanders' compound, there are large houses here also. In front of one of them a Guardian is mowing the lawn. The lawns are tidy, the façades are gracious, in good repair; they're like the beautiful pictures they used to print in the magazines about homes and gardens and interior decoration. There is the same absence of people, the same air of being asleep. The street is almost like a museum, or a street in a model town constructed to show the way people used to live. As in those pictures, those museums, those model towns, there are no children.

This is the heart of Gilead, where the war cannot intrude except on television. Where the edges are we aren't sure, they vary, according to the attacks and counterattacks; but this is the center, where nothing moves. The Republic of Gilead, said Aunt Lydia, knows no bounds. Gilead is within you.

Doctors lived here once, lawyers, university professors. There are no lawyers any more, and the university is closed.

Luke and I used to walk together, sometimes, along these streets. We used to talk about buying a house like one of these, an old big house, fixing it up. We would have a garden, swings for the children. We would have children. Although we knew it wasn't too likely we could ever afford it, it was something to talk about, a game for Sundays. Such freedom now seems almost weightless.

We turn the corner onto a main street, where there's more traffic. Cars go by, black most of them, some gray and brown. There are other women with baskets, some in red, some in the dull green of the Marthas, some in the striped dresses, red and blue and green and cheap and skimpy, that mark the women of the poorer men. Econowives, they're called. These women are not divided into functions. They have to do everything; if they can. Sometimes there is a

▷ **1** *dumpy:* dull, unattractive **31** *surreptitious:* secret **38** *compound:* group of houses that belong together **50** *bounds:* boundaries **64** *skimpy:* simple, not elegant

woman all in black, a widow. There used to be more of them, but they seem to be diminishing. You don't see the Commanders' Wives on the sidewalks. Only in cars.

The sidewalks here are cement. Like a child, I avoid stepping on the cracks. I'm remembering my feet on these sidewalks, in the time before, and what I used to wear on them. Sometimes it was shoes for running, with cushioned soles and breathing holes, and stars of fluorescent fabric that reflected light in the darkness. Though I never ran at night; and in the daytime, only beside well-frequented roads.

Women were not protected then. I remember the rules, rules that were never spelled out but that every woman knew: don't open your door to a stranger, even if he says he is the police. Make him slide his ID under the door. Don't stop on the road to help a motorist pretending to be in trouble. Keep the locks on and keep going. If anyone whistles, don't turn to look. Don't go into a laundromat, by yourself, at night.

I think about laundromats. What I wore to them: shorts, jeans, jogging pants. What I put into them: my own clothes, my own soap, my own money, money I had earned myself. I think about having such control.

Now we walk along the same street, in red pairs, and no man shouts obscenities at us, speaks to us, touches us. No one whistles.

There is more than one kind of freedom, said Aunt Lydia. Freedom to and freedom from. In the days of anarchy, it was freedom to. Now you are being given freedom from. Don't underrate it.

In front of us, to the right, is the store where we order dresses. Some people call them *habits*, a good word for them. Habits are hard to break. The store has a huge wooden sign outside it, in the shape of a golden lily; Lilies of the Field, it's called. You can see the place, under the lily, where the lettering was painted out, when they decided that even the names of shops were too much temptation for us. Now places are known by their signs alone.

Lilies used to be a movie theater, before. Students went there a lot; every spring they had a Humphrey Bogart festival, with Lauren Bacall or Katherine Hepburn, women on their own, making up their minds. They wore blouses with buttons down the front that suggested the possibilities of the word *undone*. These women could be undone; or not.

They seemed to be able to choose. We seemed to be able to choose, then. We were a society dying, said Aunt Lydia, of too much choice.

I don't know when they stopped having the festival. I must have been grown up. So I didn't notice.

We don't go into Lilies, but across the road and along a sidestreet. Our first stop is at a store with another wooden sign: three eggs, a bee, a cow. Milk and Honey. There's a line, and we wait our turn, two by two. I see they have oranges today. Ever since Central America was lost to the Libertheos, oranges have been hard to get: sometimes they are there, sometimes not. The war interferes with the oranges from California, and even Florida isn't dependable, when there are roadblocks or when the train tracks have been blown up. I look at the oranges, longing for one. But I haven't brought any tokens for oranges. I'll go back and tell Rita about them, I think. She'll be pleased. It will be something, a small achievement, to have made oranges happen.

Those who've reached the counter hand their tokens across it, to the two men in Guardian uniforms who stand on the other side. Nobody talks much, though there is a rustling, and the women's heads move furtively from side to side: here, shopping, is where you might see someone you know, someone you've known in the time before, or at the Red Center. Just to catch sight of a face like that is an encouragement. If I could see Moira, just see her, know she still exists. It's hard to imagine now, having a friend.

But Ofglen, beside me, isn't looking. Maybe she doesn't know anyone any more. Maybe they have all vanished, the women she knew. Or maybe she doesn't want to be seen. She stands in silence, head down.

As we wait in our double line, the door opens and two more women come in, both in the red dresses and white wings of the Handmaids. One of them is vastly pregnant; her belly, under her loose garment, swells triumphantly. There is a shifting in the room, a

▷ **13** *ID:* identification card **26** *underrate sth.:* etwas unterschätzen **28** *habit:* a nun's or monk's special dress; something you are used to doing **32** *temptation:* Versuchung **35–36** *Humphrey Bogart, Lauren Bacall, Katherine Hepburn:* US film stars **58** *furtive:* secret **70** *shifting* (n): nervous movement

murmur, an escape of breath; despite ourselves we turn our heads, blatantly, to see better; our fingers itch to touch her. She's a magic presence to us, an object of envy and desire, we covet her. She's a flag on a hilltop, showing us what can still be done: we too can be saved.

The women in the room are whispering, almost talking, so great is their excitement.

"Who is it?" I hear behind me.

"Ofwayne. No. Ofwarren."

"Show-off," a voice hisses, and this is true. A woman that pregnant doesn't have to go out, doesn't have to go shopping. The daily walk is no longer prescribed, to keep her abdominal muscles in working order. She needs only the floor exercises, the breathing drill. She could stay at her house. And it's dangerous for her to be out, there must be a Guardian standing outside the door, waiting for her. Now that she's the carrier of life, she is closer to death, and needs special security. Jealousy could get her, it's happened before. All children are wanted now, but not by everyone.

But the walk may be a whim of hers, and they humor whims, when something has gone this far and there's been no miscarriage. Or perhaps she's one of those, *Pile it on, I can take it*, a martyr. I catch a glimpse of her face, as she raises it to look around. The voice behind me was right. She's come to display herself. She's glowing, rosy, she's enjoying every minute of this.

"Quiet," says one of the Guardians behind the counter, and we hush like schoolgirls.

Ofglen and I have reached the counter. We hand over our tokens, and one Guardian enters the numbers on them into the Compubite while the other gives us our purchases, the milk, the eggs. We put them into our baskets and go out again, past the pregnant woman and her partner, who beside her looks spindly, shrunken; as we all do. The pregnant woman's belly is like a huge fruit. *Humungous*, word of my childhood. Her hands rest on it as if to defend it, or as if they're gathering something from it, warmth and strength.

As I pass she looks full at me, into my eyes, and I know who she is. She was at the Red Center with me, one of Aunt Lydia's pets. I never liked her. Her name, in the time before, was Janine.

Janine looks at me, then, and around the corners of her mouth there is the trace of a smirk. She glances down to where my own belly lies flat under my red robe, and the wings cover her face. I can see only a little of her forehead, and the pinkish tip of her nose.

Next we go into All Flesh, which is marked by a large wooden pork chop hanging from two chains. There isn't so much of a line here: meat is expensive, and even the Commanders don't have it every day. Ofglen gets steak, though, and that's the second time this week. I'll tell that to the Marthas: it's the kind of thing they enjoy hearing about. They are very interested in how other households are run; such bits of petty gossip give them an opportunity for pride or discontent.

I take the chicken, wrapped in butcher's paper and trussed with string. Not many things are plastic, any more. I remember those endless white plastic shopping bags, from the supermarket; I hated to waste them and would stuff them in under the sink, until the day would come when there would be too many and I would open the cupboard door and they would bulge out, sliding over the floor. Luke used to complain about it. Periodically he would take all the bags and throw them out.

She could get one of those over her head, he'd say. You know how kids like to play. She never would, I'd say. She's too old. (Or too smart, or too lucky.) But I would feel a chill of fear, and then guilt for having been so careless. It was true, I took too much for granted; I trusted fate, back then. I'll keep them in a higher cupboard, I'd say. Don't keep them at all, he'd say. We never use them for anything. Garbage bags, I'd say. He'd say ...

Not here and now. Not where people are looking. I turn, see my silhouette in the plate-glass window. We have come outside then, we are on the street.

A group of people is coming towards us. They're tourists, from Japan it looks like, a trade delegation perhaps, on a tour of the historic land-

▷ **2** *blatant* ['bleɪtnt]: done in an obvious and open way **3** *covet sth.* ['kʌvət] (fml): want sth. very much **18** *whim:* Laune • *humor sb.:* go along with sb.'s wishes concerning sth. even if you disagree with them **19** *miscarriage:* Fehlgeburt **30** *spindly* (adj): long, thin and not strong **31** *humungous* (infml, esp. used by children): huge **38** *smirk:* unpleasant smile **47** *petty:* unimportant **48** *trussed:* tied together

marks or out for local color. They're diminutive and neatly turned out; each has his or her camera, his or her smile. They look around, bright-eyed, cocking their heads to one side like robins, their very cheerfulness aggressive, and I can't help staring. It's been a long time since I've seen skirts that short on women. The skirts reach just below the knee and the legs come out from beneath them, nearly naked in their thin stockings, blatant, the high-heeled shoes with their straps attached to the feet like delicate instruments of torture. The women teeter on their spiked feet as if on stilts, but off balance; their backs arch at the waist, thrusting the buttocks out. Their heads are uncovered and their hair too is exposed, in all its darkness and sexuality. They wear lipstick, red, outlining the damp cavities of their mouths, like scrawls on a washroom wall, of the time before.

I stop walking. Ofglen stops beside me and I know that she too cannot take her eyes off these women. We are fascinated, but also repelled. They seem undressed. It has taken so little time to change our minds, about things like this.

Then I think: I used to dress like that. That was freedom.

Westernized, they used to call it.

The Japanese tourists come towards us, twittering, and we turn our heads away too late: our faces have been seen.

There's an interpreter, in the standard blue suit and red-patterned tie, with the winged-eye tie pin. He's the one who steps forward, out of the group, in front of us, blocking our way. The tourists bunch behind him; one of them raises a camera.

"Excuse me," he says to both of us, politely enough. "They're asking if they can take your picture."

I look down at the sidewalk, shake my head for No. What they must see is the white wings only, a scrap of face, my chin and part of my mouth. Not the eyes. I know better than to look the interpreter in the face. Most of the interpreters are Eyes, or so it's said.

I also know better than to say Yes. Modesty is invisibility, said Aunt Lydia. Never forget it. To be seen – to be *seen* – is to be – her voice trembled – penetrated. What you must be, girls, is impenetrable. She called us girls.

Beside me, Ofglen is also silent. She's tucked her red-gloved hands up into her sleeves, to hide them.

The interpreter turns back to the group, chatters at them in staccato. I know what he'll be saying, I know the line. He'll be telling them that the women here have different customs, that to stare at them through the lens of a camera is, for them, an experience of violation.

I'm looking down, at the sidewalk, mesmerized by the women's feet. One of them is wearing open-toed sandals, the toenails painted pink. I remember the smell of nail polish, the way it wrinkled if you put the second coat on too soon, the satiny brushing of sheer pantyhose against the skin, the way the toes felt, pushed towards the opening in the shoe by the whole weight of the body. The woman with painted toes shifts from one foot to the other. I can feel her shoes, on my own feet. The smell of nail polish has made me hungry.

"Excuse me," says the interpreter again, to catch our attention.

I nod, to show I've heard him.

"He asks, are you happy," says the interpreter. I can imagine it, their curiosity: *Are they happy? How can they be happy?* I can feel their bright black eyes on us, the way they lean a little forward to catch our answers, the women especially, but the men too: we are secret, forbidden, we excite them.

Ofglen says nothing. There is a silence. But sometimes it's as dangerous not to speak.

"Yes, we are very happy," I murmur. I have to say something. What else can I say?

▷ **1** *diminutive:* very small **1–2** *turned out:* dressed **3** *robin:* Rotkehlchen **13** *washroom:* toilet **16** *repelled:* disgusted **43** *mesmerized:* fascinated **46** *sheer:* very thin and light

CHAPTER 6

A block past All Flesh, Ofglen pauses, as if hesitant about which way to go. We have a choice. We could go straight back, or we could walk the long way around. We already know which way we will take, because we always take it.

"I'd like to pass by the church," says Ofglen, as if piously.

"All right," I say, though I know as well as she does what she's really after.

We walk, sedately. The sun is out, in the sky there are white fluffy clouds, the kind that look like headless sheep. Given our wings, our blinkers, it's hard to look up, hard to get the full view, of the sky, of anything. But we can do it, a little at a time, a quick move of the head, up and down, to the side and back. We have learned to see the world in gasps.

To the right, if you could walk along, there's a street that would take you down towards the river. There's a boathouse, where they kept the sculls once, and some bridges; trees, green banks, where you could sit and watch the water, and the young men with their naked arms, their oars lifting into the sunlight as they played at winning. On the way to the river are the old dormitories, used for something else now, with their fairytale turrets, painted white and gold and blue. When we think of the past it's the beautiful things we pick out. We want to believe it was all like that.

The football stadium is down there too, where they hold the Men's Salvagings. As well as the football games. They still have those.

I don't go to the river any more, or over bridges. Or on the subway, although there's a station right there. We're not allowed on, there are Guardians now, there's no official reason for us to go down those steps, ride on the trains under the river, into the main city. Why would we want to go from here to there? We would be up to no good and they would know it.

The church is a small one, one of the first erected here, hundreds of years ago. It isn't used any more, except as a museum. Inside it you can see paintings, of women in long sombre dresses, their hair covered by white caps, and of upright men, darkly clothed and unsmiling. Our ancestors. Admission is free.

We don't go in, though, but stand on the path, looking at the churchyard. The old gravestones are still there, weathered, eroding, with their skulls and crossed bones, *memento mori*, their dough-faced angels, their winged hourglasses to remind us of the passing of mortal time, and, from a later century, their urns and willow trees, for mourning.

They haven't fiddled with the gravestones, or the church either. It's only the more recent history that offends them.

Ofglen's head is bowed, as if she's praying. She does this every time. Maybe, I think, there's someone, someone in particular gone, for her too; a man, a child. But I can't entirely believe it. I think of her as a woman for whom every act is done for show, is acting rather than a real act. She does such things to look good, I think. She's out to make the best of it.

But that is what I must look like to her, as well. How can it be otherwise?

Now we turn our backs on the church and there is the thing we've in truth come to see: the Wall.

The Wall is hundreds of years old too; or over a hundred, at least. Like the sidewalks, it's red brick, and must once have been plain but handsome. Now the gates have sentries and there are ugly new floodlights mounted on metal posts above it, and barbed wire along the bottom and broken glass set in concrete along the top.

No one goes through those gates willingly. The precautions are for those trying to get out, though to make it even as far as the Wall, from the inside, past the electronic alarm system, would be next to impossible.

Beside the main gateway there are six more bodies hanging, by the necks, their hands tied in front of them, their heads in white bags tipped sideways onto their shoulders. There must have been a Men's Salvaging early this morning. I didn't hear the bells. Perhaps I've become used to them.

▷ **5** *pious* ['paɪəs]: fromm **8** *sedately:* without hurrying **10** *blinkers:* eye-shields used to prevent a horse from looking right or left in traffic **13** *in gasps:* in short breaths **16** *sculls:* type of oars (= Riemen) **19** *dormitory:* building where university students live and sleep **37** *erode:* zerfallen **42** *fiddle with sth.* (infml): change sth. to fit your needs **56** *sentry:* soldier on guard **59** *precautions:* Vorsichtsmaßnahmen

We stop, together as if on signal, and stand and look at the bodies. It doesn't matter if we look. We're supposed to look: this is what they are there for, hanging on the Wall. Sometimes they'll be there for days, until there's a new batch, so as many people as possible will have the chance to see them.

What they are hanging from is hooks. The hooks have been set into the brickwork of the Wall, for this purpose. Not all of them are occupied. The hooks look like appliances for the armless. Or steel question marks, upside-down and sideways.

It's the bags over the heads that are the worst, worse than the faces themselves would be. It makes the men look like dolls on which faces have not yet been painted; like scarecrows, which in a way is what they are, since they are meant to scare. Or as if their heads are sacks, stuffed with some undifferentiated material, like flour or dough. It's the obvious heaviness of the heads, their vacancy, the way gravity pulls them down and there's no life any more to hold them up. The heads are zeros.

Though if you look and look, as we are doing, you can see the outlines of the features under the white cloth, like gray shadows. The heads are the heads of snowmen, with the coal eyes and the carrot noses fallen out. The heads are melting.

But on one bag there's blood, which has seeped through the white cloth, where the mouth must have been. It makes another mouth, a small red one, like the mouths painted with thick brushes by kindergarten children. A child's idea of a smile. This smile of blood is what fixes the attention, finally. These are not snowmen after all.

The men wear white coats, like those worn by doctors or scientists. Doctors and scientists aren't the only ones, there are others, but they must have had a run on them this morning. Each has a placard hung around his neck to show why he has been executed: a drawing of a human foetus. They were doctors, then, in the time before, when such things were legal. Angel makers, they used to call them: or was that something else? They've been turned up now by the searches through hospital records, or – more likely, since most hospitals destroyed such records once it became clear what was going to happen – by informants: ex-nurses perhaps, or a pair of them, since evidence from a single woman is no longer admissible; or another doctor, hoping to save his own skin; or someone already accused, lashing out at an enemy, or at random, in some desperate bid for safety. Though informants are not always pardoned.

These men, we've been told, are like war criminals. It's no excuse that what they did was legal at the time: their crimes are retroactive. They have committed atrocities, and must be made into examples, for the rest. Though this is hardly needed. No woman in her right mind, these days, would seek to prevent a birth, should she be so lucky as to conceive.

What we are supposed to feel towards these bodies is hatred and scorn. This isn't what I feel. These bodies hanging on the Wall are time travellers, anachronisms. They've come here from the past.

What I feel towards them is blankness. What I feel is that I must not feel. What I feel is partly relief, because none of these men is Luke. Luke wasn't a doctor. Isn't.

I look at the one red smile. The red of the smile is the same as the red of the tulips in Serena Joy's garden, towards the base of the flowers where they are beginning to heal. The red is the same but there is no connection. The tulips are not tulips of blood, the red smiles are not flowers, neither thing makes a comment on the other. The tulip is not a reason for disbelief in the hanged man, or vice versa. Each thing is valid and really there. It is through a field of such valid objects that I must pick my way, every day and in every way. I put a lot of effort into making such distinctions. I need to make them. I need to be very clear, in my own mind.

I feel a tremor in the woman beside me. Is she crying? In what way could it make her look good? I can't afford to know. My own hands are clenched, I note, tight around the handle of my basket. I won't give anything away.

Ordinary, said Aunt Lydia, is what you are used to. This may not seem ordinary to you now, but after a time it will. It will become ordinary.

▷ **4** *batch:* Ladung **12** *scarecrow:* Vogelscheuche **29** *have a run on sb.:* (here) find and kill sb. **38** *lash out at sb.:* hurt sb. by saying unpleasant things about them **43** *atrocity* [ə'trɑːsəti]: terrible deed **46** *conceive:* become pregnant **50** *blankness:* indifference, no feeling at all **63** *tremor:* shaking

III

Night

CHAPTER 7

The night is mine, my own time, to do with as I will, as long as I am quiet. As long as I don't move. As long as I lie still. The difference between *lie* and *lay*. Lay is always passive. Even men used to say, I'd like to get laid. Though sometimes they said, I'd like to lay her. All this is pure speculation. I don't really know what men used to say. I had only their words for it.

I lie, then, inside the room, under the plaster eye in the ceiling, behind the white curtains, between the sheets, neatly as they, and step sideways out of my own time. Out of time. Though this is time, nor am I out of it.

But the night is my time out. Where should I go?

Somewhere good.

Moira, sitting on the edge of my bed, legs crossed, ankle on knee, in her purple overalls, one dangly earring, the gold fingernail she wore to be eccentric, a cigarette between her stubby yellow-ended fingers. Let's go for a beer.

You're getting ashes in my bed, I said.

If you'd make it you wouldn't have this problem, said Moira.

In half an hour, I said. I had a paper due the next day. What was it? Psychology, English, Economics. We studied things like that, then. On the floor of the room there were books, open face down, this way and that, extravagantly.

Now, said Moira. You don't need to paint your face, it's only me. What's your paper on? I just did one on date rape.

Date rape, I said. You're so trendy. It sounds like some kind of dessert. *Date Rapé*.

Ha ha, said Moira. Get your coat.

She got it herself and tossed it at me. I'm borrowing five bucks off you, okay?

*

▷ **19** *due:* supposed to be ready

Or in a park somewhere, with my mother. How old was I? It was cold, our breaths came out in front of us, there were no leaves on the trees; gray sky, two ducks in the pond, disconsolate. Bread crumbs under my fingers, in my pocket. That's it: she said we were going to feed the ducks.

But there were some women burning books, that's what she was really there for. To see her friends; she'd lied to me, Saturdays were supposed to be my day. I turned away from her, sulking, towards the ducks, but the fire drew me back.

There were some men, too, among the women, and the books were magazines. They must have poured gasoline, because the flames shot high, and then they began dumping the magazines, from boxes, not too many at a time. Some of them were chanting; onlookers gathered.

Their faces were happy, ecstatic almost. Fire can do that. Even my mother's face, usually pale, thinnish, looked ruddy and cheerful, like a Christmas card; and there was another woman, large, with a soot smear down her cheek and an orange knitted cap, I remember her.

You want to throw one on, honey? she said. How old was I?

Good riddance to bad rubbish, she said, chuckling. It okay? she said to my mother.

If she wants to, my mother said; she had a way of talking about me to others as if I couldn't hear.

The woman handed me one of the magazines. It had a pretty woman on it, with no clothes on, hanging from the ceiling by a chain wound around her hands. I looked at it with interest. It didn't frighten me. I thought she was swinging, like Tarzan from a vine, on the TV.

Don't let her see it, said my mother. Here, she said to me, toss it in, quick.

I threw the magazine into the flames. It riffled open in the wind of its burning; big flakes of paper came loose, sailed into the air, still on fire, parts of women's bodies, turning to black ash in the air, before my eyes.

But then what happens, but then what happens?

I know I lost time.

There must have been needles, pills, something like that. I couldn't have lost that much time without help. You have had a shock, they said.

I would come up through a roaring and confusion, like surf boiling. I can remember feeling quite calm. I can remember screaming, it felt like screaming though it may have been only a whisper, *Where is she? What have you done with her?*

There was no night or day; only a flickering. After a while there were chairs again, and a bed, and after that a window.

She's in good hands, they said. With people who are fit. You are unfit, but you want the best for her. Don't you?

They showed me a picture of her, standing outside on a lawn, her face a closed oval. Her light hair was pulled back tight behind her head. Holding her hand was a woman I didn't know. She was only as tall as the woman's elbow.

You've killed her, I said. She looked like an angel, solemn, compact, made of air.

She was wearing a dress I'd never seen, white and down to the ground.

I would like to believe this is a story I'm telling. I need to believe it. I must believe it. Those who can believe that such stories are only stories have a better chance.

If it's a story I'm telling, then I have control over the ending. Then there will be an ending, to the story, and real life will come after it. I can pick up where I left off.

It isn't a story I'm telling.

It's also a story I'm telling, in my head, as I go along.

Tell, rather than write, because I have nothing to write with and writing is in any case forbidden. But if it's a story, even in my head, I must be telling it to someone. You don't tell a story only to yourself. There's always someone else.

Even when there is no one.

A story is like a letter. *Dear You*, I'll say. Just *you*, without a name. Attaching a name attaches *you* to the world of fact, which is riskier, more hazardous: who knows what the chances are out there, of survival, yours? I will say *you*, *you*, like an old love song. *You* can mean more than one.

▷ **3** *disconsolate:* unhappy **8** *sulk:* schmollen **29** *riffle open:* (of pages) open up quickly one by one **69** *hazardous* ['hæzərdəs]: dangerous

You can mean thousands.
I'm not in any immediate danger, I'll say to you.
I'll pretend you can hear me.
But it's no good, because I know you can't.

IV

Waiting Room

CHAPTER 8

The good weather holds. It's almost like June, when we would get out our sundresses and our sandals and go for an ice-cream cone. There are three new bodies on the Wall. One is a priest, still wearing the black cassock. That's been put on him, for the trial, even though they gave up wearing those years ago, when the sect wars first began; cassocks made them too conspicuous. The two others have purple placards hung around their necks: Gender Treachery. Their bodies still wear the Guardian uniforms. Caught together, they must have been, but where? A barracks, a shower? It's hard to say. The snowman with the red smile is gone.

"We should go back," I say to Ofglen. I'm always the one to say this. Sometimes I feel that if I didn't say it, she would stay here forever. But is she mourning or gloating? I still can't tell.

Without a word she swivels, as if she's voice-activated, as if she's on little oiled wheels, as if she's on top of a music box. I resent this grace of hers. I resent her meek head, bowed as if into a heavy wind. But there is no wind.

We leave the Wall, walk back the way we came, in the warm sun.

"It's a beautiful May day," Ofglen says. I feel rather than see her head turn towards me, waiting for a reply.

"Yes," I say. "Praise be," I add as an afterthought. *Mayday* used to be a distress signal, a long time ago, in one of those wars we studied in high school. I kept getting them mixed up, but you could tell them apart by the airplanes if you paid attention. It was Luke who told me about Mayday though. *Mayday, mayday*, for pilots whose planes had been hit, and ships – was it ships too? – at sea. Maybe it was SOS for ships. I wish I could look it up. And it was something from Beethoven, for the beginning of the victory, in one of those wars.

▷ **6** *cassock:* the long black piece of clothing worn esp. by Catholic priests • *conspicuous:* easy to see or notice **7** *treachery* ['tretʃəri]: Verrat **13** *gloat:* feel pleasure at the bad luck of others **14** *swivel:* turn around **15** *resent sth.* [rɪ'zent]: dislike sth. **28** *Ludwig van Beethoven* (1770–1827): German composer, the beginning of whose Fifth Symphony is the same as the morse code for "V"; the four notes were used by the BBC when broadcasting to occupied Europe during the Second World War

Do you know what it came from? said Luke. Mayday?

No, I said. It's a strange word to use for that, isn't it?

Newspapers and coffee, on Sunday mornings, before she was born. There were still newspapers, then. We used to read them in bed.

It's French, he said. From *m'aidez.*

Help me.

Coming towards us there's a small procession, a funeral: three women, each with a black transparent veil thrown over her head-dress. An Econowife and two others, the mourners, also Econowives, her friends perhaps. Their striped dresses are worn-looking, as are their faces. Some day, when times improve, says Aunt Lydia, no one will have to be an Econowife.

The first one is the bereaved, the mother; she carries a small black jar. From the size of the jar you can tell how old it was when it foundered, inside her, flowed to its death. Two or three months, too young to tell whether or not it was an Unbaby. The older ones and those that die at birth have boxes.

We pause, out of respect, while they go by. I wonder if Ofglen feels what I do, a pain like a stab, in the belly. We put our hands over our hearts to show these stranger women that we feel with them in their loss. Beneath her veil the first one scowls at us. One of the others turns aside, spits on the sidewalk. The Econowives do not like us.

We go past the shops and come to the barrier again, and are passed through. We continue on among the large empty-looking houses, the weedless lawns. At the corner near the house where I'm posted, Ofglen stops, turns to me.

"Under His Eye," she says. The right farewell.

"Under His Eye," I reply, and she gives a little nod. She hesitates, as if to say something more, but then she turns away and walks down the street. I watch her. She's like my own reflection, in a mirror from which I am moving away.

In the driveway, Nick is polishing the Whirlwind again. He's reached the chrome at the back. I put my gloved hand on the latch of the gate, open it, push inward. The gate clicks behind me. The tulips along the border are redder than ever, opening, no longer winecups but chalices; thrusting themselves up, to what end? They are, after all, empty. When they are old they turn themselves inside out, then explode slowly, the petals thrown out like shards.

Nick looks up and begins to whistle. Then he says, "Nice walk?"

I nod, but do not answer with my voice. He isn't supposed to speak to me. Of course some of them will try, said Aunt Lydia. All flesh is weak. All flesh is grass, I corrected her in my head. They can't help it, she said, God made them that way but He did not make you that way. He made you different. It's up to you to set the boundaries. Later you will be thanked.

In the garden behind the house the Commander's Wife is sitting, in the chair she's had brought out. Serena Joy, what a stupid name. It's like something you'd put on your hair, in the other time, the time before, to straighten it. *Serena Joy*, it would say on the bottle, with a woman's head in cut-paper silhouette on a pink oval background with scalloped gold edges. With everything to choose from in the way of names, why did she pick that one? Serena Joy was never her real name, not even then. Her real name was Pam. I read that in a profile on her, in a news magazine, long after I'd first watched her singing while my mother slept in on Sunday mornings. By that time she was worthy of a profile: *Time* or *Newsweek* it was, it must have been. She wasn't singing any more by then, she was making speeches. She was good at it. Her speeches were about the sanctity of the home, about how women should stay home. Serena Joy didn't do this herself, she made speeches instead, but she presented this failure of hers as a sacrifice she was making for the good of all.

Around that time, someone tried to shoot her and missed; her secretary, who was standing right behind her, was killed instead. Someone else planted a bomb in her car but it went off too early. Though some people said she'd put the bomb in her own car, for sympathy. That's how hot things were getting.

Luke and I would watch her sometimes on the late-night news. Bathrobes, nightcaps. We'd watch her sprayed hair and her hysteria,

▷ **13** *the bereaved:* the person whose loved one has died **15** *founder* (v): fail to survive **19** *stab* (n): the act of being injured with a sharp instrument (e.g. a knife) **21** *scowl* (v): look in an unfriendly way **25** *weedless:* ohne Unkraut **36** *chalice:* Kelch **38** *shards:* Scherben **41–42** *all flesh is weak/all flesh is grass:* reference to Isaiah 40:6 and 1 Peter 1:24 (cf. also Matthew 26:41) **53** *profile:* (here) article about sb.'s life and work

and the tears she could still produce at will, and the mascara blackening her cheeks. By that time she was wearing more makeup. We thought she was funny. Or Luke thought she was funny. I only pretended to think so. Really she was a little frightening. She was in earnest.

She doesn't make speeches any more. She has become speechless. She stays in her home, but it doesn't seem to agree with her. How furious she must be, now that she's been taken at her word.

She's looking at the tulips. Her cane is beside her, on the grass. Her profile is towards me, I can see that in the quick sideways look I take at her as I go past. It wouldn't do to stare. It's no longer a flawless cut-paper profile, her face is sinking in upon itself, and I think of those towns built on underground rivers, where houses and whole streets disappear overnight, into sudden quagmires, or coal towns collapsing into the mines beneath them. Something like this must have happened to her, once she saw the true shape of things to come.

She doesn't turn her head. She doesn't acknowledge my presence in any way, although she knows I'm there. I can tell she knows, it's like a smell, her knowledge; something gone sour, like old milk.

It's not the husbands you have to watch out for, said Aunt Lydia, it's the Wives. You should always try to imagine what they must be feeling. Of course they will resent you. It is only natural. Try to feel for them. Aunt Lydia thought she was very good at feeling for other people. Try to pity them. Forgive them, for they know not what they do. Again the tremulous smile, of a beggar, the weak-eyed blinking, the gaze upwards, through the round steel-rimmed glasses, towards the back of the classroom, as if the green-painted plaster ceiling were opening and God on a cloud of Pink Pearl face powder were coming down through the wires and sprinkler plumbing. You must realize that they are defeated women. They have been unable …

Here her voice broke off, and there was a pause, during which I could hear a sigh, a collective sigh from those around me. It was a bad idea to rustle or fidget during these pauses: Aunt Lydia might look abstracted but she was aware of every twitch. So there was only the sigh.

The future is in your hands, she resumed. She held her own hands out to us, the ancient gesture that was both an offering and an invitation, to come forward, into an embrace, an acceptance. In your hands, she said, looking down at her own hands as if they had given her the idea. But there was nothing in them. They were empty. It was our hands that were supposed to be full, of the future; which could be held but not seen.

I walk around to the back door, open it, go in, set my basket down on the kitchen table. The table has been scrubbed off, cleared of flour; today's bread, freshly baked, is cooling on its rack. The kitchen smells of yeast, a nostalgic smell. It reminds me of other kitchens, kitchens that were mine. It smells of mothers; although my own mother did not make bread. It smells of me, in former times, when I was a mother.

This is a treacherous smell, and I know I must shut it out.

Rita is there, sitting at the table, peeling and slicing carrots. Old carrots they are, thick ones, over-wintered, bearded from their time in storage. The new carrots, tender and pale, won't be ready for weeks. The knife she uses is sharp and bright, and tempting. I would like to have a knife like that.

Rita stops chopping the carrots, stands up, takes the parcels out of the basket, almost eagerly. She looks forward to seeing what I've brought, although she always frowns while opening the parcels; nothing I bring fully pleases her. She's thinking she could have done better herself. She would rather do the shopping, get exactly what she wants; she envies me the walk. In this house we all envy each other something.

"They've got oranges," I say. "At Milk and Honey. There are still some left." I hold out this idea to her like an offering. I wish to ingratiate myself. I saw the oranges yesterday, but I didn't tell Rita; yesterday she was too grumpy. "I could get some, tomorrow, if you'd give me the tokens for them." I hold out the chicken to her. She wanted steak today, but there wasn't any.

Rita grunts, not revealing pleasure or acceptance. She'll think about it, the grunt says, in her own sweet time. She undoes the string on the chicken, and the glazed paper. She prods the chicken, flexes a

▷ **14** *quagmire:* soft wet ground that sucks in people or objects **24–25** *Forgive them, for they know not what they do:* reference to Luke 23:34 **25** *tremulous:* shaky **33** *rustle:* cause a noise by moving paper or your clothes • *fidget:* move around in your seat as if nervous **46** *yeast:* Hefe **49** *treacherous* ['tretʃərəs]: dangerous; that deceives **64** *ingratiate yourself:* make yourself pleasing to sb. **65** *grumpy:* mürrisch, schlecht gelaunt

wing, pokes a finger into the cavity, fishes out the giblets. The chicken lies there, headless and without feet, goose-pimpled as though shivering.

"Bath day," Rita says, without looking at me.

Cora comes into the kitchen, from the pantry at the back, where they keep the mops and brooms. "A chicken," she says, almost with delight.

"Scrawny," says Rita, "but it'll have to do."

"There wasn't much else," I say. Rita ignores me.

"Looks big enough to me," says Cora. Is she standing up for me? I look at her, to see if I should smile; but no, it's only the food she's thinking of. She's younger than Rita; the sunlight, coming slant now through the west window, catches her hair, parted and drawn back. She must have been pretty, quite recently. There's a little mark, like a dimple, in each of her ears, where the punctures for earrings have grown over.

"Tall," says Rita, "but bony. You should speak up," she says to me, looking directly at me for the first time. "Ain't like you're common." She means the Commander's rank. But in the other sense, her sense, she thinks I am common. She is over sixty, her mind's made up.

She goes to the sink, runs her hands briefly under the tap, dries them on the dishtowel. The dishtowel is white with blue stripes. Dishtowels are the same as they always were. Sometimes these flashes of normality come at me from the side, like ambushes. The ordinary, the usual, a reminder, like a kick. I see the dishtowel, out of context, and I catch my breath. For some, in some ways, things haven't changed that much.

"Who's doing the bath?" says Rita, to Cora, not to me. "I got to tenderize this bird."

"I'll do it later," says Cora, "after the dusting."

"Just so it gets done," says Rita.

They're talking about me as though I can't hear. To them I'm a household chore, one among many.

I've been dismissed. I pick up the basket, go through the kitchen door and along the hall towards the grandfather clock. The sitting-room door is closed. Sun comes through the fanlight, falling in colors across the floor: red and blue, purple. I step into it briefly, stretch out my hands; they fill with flowers of light. I go up the stairs, my face, distant and white and distorted, framed in the hall mirror, which bulges outward like an eye under pressure. I follow the dusty-pink runner down the long upstairs hallway, back to the room.

There's someone standing in the hall, near the door to the room where I stay. The hall is dusky, this is a man, his back to me; he's looking into the room, dark against its light. I can see now, it's the Commander, he isn't supposed to be here. He hears me coming, turns, hesitates, walks forward. Towards me. He is violating custom, what do I do now?

I stop, he pauses, I can't see his face, he's looking at me, what does he want? But then he moves forward again, steps to the side to avoid touching me, inclines his head, is gone.

Something has been shown to me, but what is it? Like the flag of an unknown country, seen for an instant above a curve of hill, it could mean attack, it could mean parley, it could mean the edge of something, a territory. The signals animals give one another: lowered blue eyelids, ears laid back, raised hackles. A flash of bared teeth, what in hell does he think he's doing? Nobody else has seen him. I hope. Was he invading? Was he in my room?

I called it *mine*.

▷ **1** *giblets* ['dʒɪbləts]: Innereien **8** *scrawny:* thin; lacking meat **24** *ambush:* secret attack **33** *chore:* unpleasant and boring (household) task **43** *dusky:* half-dark **53** *parley:* discussion between enemies in order to make a peace deal **55** *raised hackles:* aufgestellte Nackenhaare • *bare sth.:* etwas entblößen **57** *invade sth.:* enter sth. (esp. a place) without permission

CHAPTER 9

My room, then. There has to be some space, finally, that I claim as mine, even in this time.

I'm waiting, in my room, which right now is a waiting room. When I go to bed it's a bedroom. The curtains are still wavering in the small wind, the sun outside is still shining, though not in through the window directly. It has moved west. I am trying not to tell stories, or at any rate not this one.

Someone has lived in this room, before me. Someone like me, or I prefer to believe so.

I discovered it three days after I was moved here.

I had a lot of time to pass. I decided to explore the room. Not hastily, as one would explore a hotel room, expecting no surprise, opening and shutting the desk drawers, the cupboard doors, unwrapping the tiny individually wrapped bar of soap, prodding the pillows. Will I ever be in a hotel room again? How I wasted them, those rooms, that freedom from being seen.

Rented licence.

In the afternoons, when Luke was still in flight from his wife, when I was still imaginary for him. Before we were married and I solidified. I would always get there first, check in. It wasn't that many times, but it seems now like a decade, an era; I can remember what I wore, each blouse, each scarf. I would pace, waiting for him, turn the television on and then off, dab behind my ears with perfume, Opium it was. It came in a Chinese bottle, red and gold.

I was nervous. How was I to know he loved me? It might be just an affair. Why did we ever say *just*? Though at that time men and women tried each other on, casually, like suits, rejecting whatever did not fit.

The knock would come at the door; I'd open, with relief, desire. He was so momentary, so condensed. And yet there seemed no end to him. We would lie in those afternoon beds, afterwards, hands on each other, talking it over. Possible, impossible. What could be done? We thought we had such problems. How were we to know we were happy?

But now it's the rooms themselves I miss as well, even the dreadful paintings that hung on the walls, landscapes with fall foliage or snow melting in hardwoods, or women in period costume, with china-doll faces and bustles and parasols, or sad-eyed clowns, or bowls of fruit, stiff and chalky-looking. The fresh towels ready for spoilage, the wastebaskets gaping their invitations, beckoning in the careless junk. Careless. I was careless, in those rooms. I could lift the telephone and food would appear on a tray, food I had chosen. Food that was bad for me, no doubt, and drink too. There were Bibles in the dresser drawers, put there by some charitable society, though probably no one read them very much. There were postcards, too, with pictures of the hotel on them, and you could write on the postcards and send them to anyone you wanted. It seems like such an impossible thing, now; like something you'd make up.

So. I explored this room, not hastily, then, like a hotel room, wasting it. I didn't want to do it all at once, I wanted to make it last. I divided the room into sections, in my head; I allowed myself one section a day. This one section I would examine with the greatest minuteness: the unevenness of the plaster under the wallpaper, the scratches in the paint of the baseboard and the windowsill, under the top coat of paint, the stains on the mattress, for I went so far as to lift the blankets and sheets from the bed, fold them back, a little at a time, so they could be replaced quickly if anyone came.

The stains on the mattress. Like dried flower petals. Not recent. Old love; there's no other kind of love in this room now.

When I saw that, that evidence left by two people, of love or something like it, desire at least, at least touch, between two people now perhaps old or dead, I covered the bed again and lay down on it. I looked up at the blind plaster eye in the ceiling. I wanted to feel Luke lying beside me. I have them, these attacks of the past, like faintness, a wave sweeping over my head. Sometimes it can hardly be borne. What is to be done, what is to be done, I thought. There is nothing to be done. They also serve who only stand and wait. Or lie down and

▷ **17** *licence:* permission to do sth. which is actually forbidden **36** *fall foliage* (AE): autumn leaves **37** *period costume:* the way of dressing of a certain time (= period) in history **38** *bustle:* 19th century dress **40** *gape:* look with wide open eyes **43** *dresser:* piece of furniture with drawers (= Schubladen) **53** *minuteness* [maɪ'nu:tnəs]: care for detail **55** *coat of paint:* Farbanstrich

wait. I know why the glass in the window is shatterproof, and why they took down the chandelier. I wanted to feel Luke lying beside me, but there wasn't room.

I saved the cupboard until the third day. I looked carefully over the door first, inside and out, then the walls with their brass hooks – how could they have overlooked the hooks? Why didn't they remove them? Too close to the floor? But still, a stocking, that's all you'd need. And the rod with the plastic hangers, my dresses hanging on them, the red woollen cape for cold weather, the shawl. I knelt to examine the floor, and there it was, in tiny writing, quite fresh it seemed, scratched with a pin or maybe just a fingernail, in the corner where the darkest shadow fell: *Nolite te bastardes carborundorum.*

I didn't know what it meant, or even what language it was in. I thought it might be Latin, but I didn't know any Latin. Still, it was a message, and it was in writing, forbidden by that very fact, and it hadn't yet been discovered. Except by me, for whom it was intended. It was intended for whoever came next.

It pleases me to ponder this message. It pleases me to think I'm communing with her, this unknown woman. For she is unknown; or if known, she has never been mentioned to me. It pleases me to know that her taboo message made it through, to at least one other person, washed itself up on the wall of my cupboard, was opened and read by me. Sometimes I repeat the words to myself. They give me a small joy. When I imagine the woman who wrote them, I think of her as about my age, maybe a little younger. I turn her into Moira, Moira as she was when she was in college, in the room next to mine: quirky, jaunty, athletic, with a bicycle once, and a knapsack for hiking. Freckles, I think; irreverent, resourceful.

I wonder who she was or is, and what's become of her.

I tried that out on Rita, the day I found the message.

Who was the woman who stayed in that room? I said. Before me? If I'd asked it differently, if I'd said, Was there a woman who stayed in that room before me? I might not have got anywhere.

Which one? she said; she sounded grudging, suspicious, but then, she almost always sounds like that when she speaks to me.

So there have been more than one. Some haven't stayed their full term of posting, their full two years. Some have been sent away, for one reason or another. Or maybe not sent; gone?

The lively one. I was guessing. The one with freckles.

You knew her? Rita asked, more suspicious than ever.

I knew her before, I lied. I heard she was here.

Rita accepted this. She knows there must be a grapevine, an underground of sorts.

She didn't work out, she said.

In what way? I asked, trying to sound as neutral as possible.

But Rita clamped her lips together. I am like a child here, there are some things I must not be told. What you don't know won't hurt you, was all she would say.

▷ **19** *commune with sb.:* share your feelings with sb. without speaking **26** *quirky:* having strange behavior **27** *freckles:* Sommersprossen **28** *irreverent:* disrespectful • *resourceful:* good at finding ways of doing things and solving problems **42** *grapevine:* informal way of sharing information about lots of people

CHAPTER 10

Sometimes I sing to myself, in my head; something lugubrious, mournful, presbyterian:

Amazing grace, how sweet the sound
Could save a wretch like me,
Who once was lost, but now am found,
Was bound, but now am free.

I don't know if the words are right. I can't remember. Such songs are not sung any more in public, especially the ones that use words like free. They are considered too dangerous. They belong to outlawed sects.

I feel so lonely, baby,
I feel so lonely, baby,
I feel so lonely I could die.

This too is outlawed. I know it from an old cassette tape, of my mother's; she had a scratchy and untrustworthy machine, too, that could still play such things. She used to put the tape on when her friends came over and they'd had a few drinks.

I don't sing like this often. It makes my throat hurt.

There isn't much music in this house, except what we hear on the TV. Sometimes Rita will hum, while kneading or peeling; a wordless humming, tuneless, unfathomable. And sometimes from the front sitting room there will be the thin sound of Serena's voice, from a disc made long ago and played now with the volume low, so she won't be caught listening as she sits there knitting, remembering her own former and now amputated glory: *Hallelujah*.

It's warm for this time of year. Houses like this heat up in the sun, there's not enough insulation. Around me the air is stagnant, despite the little current, the breath coming in past the curtains. I'd like to be able to open the window as wide as it could go. Soon we'll be allowed to change into the summer dresses.

The summer dresses are unpacked and hanging in the closet, two of them, pure cotton, which is better than synthetics like the cheaper ones, though even so, when it's muggy, in July and August, you sweat inside them. No worry about sunburn though, said Aunt Lydia. The spectacles women used to make of themselves. Oiling themselves like roast meat on a spit, and bare backs and shoulders, on the street, in public, and legs, not even stockings on them, no wonder those things used to happen. *Things*, the word she used when whatever it stood for was too distasteful or filthy or horrible to pass her lips. A successful life for her was one that avoided *things*, excluded *things*. Such *things* do not happen to nice women. And not good for the complexion, not at all, wrinkle you up like a dried apple. But we weren't supposed to care about our complexions any more, she'd forgotten that.

In the park, said Aunt Lydia, lying on blankets, men and women together sometimes, and at that she began to cry, standing up there in front of us, in full view.

I'm doing my best, she said. I'm trying to give you the best chance you can have. She blinked, the light was too strong for her, her mouth trembled, around her front teeth, teeth that stuck out a little and were long and yellowish, and I thought about the dead mice we would find on our doorstep, when we lived in a house, all three of us, four counting our cat, who was the one making these offerings.

Aunt Lydia pressed her hand over her mouth of a dead rodent. After a minute she took her hand away. I wanted to cry too because she reminded me. If only she wouldn't eat half of them first, I said to Luke.

Don't think it's easy for me either, said Aunt Lydia.

Moira, breezing into my room, dropping her denim jacket on the floor. Got any cigs, she said.

In my purse, I said. No matches though.

Moira rummages in my purse. You should throw out some of this junk, she says. I'm giving an underwhore party.

A what? I say. There's no point trying to work, Moira won't allow it, she's like a cat that crawls onto the page when you're trying to read.

▷ **1** *lugubrious* [lə'gu:briəs]: sad, gloomy **2** *presbyterian:* belonging to a certain Protestant faith **21** *unfathomable* [ʌn'fæðəməbəl]: unergründlich **42** *complexion:* skin of a person's face **59** *breeze:* move lightly and easily **63** *underwhore:* word coined from "underwear" and "whore"

You know, like Tupperware, only with underwear. Tarts' stuff. Lace crotches, snap garters. Bras that push your tits up. She finds my lighter, lights the cigarette she's extracted from my purse. Want one? Tosses the package, with great generosity considering they're mine.

Thanks piles, I say sourly. You're crazy. Where'd you get an idea like that?

Working my way through college, says Moira. I've got connections. Friend of my mother's. It's big in the suburbs, once they start getting age spots they figure they've got to beat the competition. The Pornomarts and what have you.

I'm laughing. She always made me laugh.

But here? I say. Who'll come? Who needs it?

You're never too young to learn, she says. Come on, it'll be great. We'll all pee our pants laughing.

Is that how we lived then? But we lived as usual. Everyone does, most of the time. Whatever is going on is as usual. Even this is as usual, now.

We lived, as usual, by ignoring. Ignoring isn't the same as ignorance, you have to work at it.

Nothing changes instantaneously: in a gradually heating bathtub you'd be boiled to death before you knew it. There were stories in the newspapers, of course, corpses in ditches or the woods, bludgeoned to death or mutilated, interfered with as they used to say, but they were about other women, and the men who did such things were other men. None of them were the men we knew. The newspaper stories were like dreams to us, bad dreams dreamt by others. How awful, we would say, and they were, but they were awful without being believable. They were too melodramatic, they had a dimension that was not the dimension of our lives.

We were the people who were not in the papers. We lived in the blank white spaces at the edges of print. It gave us more freedom.

We lived in the gaps between the stories.

From below, from the driveway, comes the sound of the car being started. It's quiet in this area, there isn't a lot of traffic, you can hear things like that very clearly: car motors, lawn mowers, the clipping of a hedge, the slam of a door. You could hear a shout clearly, or a shot, if such noises were ever made here. Sometimes there are distant sirens.

I go to the window and sit on the window seat, which is too narrow for comfort. There's a hard little cushion on it, with a petit-point cover: FAITH, in square print, surrounded by a wreath of lilies. FAITH is a faded blue, the leaves of the lilies a dingy green. This is a cushion once used elsewhere, worn but not enough to throw out. Somehow it's been overlooked.

I can spend minutes, tens of minutes, running my eyes over the print: FAITH. It's the only thing they've given me to read. If I were caught doing it, would it count? I didn't put the cushion here myself.

The motor turns, and I lean forward, pulling the white curtain across my face, like a veil. It's semi-sheer, I can see through it. If I press my forehead against the glass and look down, I can see the back half of the Whirlwind. Nobody is there, but as I watch I see Nick come around to the back door of the car, open it, stand stiffly beside it. His cap is straight now and his sleeves rolled down and buttoned. I can't see his face because I'm looking down on him.

Now the Commander is coming out. I glimpse him only for an instant, foreshortened, walking to the car. He doesn't have his hat on, so it's not a formal event he's going to. His hair is gray. Silver, you might call it if you were being kind. I don't feel like being kind. The one before this was bald, so I suppose he's an improvement.

If I could spit, out the window, or throw something, the cushion for instance, I might be able to hit him.

Moira and I, with paper bags filled with water. Water bombs, they were called. Leaning out my dorm window, dropping them on the heads of the boys below. It was Moira's idea. What were they trying to do? Climb a ladder, for something. For our underwear.

That dormitory had once been co-educational, there were still urinals in one of the washrooms on our floor. But by the time I'd got there they'd put the men and women back the way they were.

▷ **1** *tart* (infml): prostitute **2** *crotch*: the part of underwear or the body between the legs • *snap garter:* elastisches Strumpfband **5** *thanks piles:* thanks a lot (for sth. negative) **22** *bludgeon sb.* ['blʌdʒən]: beat sb. hard with a dull instrument **35** *clip sth.*: cut sth. a little bit **63** *dorm* = *dormitory* (cf. p. 36, l. 19) **67** *urinal:* Pissoir

The Commander stoops, gets into the car, disappears, and Nick shuts the door. A moment later the car moves backwards, down the driveway and onto the street, and vanishes behind the hedge.

I ought to feel hatred for this man. I know I ought to feel it, but it isn't what I do feel. What I feel is more complicated than that. I don't know what to call it. It isn't love.

CHAPTER 11

Yesterday morning I went to the doctor. Was taken, by a Guardian, one of those with the red armbands who are in charge of such things. We rode in a red car, him in the front, me in the back. No twin went with me; on these occasions I'm solitaire.

I'm taken to the doctor's once a month, for tests: urine, hormones, cancer smear, blood test; the same as before, except that now it's obligatory.

The doctor's office is in a modern office building. We ride up in the elevator, silently, the Guardian facing me. In the black mirror wall of the elevator I can see the back of his head. At the office itself, I go in; he waits, outside in the hall, with the other Guardians, on one of the chairs placed there for that purpose.

Inside the waiting room there are other women, three of them, in red: this doctor is a specialist. Covertly we regard each other, sizing up each other's bellies: is anyone lucky? The nurse records our names and the numbers from our passes on the Compudoc, to see if we are who we are supposed to be. He's six feet tall, about forty, a diagonal scar across his cheek; he sits typing, his hands too big for the keyboard, still wearing his pistol in the shoulder holster.

When I'm called I go through the doorway into the inner room. It's white, featureless, like the outer one, except for a folding screen, red cloth stretched on a frame, a gold eye painted on it, with a snake-twined sword upright beneath it, like a sort of handle. The snakes and the sword are bits of broken symbolism left over from the time before.

After I've filled the small bottle left ready for me in the little washroom, I take off my clothes, behind the screen, and leave them folded on the chair. When I'm naked I lie down on the examining table, on the sheet of chilly crackling disposable paper. I pull the second sheet, the cloth one, up over my body. At neck level there's another sheet, suspended from the ceiling. It intersects me so that the doctor will never see my face. He deals with a torso only.

▷ **20** *covert:* secret **20–21** *size sth. up:* look to find out how big sth. is **25** *holster:* kind of pocket for a gun

When I'm arranged I reach my hand out, fumble for the small lever at the right side of the table, pull it back. Somewhere else a bell rings, unheard by me. After a minute the door opens, footsteps come in, there is breathing. He isn't supposed to speak to me except when it's absolutely necessary. But this doctor is talkative.

"How are we getting along?" he says, some tic of speech from the other time. The sheet is lifted from my skin, a draft pimples me. A cold finger, rubber-clad and jellied, slides into me, I am poked and prodded. The finger retreats, enters otherwise, withdraws.

"Nothing wrong with you," the doctor says, as if to himself. "Any pain, honey?" He calls me *honey*.

"No," I say.

My breasts are fingered in their turn, a search for ripeness, rot. The breathing comes nearer, I smell old smoke, aftershave, tobacco dust on hair. Then the voice, very soft, close to my head: that's him, bulging the sheet.

"I could help you," he says. Whispers.

"What?" I say.

"Shh," he says. "I could help you. I've helped others."

"Help me?" I say, my voice as low as his. "How?" Does he know something, has he seen Luke, has he found, can he bring back?

"How do you think?" he says, still barely breathing it. Is that his hand, sliding up my leg? He's taken off the glove.

"The door's locked. No one will come in. They'll never know it isn't his."

He lifts the sheet. The lower part of his face is covered by the white gauze mask, regulation. Two brown eyes, a nose, a head with brown hair on it. His hand is between my legs.

"Most of those old guys can't make it any more," he says. "Or they're sterile."

I almost gasp: he's said a forbidden word. *Sterile*. There is no such thing as a sterile man any more, not officially. There are only women who are fruitful and women who are barren, that's the law.

"Lots of women do it," he goes on. "You want a baby, don't you?"

"Yes," I say. It's true, and I don't ask why, because I know. *Give me children, or else I die*. There's more than one meaning to it.

"You're soft," he says. "It's time. Today or tomorrow would do it, why waste it? It'd only take a minute, honey." What he called his wife, once; maybe still does, but really it's a generic term. We are all *honey*.

I hesitate. He's offering himself to me, his services, at some risk to himself.

"I hate to see what they put you through," he murmurs. It's genuine, genuine sympathy; and yet he's enjoying this, sympathy and all. His eyes are moist with compassion, his hand is moving on me, nervously and with impatience.

"It's too dangerous," I say. "No. I can't." The penalty is death. But they have to catch you in the act, with two witnesses. What are the odds, is the room bugged, who's waiting just outside the door?

His hand stops. "Think about it," he says. "I've seen your chart. You don't have a lot of time left. But it's your life."

"Thank you," I say. I must leave the impression that I'm not offended, that I'm open to suggestion. He takes his hand away, lazily almost, lingeringly, this is not the last word as far as he's concerned. He could fake the tests, report me for cancer, for infertility, have me shipped off to the Colonies, with the Unwomen. None of this has been said, but the knowledge of his power hangs nevertheless in the air as he pats my thigh, withdraws himself behind the hanging sheet.

"Next month," he says.

I put on my clothes again, behind the screen. My hands are shaking. Why am I frightened? I've crossed no boundaries, I've given no trust, taken no risk, all is safe. It's the choice that terrifies me. A way out, a salvation.

▷ **7** *draft:* Luftzug • *pimple sth.:* (here) cause bumps (*goose pimples:* Gänsehaut) on sth. (esp. the skin) **15** *bulge sth.:* cause sth. (e.g. a cloth or a sheet) to move forward **33** *barren:* unable to have children **35–36** *Give me children, or else I die:* reference to Genesis 30:1 **39** *generic term:* word applied to any member of a certain group (here: women)

CHAPTER 12

The bathroom is beside the bedroom. It's papered in small blue flowers, forget-me-nots, with curtains to match. There's a blue bathmat, a blue fake-fur cover on the toilet seat; all this bathroom lacks from the time before is a doll whose skirt conceals the extra roll of toilet paper. Except that the mirror over the sink has been taken out and replaced by an oblong of tin, and the door has no lock, and there are no razors, of course. There were incidents in bathrooms at first; there were cuttings, drownings. Before they got all the bugs ironed out. Cora sits on a chair outside in the hall, to see that no one else goes in. In a bathroom, in a bathtub, you are vulnerable, said Aunt Lydia. She didn't say to what.

The bath is a requirement, but it is also a luxury. Merely to lift off the heavy white wings and the veil, merely to feel my own hair again, with my hands, is a luxury. My hair is long now, untrimmed. Hair must be long but covered. Aunt Lydia said: Saint Paul said it's either that or a close shave. She laughed, that held-back neighing of hers, as if she'd told a joke.

Cora has run the bath. It steams like a bowl of soup. I take off the rest of my clothes, the overdress, the white shift and petticoat, the red stockings, the loose cotton pantaloons. Pantyhose gives you crotch rot, Moira used to say. Aunt Lydia would never have used an expression like *crotch rot. Unhygenic* was hers. She wanted everything to be very hygenic.

My nakedness is strange to me already. My body seems outdated. Did I really wear bathing suits, at the beach? I did, without thought, among men, without caring that my legs, my arms, my thighs and back were on display, could be seen. *Shameful, immodest.* I avoid looking down at my body, not so much because it's shameful or immodest but because I don't want to see it. I don't want to look at something that determines me so completely.

I step into the water, lie down, let it hold me. The water is soft as hands. I close my eyes, and she's there with me, suddenly, without warning, it must be the smell of the soap. I put my face against the soft hair at the back of her neck and breathe her in, baby powder and child's washed flesh and shampoo, with an undertone, the faint scent of urine. This is the age she is when I'm in the bath. She comes back to me at different ages. This is how I know she's not really a ghost. If she were a ghost she would be the same age always.

One day, when she was eleven months old, just before she began to walk, a woman stole her out of a supermarket cart. It was a Saturday, which was when Luke and I did the week's shopping, because both of us had jobs. She was sitting in the little baby seats they had then, in supermarket carts, with holes for the legs. She was happy enough, and I'd turned my back, the cat-food section I think it was; Luke was over at the side of the store, out of sight, at the meat counter. He liked to choose what kind of meat we were going to eat during the week. He said men needed more meat than women did, and that it wasn't a superstition and he wasn't being a jerk, studies had been done. There are some differences, he said. He was fond of saying that, as if I was trying to prove there weren't. But mostly he said it when my mother was there. He liked to tease her.

I heard her start to cry. I turned around and she was disappearing down the aisle, in the arms of a woman I'd never seen before. I screamed, and the woman was stopped. She must have been about thirty-five. She was crying and saying it was her baby, the Lord had given it to her, he'd sent her a sign. I felt sorry for her. The store manager apologized and they held her until the police came.

She's just crazy, Luke said.

I thought it was an isolated incident, at the time.

She fades, I can't keep her here with me, she's gone now. Maybe I do think of her as a ghost, the ghost of a dead girl, a little girl who died when she was five. I remember the pictures of us I had once, me holding her, standard poses, mother and baby, locked in a frame, for safety. Behind my closed eyes I can see myself as I am now, sitting beside an open drawer, or a trunk, in the cellar, where the baby

▷ **6** *oblong:* shape that is longer than it is wide **8** *bug:* (here) thing that is not working correctly **15** *Saint Paul:* reference to 1 Corinthians 11:5–6 **16** *a close shave:* pun on "have very short hair" and "situation in which you just manage to avoid sth. dangerous" **21** *rot:* Fäulnis **48** *jerk* (infml): idiot **53** *aisle* [aɪl]: walkway between rows **65** *trunk:* Schrankkoffer

clothes are folded away, a lock of hair, cut when she was two, in an envelope, white blonde. It got darker later.

I don't have those things any more, the clothes and hair. I wonder what happened to all our things. Looted, dumped out, carried away. Confiscated.

I've learned to do without a lot of things. If you have a lot of things, said Aunt Lydia, you get too attached to this material world and you forget about spiritual values. You must cultivate poverty of spirit. Blessed are the meek. She didn't go on to say anything about inheriting the earth.

I lie, lapped by the water, beside an open drawer that does not exist, and think about a girl who did not die when she was five; who still does exist, I hope, though not for me. Do I exist for her? Am I a picture somewhere, in the dark at the back of her mind?

They must have told her I was dead. That's what they would think of doing. They would say it would be easier for her to adjust.

Eight, she must be now. I've filled in the time I lost, I know how much there's been. They were right, it's easier, to think of her as dead. I don't have to hope then, or make a wasted effort. Why bash your head, said Aunt Lydia, against a wall? Sometimes she had a graphic way of putting things.

"I ain't got all day," says Cora's voice outside the door. It's true, she hasn't. She hasn't got all of anything. I must not deprive her of her time. I soap myself, use the scrub brush and the piece of pumice for sanding off dead skin. Such puritan aids are supplied. I wish to be totally clean, germless, without bacteria, like the surface of the moon. I will not be able to wash myself, this evening, not afterwards, not for a day. It interferes, they say, and why take chances?

I cannot avoid seeing, now, the small tattoo on my ankle. Four digits and an eye, a passport in reverse. It's supposed to guarantee that I will never be able to fade, finally, into another landscape. I am too important, too scarce, for that. I am a national resource.

I pull the plug, dry myself, put on my red terrycloth robe. I leave today's dress here, where Cora will pick it up to be washed. Back in the room I dress again. The white headdress isn't necessary for the evening, because I won't be going out. Everyone in this house knows what my face looks like. The red veil goes on, though, covering my damp hair, my head, which has not been shaved. Where did I see that film, about the women, kneeling in the town square, hands holding them, their hair falling in clumps? What had they done? It must have been a long time ago, because I can't remember.

Cora brings my supper, covered, on a tray. She knocks at the door before entering. I like her for that. It means she thinks I have some of what we used to call privacy left.

"Thank you," I say, taking the tray from her, and she actually smiles at me, but she turns away without answering. When we're alone together she's shy of me.

I put the tray on the small white-painted table and draw the chair up to it. I take the cover off the tray. The thigh of a chicken, overcooked. It's better than bloody, which is the other way she does it. Rita has ways of making her resentment felt. A baked potato, green beans, salad. Canned pears for dessert. It's good enough food, though bland. Healthy food. You have to get your vitamins and minerals, said Aunt Lydia coyly. You must be a worthy vessel. No coffee or tea though, no alcohol. Studies have been done. There's a paper napkin, as in cafeterias.

I think of the others, those without. This is the heartland, here, I'm leading a pampered life, may the Lord make us truly grateful, said Aunt Lydia, or was it thankful, and I start to eat the food. I'm not hungry tonight. I feel sick to my stomach. But there's no place to put the food, no potted plants, and I won't chance the toilet. I'm too nervous, that's what it is. Could I leave it on the plate, ask Cora not to report me? I chew and swallow, chew and swallow, feeling the sweat come out. In my stomach the food balls itself together, a handful of damp cardboard, squeezed.

Downstairs, in the dining room, there will be candles on the large mahogany table, a white cloth, silver, flowers, wine glasses with wine in them. There will be a click of knives against china, a clink as she

▷ **5** *confiscated:* taken away by sb. in authority **8–10** *poverty of spirit/blessed are the meek/inheriting the earth:* reference to the Beatitudes (= Seligpreisungen) (cf. Matthew 5:3–11) **23** *deprive sb. of sth.:* take sth. valuable away from sb. **24** *pumice* ['pʌmɪs]: Bimsstein **28** *interfere (with sth.):* change the development of sth. **51** *resentment:* dislike **53** *bland:* tasteless **54** *coy:* pretending to be innocent • *vessel:* container **58** *pampered:* be taken care of very well **58–59** *may the Lord make us truly … thankful:* reference to the grace (= Tischgebet) "For what we are about to receive, may the Lord make us truly thankful"

sets down her fork, with a barely audible sigh, leaving half the contents of her plate untouched. Possibly she will say she has no appetite. Possibly she won't say anything. If she says something, does he comment? If she doesn't say anything, does he notice? I wonder how she manages to get herself noticed. I think it must be hard.

There's a pat of butter on the side of the plate. I tear off a corner of the paper napkin, wrap the butter in it, take it to the cupboard and slip it into the toe of my right shoe, from the extra pair, as I have done before. I crumple up the rest of the napkin: no one, surely, will bother to smooth it out, to check if any is missing. I will use the butter later tonight. It would not do, this evening, to smell of butter.

I wait. I compose myself. My self is a thing I must now compose, as one composes a speech. What I must present is a made thing, not something born.

V

Nap

CHAPTER 13

There's time to spare. This is one of the things I wasn't prepared for – the amount of unfilled time, the long parentheses of nothing. Time as white sound. If only I could embroider. Weave, knit, something to do with my hands. I want a cigarette. I remember walking in art galleries, through the nineteenth century: the obsession they had then with harems. Dozens of paintings of harems, fat women lolling on divans, turbans on their heads or velvet caps, being fanned with peacock tails, a eunuch in the background standing guard. Studies of sedentary flesh, painted by men who'd never been there. These pictures were supposed to be erotic, and I thought they were, at the time; but I see now what they were really about. They were paintings about suspended animation; about waiting, about objects not in use. They were paintings about boredom.

But maybe boredom is erotic, when women do it, for men.

I wait, washed, brushed, fed, like a prize pig. Sometime in the eighties they invented pig balls, for pigs who were being fattened in pens. Pig balls were large colored balls; the pigs rolled them around with their snouts. The pig marketers said this improved their muscle tone; the pigs were curious, they liked to have something to think about.

I read about that in Introduction to Psychology; that, and the chapter on caged rats who'd give themselves electric shocks for something to do. And the one on the pigeons, trained to peck a button which made a grain of corn appear. Three groups of them: the first got one grain per peck, the second one grain every other peck, the third was random. When the man in charge cut off the grain, the first group gave up quite soon, the second group a little later. The third group never gave up. They'd peck themselves to death, rather than quit. Who knew what worked?

I wish I had a pig ball.

*

▷ **2** *parenthesis* (pl *parentheses* [pəˈrenθəsiːz]): (here) space or time in between other things **8–9** *sedentary* [ˈsedənteri]: (used to) sitting down **16** *pen:* small enclosure in which farm animals are kept **25** *random:* done without a fixed plan

I lie down on the braided rug. You can always practise, said Aunt Lydia. Several sessions a day, fitted into your daily routine. Arms at the sides, knees bent, lift the pelvis, roll the backbone down. Tuck. Again. Breathe in to the count of five, hold, expel. We'd do that in what used to be the Domestic Science room, cleared now of sewing machines and washerdryers; in unison, lying on little Japanese mats, a tape playing, *Les Sylphides*. That's what I hear now, in my head, as I lift, tilt, breathe. Behind my closed eyes thin white dancers flit gracefully among the trees, their legs fluttering like the wings of held birds.

In the afternoons we lay on our beds for an hour in the gymnasium, between three and four. They said it was a period of rest and meditation. I thought then they did it because they wanted some time off themselves, from teaching us, and I know the Aunts not on duty went off to the teachers' room for a cup of coffee, or whatever they called by that name. But now I think that the rest also was practice. They were giving us a chance to get used to blank time.

A catnap, Aunt Lydia called it, in her coy way.

The strange thing is we needed a rest. Many of us went to sleep. We were tired there, a lot of the time. We were on some kind of pill or drug I think, they put it in the food, to keep us calm. But maybe not. Maybe it was the place itself. After the first shock, after you'd come to terms, it was better to be lethargic. You could tell yourself you were saving up your strength.

I must have been there three weeks when Moira came. She was brought into the gymnasium by two of the Aunts, in the usual way, while we were having our nap. She still had her clothes on, jeans and a blue sweatshirt – her hair was short, she'd defied fashion as usual – so I recognized her at once. She saw me too, but she turned away, she already knew what was safe. There was a bruise on her left cheek, turning purple. The Aunts took her to a vacant bed where the red dress was already laid out. She undressed, began to dress again, in silence, the Aunts standing at the end of the bed, the rest of us watching from inside our slitted eyes. As she bent over I could see the knobs on her spine. I couldn't talk to her for several days; we looked only, small glances, like sips. Friendships were suspicious, we knew it, we avoided each other during the mealtime lineups in the cafeteria and in the halls between classes. But on the fourth day she was beside me during the walk, two by two around the football field. We weren't given the white wings until we graduated, we had only the veils; so we could talk, as long as we did it quietly and didn't turn to look at one another. The Aunts walked at the head of the line and at the end, so the only danger was from the others. Some were believers and might report us.

This is a loony bin, Moira said.

I'm so glad to see you, I said.

Where can we talk? said Moira.

Washroom, I said. Watch the clock. End stall, two-thirty.

That was all we said.

It makes me feel safer, that Moira is here. We can go to the washroom if we put our hands up, though there's a limit to how many times a day, they mark it down on a chart. I watch the clock, electric and round, at the front over the green blackboard. Two-thirty comes during Testifying. Aunt Helena is here, as well as Aunt Lydia, because Testifying is special. Aunt Helena is fat, she once headed a Weight Watchers' franchise operation in Iowa. She's good at Testifying.

It's Janine, telling about how she was gang-raped at fourteen and had an abortion. She told the same story last week. She seemed almost proud of it, while she was telling. It may not even be true. At Testifying, it's safer to make things up than to say you have nothing to reveal. But since it's Janine, it's probably more or less true.

But *whose* fault was it? Aunt Helena says, holding up one plump finger.

Her fault, *her* fault, *her* fault, we chant in unison.

Who led them on? Aunt Helena beams, pleased with us.

She did. *She* did. *She* did.

Why did God allow such a terrible thing to happen?

Teach her a *lesson*. Teach her a *lesson*. Teach her a *lesson*.

▷ **3** *pelvis:* Becken **6** *in unison:* all together at the same time **7** *Les Sylphides:* ballet music based on music by Frédéric Chopin **17** *blank:* empty **18** *catnap:* short sleep **28** *defy sth.:* refuse to follow normal rules of sth. **30** *bruise* [bru:z]: a blue, brown or purple mark that appears on the skin after an injury **34** *slitted eyes:* eyes that are only barely opened; (here) eyes that do not have a full view of sth. **45** *loony bin* (sl, derog): hospital for mentally sick people **48** *end stall:* letzte Kabine

Last week, Janine burst into tears. Aunt Helena made her kneel at the front of the classroom, hands behind her back, where we could all see her, her red face and dripping nose. Her hair dull blonde, her eyelashes so light they seemed not there, the lost eyelashes of someone who's been in a fire. Burned eyes. She looked disgusting: weak, squirmy, blotchy, pink, like a newborn mouse. None of us wanted to look like that, ever. For a moment, even though we knew what was being done to her, we despised her.

Crybaby. Crybaby. Crybaby.

We meant it, which is the bad part.

I used to think well of myself. I didn't then.

That was last week. This week Janine doesn't wait for us to jeer at her. It was my fault, she says. It was my own fault. I led them on. I deserved the pain.

Very good, Janine, says Aunt Lydia. You are an example.

I have to wait until this is over before I put up my hand. Sometimes, if you ask at the wrong moment, they say No. If you really have to go that can be crucial. Yesterday Dolores wet the floor. Two Aunts hauled her away, a hand under each armpit. She wasn't there for the afternoon walk, but at night she was back in her usual bed. All night we could hear her moaning, off and on.

What did they do to her? we whispered, from bed to bed.

I don't know.

Not knowing makes it worse.

I raise my hand, Aunt Lydia nods. I stand up and walk out into the hall, as inconspicuously as possible. Outside the washroom Aunt Elizabeth is standing guard. She nods, signalling that I can go in.

This washroom used to be for boys. The mirrors have been replaced here too by oblongs of dull gray metal, but the urinals are still there, on one wall, white enamel with yellow stains. They look oddly like babies' coffins. I marvel again at the nakedness of men's lives: the showers right out in the open, the body exposed for inspection and comparison, the public display of privates. What is it for? What purposes of reassurance does it serve? The flashing of a badge, look, everyone, all is in order, I belong here. Why don't women have to prove to one another that they are women? Some form of unbuttoning, some split-crotch routine, just as casual. A dog-like sniffing.

The high school is old, the stalls are wooden, some kind of chipboard. I go into the second one from the end, swing the door to. Of course there are no longer any locks. In the wood there's a small hole, at the back, next to the wall, about waist height, souvenir of some previous vandalism or legacy of an ancient voyeur. Everyone in the Center knows about this hole in the woodwork; everyone except the Aunts.

I'm afraid I am too late, held up by Janine's Testifying: maybe Moira has been here already, maybe she's had to go back. They don't give you much time. I look carefully down, aslant under the stall wall, and there are two red shoes. But how can I tell who it is?

I put my mouth to the wooden hole. Moira? I whisper.

Is that you? she says.

Yes, I say. Relief goes through me.

God, do I need a cigarette, says Moira.

Me too, I say.

I feel ridiculously happy.

I sink down into my body as into a swamp, fenland, where only I know the footing. Treacherous ground, my own territory. I become the earth I set my ear against, for rumors of the future. Each twinge, each murmur of slight pain, ripples of sloughed-off matter, swellings and diminishings of tissue, the droolings of the flesh, these are signs, these are the things I need to know about. Each month I watch for blood, fearfully, for when it comes it means failure. I have failed once again to fulfil the expectations of others, which have become my own.

I used to think of my body as an instrument, of pleasure, or a means of transportation, or an implement for the accomplishment of my will. I could use it to run, push buttons, of one sort or another, make

▷ **6** *squirmy:* nervous, uncomfortable **12** *jeer at sb.:* laugh or shout rude remarks at sb. to show that you do not respect them **26** *inconspicuous:* trying not to attract any attention **33** *privates = private parts:* Geschlechtsteile **34** *flash sth.:* show sth. (here: genitals) to sb. suddenly and unexpectedly • *badge:* small piece of metal, fabric or plastic with a design or words on it showing that a person belongs to an organization **40** *chipboard:* Spanholzplatte **48** *aslant* [ə'slænt]: not straight, but across at an angle **56** *fenland:* area of low flat wet land **57** *footing* (n): Halt, Tritt **58** *twinge:* slight feeling of pain **59** *ripple:* small wave • *sloughed-off matter* [slʌft]: bits of dead tissue discarded by the body (esp. as done by a snake) **60** *drooling:* Gesabber

things happen. There were limits but my body was nevertheless lithe, single, solid, one with me.

Now the flesh arranges itself differently. I'm a cloud, congealed around a central object, the shape of a pear, which is hard and more real than I am and glows red within its translucent wrapping. Inside it is a space, huge as the sky at night and dark and curved like that, though black-red rather than black. Pinpoints of light swell, sparkle, burst and shrivel within it, countless as stars. Every month there is a moon, gigantic, round, heavy, an omen. It transits, pauses, continues on and passes out of sight, and I see despair coming towards me like famine. To feel that empty, again, again. I listen to my heart, wave upon wave, salty and red, continuing on and on, marking time.

I'm in our first apartment, in the bedroom. I'm standing in front of the cupboard, which has folding doors made of wood. Around me I know it's empty, all the furniture is gone, the floors are bare, no carpets even; but despite this the cupboard is full of clothes. I think they're my clothes, but they don't look like mine, I've never seen them before. Maybe they're clothes belonging to Luke's wife, whom I've also never seen; only pictures and a voice on the phone, late at night, when she was calling us, crying, accusing, before the divorce. But no, they're my clothes all right. I need a dress, I need something to wear. I pull out dresses, black, blue, purple, jackets, skirts; none of them will do, none of them even fits, they're too big or too small.

Luke is there, behind me, I turn to see him. He won't look at me, he looks down at the floor, where the cat is rubbing itself against his legs, mewing and mewing plaintively. It wants food, but how can there be any food with the apartment so empty?

Luke, I say. He doesn't answer. Maybe he doesn't hear me. It occurs to me that he may not be alive.

I'm running, with her, holding her hand, pulling, dragging her through the bracken, she's only half awake because of the pill I gave her, so she wouldn't cry or say anything that would give us away, she doesn't know where she is. The ground is uneven, rocks, dead branches, the smell of damp earth, old leaves, she can't run fast enough, by myself I could run faster, I'm a good runner. Now she's crying, she's frightened, I want to carry her but she would be too heavy. I have my hiking boots on and I think, when we reach the water I'll have to kick them off, will it be too cold, will she be able to swim that far, what about the current, we weren't expecting this. *Quiet*, I say to her angrily. I think about her drowning and this thought slows me. Then the shots come behind us, not loud, not like firecrackers, but sharp and crisp like a dry branch snapping. It sounds wrong, nothing ever sounds the way you think it will, and I hear the voice, *Down*, is it a real voice or a voice inside my head or my own voice, out loud?

I pull her to the ground and roll on top of her to cover her, shield her. *Quiet*, I say again, my face is wet, sweat or tears, I feel calm and floating, as if I'm no longer in my body; close to my eyes there's a leaf, red, turned early, I can see every bright vein. It's the most beautiful thing I've ever seen. I ease off, I don't want to smother her, instead I curl myself around her, keeping my hand over her mouth. There's breath and the knocking of my heart, like pounding, at the door of a house at night, where you thought you would be safe. *It's all right, I'm here*, I say, whisper, *Please be quiet*, but how can she? She's too young, it's too late, we come apart, my arms are held, and the edges go dark and nothing is left but a little window, a very little window, like the wrong end of a telescope, like the window on a Christmas card, an old one, night and ice outside, and within a candle, a shining tree, a family, I can hear the bells even, sleighbells, from the radio, old music, but through this window I can see, small but very clear, I can see her, going away from me, through the trees which are already turning, red and yellow, holding out her arms to me, being carried away.

The bell wakes me; and then Cora, knocking at my door. I sit up, on the rug, wipe my wet face with my sleeve. Of all the dreams this is the worst.

▷ **1** *lithe:* able to move easily **3** *congealed* [kən'dʒiːəld]: fest, erstarrt **7** *pinpoint:* sth. that is very very small **11** *famine* ['fæmɪn]: a lack of food for a long period of time in a particular region **26** *mew:* make the soft high noise of a cat • *plaintive:* sounding sad, esp. in a weak, complaining way **31** *bracken:* Farnkraut **46** *shield sb.:* protect sb. by covering them with your own body **59** *sleighbell* ['sleɪbel]: Schlittenglocke

VI

Household

CHAPTER 14

When the bell has finished I descend the stairs, a brief waif in the eye of glass that hangs on the downstairs wall. The clock ticks with its pendulum, keeping time; my feet in their neat red shoes count the way down.

The sitting-room door is wide open. I go in: so far no one else is here. I don't sit, but take my place, kneeling, near the chair with the footstool where Serena Joy will shortly enthrone herself, leaning on her cane while she lowers herself down. Possibly she'll put a hand on my shoulder, to steady herself, as if I'm a piece of furniture. She's done it before.

The sitting room would once have been called a drawing room, perhaps; then a living room. Or maybe it's a parlor, the kind with a spider and flies. But now it's officially a sitting room, because that's what is done in it, by some. For others there's standing room only. The posture of the body is important, here and now: minor discomforts are instructive.

The sitting room is subdued, symmetrical; it's one of the shapes money takes when it freezes. Money has trickled through this room for years and years, as if through an underground cavern, crusting and hardening like stalactites into these forms. Mutely the varied surfaces present themselves: the dusk-rose velvet of the drawn drapes, the gloss of the matching chairs, eighteenth century, the cow's-tongue hush of the tufted Chinese rug on the floor, with its peach-pink peonies, the suave leather of the Commander's chair, the glint of brass on the box beside it.

The rug is authentic. Some things in this room are authentic, some are not. For instance, two paintings, both of women, one on either side of the fireplace. Both wear dark dresses, like the ones in the old

▷ **1** *waif:* small, thin person (usu. a child) who looks as if they do not have enough to eat **5** *so far:* until now **12** *parlor* (old-fashioned): sitting room **15** *posture:* the position in which you hold your body **17** *subdued:* (here) not very bright or well-lit **20** *mute:* silent **22** *drapes* (AE): curtains • *matching* (adj): similar, made of the same style **22–23** *the cow's tongue hush of the tufted Chinese rug:* the fluffy Chinese rug feels like a cow's tongue and quietens the noise of a person's steps **24** *peony* ['piːəni]: Pfingstrose

church, though of a later date. The paintings are possibly authentic. I suspect that when Serena Joy acquired them, after it became obvious to her that she'd have to redirect her energies into something convincingly domestic, she had the intention of passing them off as ancestors. Or maybe they were in the house when the Commander bought it. There's no way of knowing such things. In any case, there they hang, their backs and mouths stiff, their breasts constricted, their faces pinched, their caps starched, their skin grayish-white, guarding the room with their narrowed eyes.

Between them, over the mantel, there's an oval mirror, flanked by two pairs of silver candlesticks, with a white china Cupid centered between them, its arm around the neck of a lamb. The tastes of Serena Joy are a strange blend: hard lust for quality, soft sentimental cravings. There's a dried flower arrangement on either end of the mantelpiece, and a vase of real daffodils on the polished marquetry end table beside the sofa.

The room smells of lemon oil, heavy cloth, fading daffodils, the leftover smells of cooking that have made their way from the kitchen or the dining room, and of Serena Joy's perfume: Lily of the Valley. Perfume is a luxury, she must have some private source. I breathe it in, thinking I should appreciate it. It's the scent of prepubescent girls, of the gifts young children used to give their mothers, for Mother's Day; the smell of white cotton socks and white cotton petticoats, of dusting powder, of the innocence of female flesh not yet given over to hairiness and blood. It makes me feel slightly ill, as if I'm in a closed car on a hot muggy day with an older woman wearing too much face powder. This is what the sitting room is like, despite its elegance.

I would like to steal something from this room. I would like to take some small thing, the scrolled ashtray, the little silver pillbox from the mantel perhaps, or a dried flower: hide it in the folds of my dress or in my zippered sleeve, keep it there until this evening is over, secrete it in my room, under the bed, or in a shoe, or in a slit in the hard petit-point FAITH cushion. Every once in a while I would take it out and look at it. It would make me feel that I have power.

But such a feeling would be an illusion, and too risky. My hands stay where they are, folded in my lap. Thighs together, heels tucked underneath me, pressing up against my body. Head lowered. In my mouth there's the taste of toothpaste: fake mint and plaster.

I wait, for the household to assemble. *Household*: that is what we are. The Commander is the head of the household. The house is what he holds. To have and to hold, till death do us part.

The hold of a ship. Hollow.

Cora comes in first, then Rita, wiping her hands on her apron. They too have been summoned by the bell, they resent it, they have other things to do, the dishes for instance. But they need to be here, they all need to be here, the Ceremony demands it. We are all obliged to sit through this, one way or another.

Rita scowls at me before slipping in to stand behind me. It's my fault, this waste of her time. Not mine, but my body's, if there is a difference. Even the Commander is subject to its whims.

Nick walks in, nods to all three of us, looks around the room. He too takes his place behind me, standing. He's so close that the tip of his boot is touching my foot. Is this on purpose? Whether it is or not we are touching, two shapes of leather. I feel my shoe soften, blood flows into it, it grows warm, it becomes a skin. I move my foot slightly, away.

"Wish he'd hurry up," says Cora.

"Hurry up and wait," says Nick. He laughs, moves his foot so it's touching mine again. No one can see, beneath the folds of my outspread skirt. I shift, it's too warm in here, the smell of stale perfume makes me feel a little sick. I move my foot away.

We hear Serena coming, down the stairs, along the hall, the muffled tap of her cane on the rug, thud of the good foot. She hobbles through the doorway, glances at us, counting but not seeing. She nods, at Nick, but says nothing. She's in one of her best dresses, sky-blue with embroidery in white along the edges of the veil: flowers and fretwork. Even at her age she still feels the urge to wreathe herself in

▷ **4** *pass sth. off as sth. else:* pretend that sth. is sth. else when it really is not **8** *pinched:* pale and thin • *starched:* stiff **10** *mantel*: frame around a fireplace, usu. with a mantelpiece (= shelf) above it **11** *Cupid:* mythological angel-like figure usu. associated with love and desire **13** *craving:* strong desire **15** *marquetry:* Intarsie, Einlegearbeit **19** *Lily of the Valley:* Maiglöckchen **21** *prepubescent* [ˌpri:pju'besənt]: that have not yet reached puberty **26** *muggy:* unpleasantly warm and humid **31** *secrete sth.* [-'-] (fml): hide sth. small **41** *to have … us part:* part of the marriage ceremony in the *Book of Common Prayer* **44** *summon sb.* (fml): order or call sb. to appear **48** *scowl at sb.* [skaʊl]: look at sb. in an angry or annoyed way **50** *be subject to sth.:* be dependent on (the authority of) sth. **67** *fretwork:* pattern cut into material

flowers. No use for you, I think at her, my face unmoving, you can't use them any more, you're withered. They're the genital organs of plants. I read that somewhere, once.

She makes her way to her chair and footstool, turns, lowers herself, lands ungracefully. She hoists her left foot onto the stool, fumbles in her sleeve pocket. I can hear the rustling, the click of her lighter, I smell the hot singe of the smoke, breathe it in.

"Late as usual," she says. We don't answer. There's a clatter as she gropes on the lamp table, then a click, and the television set runs through its warm-up.

A male choir, with greenish-yellow skin, the color needs adjusting, they're singing "Come to the Church in the Wildwood." *Come, come, come, come*, sing the basses. Serena clicks the channel changer. Waves, colored zigzags, a garble of sound: it's the Montreal satellite station, being blocked. Then there's a preacher, earnest, with shining dark eyes, leaning towards us across a desk. These days they look a lot like businessmen. Serena gives him a few seconds, then clicks onward.

Several blank channels, then the news. This is what she's been looking for. She leans back, inhales deeply. I on the contrary lean forward, a child being allowed up late with the grown-ups. This is the one good thing about these evenings, the evenings of the Ceremony: I'm allowed to watch the news. It seems to be an unspoken rule in this household: we always get here on time, he's always late, Serena always lets us watch the news.

Such as it is: who knows if any of it is true? It could be old clips, it could be faked. But I watch it anyway, hoping to be able to read beneath it. Any news, now, is better than none.

First, the front lines. They are not lines, really: the war seems to be going on in many places at once.

Wooded hills, seen from above, the trees a sickly yellow. I wish she'd fix the color. The Appalachian Highlands, says the voice-over, where the Angels of the Apocalypse, Fourth Division, are smoking out a pocket of Baptist guerrillas, with air support from the Twenty-first Battalion of the Angels of Light. We are shown two helicopters, black ones with silver wings painted on the sides. Below them, a clump of trees explodes.

Now a close shot of a prisoner, with a stubbled and dirty face, flanked by two Angels in their neat black uniforms. The prisoner accepts a cigarette from one of the Angels, puts it awkwardly to his lips with his bound hands. He gives a lopsided little grin. The announcer is saying something, but I don't hear it: I look into this man's eyes, trying to decide what he's thinking. He knows the camera is on him: is the grin a show of defiance, or is it submission? Is he embarrassed, at having been caught?

They show us only victories, never defeats. Who wants bad news?

Possibly he's an actor.

The anchorman comes on now. His manner is kindly, fatherly; he gazes out at us from the screen, looking, with his tan and his white hair and candid eyes, wise wrinkles around them, like everybody's ideal grandfather. What he's telling us, his level smile implies, is for our own good. Everything will be all right soon. I promise. There will be peace. You must trust. You must go to sleep, like good children.

He tells us what we long to believe. He's very convincing.

I struggle against him. He's like an old movie star, I tell myself, with false teeth and a face job. At the same time I sway towards him, like one hypnotized. If only it were true. If only I could believe.

Now he's telling us that an underground espionage ring has been cracked, by a team of Eyes, working with an inside informant. The ring has been smuggling precious national resources over the border into Canada.

"Five members of the heretical sect of Quakers have been arrested," he says, smiling blandly, "and more arrests are anticipated."

Two of the Quakers appear onscreen, a man and a woman. They look terrified, but they're trying to preserve some dignity in front of the camera. The man has a large dark mark on his forehead; the woman's veil has been torn off, and her hair falls in strands over her face. Both of them are about fifty.

Now we can see a city, again from the air. This used to be Detroit. Under the voice of the announcer there's the thunk of artillery. From the skyline columns of smoke ascend.

▷ **2** *withered:* welk **9** *grope:* try to reach or find sth. by using your hand **14** *garble:* muddle, confusion **40** *awkward* ['ɔːkwərd]: (here) with difficulty **41** *lopsided:* with one side lower than the other **50** *candid:* open and honest **60** *precious* ['preʃəs]: rare and worth a lot of money **62** *heretical:* ketzerisch • *Quakers:* a Christian religious group that meets without any formal ceremony and is strongly opposed to violence and war **63** *bland:* showing no strong emotions or excitement **70** *thunk* (AE): sudden, low sound

"Resettlement of the Children of Ham is continuing on schedule," says the reassuring pink face, back on the screen. "Three thousand have arrived this week in National Homeland One, with another two thousand in transit." How are they transporting that many people at once? Trains, buses? We are not shown any pictures of this. National Homeland One is in North Dakota. Lord knows what they're supposed to do, once they get there. Farm, is the theory.

Serena Joy has had enough of the news. Impatiently she clicks the button for a station change, comes up with an aging bass baritone, his cheeks like emptied udders. "Whispering Hope" is what he's singing. Serena turns him off.

We wait, the clock in the hall ticks, Serena lights another cigarette, I get into the car. It's a Saturday morning, it's a September, we still have a car. Other people have had to sell theirs. My name isn't Offred, I have another name, which nobody uses now because it's forbidden. I tell myself it doesn't matter, your name is like your telephone number, useful only to others; but what I tell myself is wrong, it does matter. I keep the knowledge of this name like something hidden, some treasure I'll come back to dig up, one day. I think of this name as buried. This name has an aura around it, like an amulet, some charm that's survived from an unimaginably distant past. I lie in my single bed at night, with my eyes closed, and the name floats there behind my eyes, not quite within reach, shining in the dark.

It's a Saturday morning in September, I'm wearing my shining name. The little girl who is now dead sits in the back seat, with her two best dolls, her stuffed rabbit, mangy with age and love. I know all the details. They are sentimental details but I can't help that. I can't think about the rabbit too much though, I can't start to cry, here on the Chinese rug, breathing in the smoke that has been inside Serena's body. Not here, not now, I can do that later.

She thought we were going on a picnic, and in fact there is a picnic basket on the back seat, beside her, with real food in it, hard-boiled eggs, thermos and all. We didn't want her to know where we were really going, we didn't want her to tell, by mistake, reveal anything, if we were stopped. We didn't want to lay upon her the burden of our truth.

I wore my hiking boots, she had on her sneakers. The laces of the sneakers had a design of hearts on them, red, purple, pink, and yellow. It was warm for the time of year, the leaves were turning already, some of them; Luke drove, I sat beside him, the sun shone, the sky was blue, the houses as we passed them looked comforting and ordinary, each house as it was left behind vanishing into past time, crumbling in an instant as if it had never been, because I would never see it again, or so I thought then.

We have almost nothing with us, we don't want to look as if we're going anywhere far or permanent. We have the forged passports, guaranteed, worth the price. We couldn't pay in money, of course, or put it on the Compucount: we used other things, some jewellery that was my grandmother's, a stamp collection Luke inherited from his uncle. Such things can be exchanged, for money, in other countries. When we get to the border we'll pretend we're just going over on a day trip; the fake visas are for a day. Before that I'll give her a sleeping pill so she'll be asleep when we cross. That way she won't betray us. You can't expect a child to lie convincingly.

And I don't want her to feel frightened, to feel the fear that is now tightening my muscles, tensing my spine, pulling me so taut that I'm certain I would break if touched. Every stoplight is an ordeal. We'll spend the night at a motel, or, better, sleeping in the car on a sideroad so there will be no suspicious questions. We'll cross in the morning, drive over the bridge, easily, just like driving to the supermarket.

We turn onto the freeway, head north, flowing with not much traffic. Since the war started, gas is expensive and in short supply. Outside the city we pass the first checkpoint.

All they want is a look at the licence, Luke does it well. The licence matches the passport: we thought of that.

Back on the road, he squeezes my hand, glances over at me. You're white as a sheet, he says.

That is how I feel: white, flat, thin. I feel transparent. Surely they will be able to see through me. Worse, how will I be able to hold on to Luke, to her, when I'm so flat, so white? I feel as if there's not much

▷ **1** *the Children of Ham:* black people; cf. Genesis 9:22–27 (due to the mention of slavery, black people were considered by white Americans to be the descendants of Ham) **10** *udder:* Euter **20** *aura* ['ɔːrə]: feeling or a particular quality that is noticeable **21** *charm:* small object (worn on a chain or bracelet) that is supposed to bring good luck **26** *mangy* ['meɪndʒi]: dirty and in a bad condition **43** *crumbling:* (here: as if) breaking into small pieces **46** *forged:* false **56** *taut* [tɑːt]: stretched tight due to anxiety **57** *ordeal:* difficult and unpleasant experience

left of me; they will slip through my arms, as if I'm made of smoke, as if I'm a mirage, fading before their eyes. *Don't think that way*, Moira would say. *Think that way and you'll make it happen*.

Cheer up, says Luke. He's driving a little too fast now. The adrenalin's gone to his head. Now he's singing. Oh what a beautiful morning, he sings.

Even his singing worries me. We've been warned not to look too happy.

CHAPTER 15

The Commander knocks at the door. The knock is prescribed: the sitting room is supposed to be Serena Joy's territory, he's supposed to ask permission to enter it. She likes to keep him waiting. It's a little thing, but in this household little things mean a lot. Tonight, however, she doesn't even get that, because before Serena Joy can speak he steps forward into the room anyway. Maybe he's just forgotten the protocol, but maybe it's deliberate. Who knows what she said to him, over the silver-encrusted dinner table? Or didn't say.

The Commander has on his black uniform, in which he looks like a museum guard. A semi-retired man, genial but wary, killing time. But only at first glance. After that he looks like a midwestern bank president, with his straight neatly brushed silver hair, his sober posture, shoulders a little stooped. And after that there is his moustache, silver also, and after that his chin, which really you can't miss. When you get down as far as the chin he looks like a vodka ad, in a glossy magazine, of times gone by.

His manner is mild, his hands large, with thick fingers and acquisitive thumbs, his blue eyes uncommunicative, falsely innocuous. He looks us over as if taking inventory. One kneeling woman in red, one seated woman in blue, two in green, standing, a solitary man, thin-faced, in the background. He manages to appear puzzled, as if he can't quite remember how we all got in here. As if we are something he inherited, like a Victorian pump organ, and he hasn't figured out what to do with us. What we are worth.

He nods, in the general direction of Serena Joy, who does not make a sound. He crosses to the large leather chair reserved for him, takes the key out of his pocket, fumbles with the ornate brass-bound leather-covered box that stands on the table beside the chair. He inserts the key, opens the box, lifts out the Bible, an ordinary copy, with a black cover and gold-edged pages. The Bible is kept locked up,

▷ **2** *mirage* [mə'rɑːʒ]: Fata Morgana **15** *deliberate* [dɪ'lɪbərət] (adj): on purpose **18** *genial* ['dʒiːnjəl]: friendly • *wary* ['weri]: careful, cautious **20** *sober:* serious **21** *stooped:* bent forward **25–26** *acquisitive* (fml, derog): wanting very much to get sth. **26** *innocuous* (fml): not intending to upset anyone

the way people once kept tea locked up, so the servants wouldn't steal it. It is an incendiary device: who knows what we'd make of it, if we ever got our hands on it? We can be read to from it, by him, but we cannot read. Our heads turn towards him, we are expectant, here comes our bedtime story.

The Commander sits down and crosses his legs, watched by us. The bookmarks are in place. He opens the book. He clears his throat a little, as if embarrassed.

"Could I have a drink of water?" he says to the air. "Please," he adds.

Behind me, one of them, Cora or Rita, leaves her space in the tableau and pads off towards the kitchen. The Commander sits, looking down. The Commander sighs, takes out a pair of reading glasses from his inside jacket pocket, gold rims, slips them on. Now he looks like a shoemaker in an old fairytale book. Is there no end to his disguises, of benevolence?

We watch him: every inch, every flicker.

To be a man, watched by women. It must be entirely strange. To have them watching him all the time. To have them wondering, What's he going to do next? To have them flinch when he moves, even if it's a harmless enough move, to reach for an ashtray perhaps. To have them sizing him up. To have them thinking, he can't do it, he won't do, he'll have to do, this last as if he were a garment, out of style or shoddy, which must nevertheless be put on because there's nothing else available.

To have them putting him on, trying him on, trying him out, while he himself puts them on, like a sock over a foot, onto the stub of himself, his extra, sensitive thumb, his tentacle, his delicate stalked slug's eye, which extrudes, expands, winces, and shrivels back into himself when touched wrongly, grows big again, bulging a little at the tip, travelling forward as if along a leaf, into them, avid for vision. To achieve vision in this way, this journey into a darkness that is composed of women, a woman, who can see in darkness while he himself strains blindly forward.

She watches him from within. We're all watching him. It's one thing we can really do, and it's not for nothing: if he were to falter, fail or die, what would become of us? No wonder he's like a boot, hard on the outside, giving shape to a pulp of tenderfoot. That's just a wish.

I've been watching him for some time and he's given no evidence, of softness.

But watch out, Commander, I tell him in my head. I've got my eye on you. One false move and I'm dead.

Still, it must be hell, to be a man, like that.

It must be just fine.

It must be hell.

It must be very silent.

The water appears, the Commander drinks it. "Thank you," he says. Cora rustles back into place.

The Commander pauses, looking down, scanning the page. He takes his time, as if unconscious of us. He's like a man toying with a steak, behind a restaurant window, pretending not to see the eyes watching him from hungry darkness not three feet from his elbow. We lean towards him a little, iron filings to his magnet. He has something we don't have, he has the word. How we squandered it, once.

The Commander, as if reluctantly, begins to read. He isn't very good at it. Maybe he's merely bored.

It's the usual story, the usual stories. God to Adam, God to Noah. *Be fruitful, and multiply, and replenish the earth*. Then comes the moldy old Rachel and Leah stuff we had drummed into us at the Center. *Give me children, or else I die. Am I in God's stead, who hath withheld from thee the fruit of the womb? Behold my maid Bilhah. She shall bear upon my knees, that I may also have children by her.* And so on and so forth. We had it read to us every breakfast, as we sat in the high-school cafeteria, eating porridge with cream and brown sugar. You're getting the best, you know, said Aunt

▷ **2** *incendiary device:* sth. that could cause a fire **12** *tableau:* a kind of living picture or scene • *pad off:* walk away with quiet steps **16** *disguise:* change of appearance so that people do not recognize you • *benevolence* [-'---]: kind, helpful, generous attitude and behavior **20** *flinch:* make a sudden movement with your face or body because of surprise, fear or pain **22** *size sb. up* (infml): form a judgement or opinion about sb. **23** *garment* (fml): piece of clothing • *shoddy:* not in good condition **27** *stub:* Stummel, Stumpf **28–29** *stalked slug's eye:* Stielauge einer Nacktschnecke **29** *wince:* zusammenzucken **36** *falter:* become weak or less effective **53** *iron filings:* Eisenspäne **54** *squander sth.:* waste sth. **58** *be fruitful … the earth:* reference to Genesis 9:1 **59** *moldy:* (here) boring because it is well-known **60–63** *Give me … by her:* reference to Genesis 30:1–3

Lydia. There's a war on, things are rationed. You are spoiled girls, she twinkled, as if rebuking a kitten. Naughty puss.

For lunch it was the Beatitudes. Blessed be this, blessed be that. They played it from a disc, the voice was a man's. *Blessed be the poor in spirit, for theirs is the kingdom of heaven. Blessed are the merciful. Blessed are the meek. Blessed are the silent.* I knew they made that up, I knew it was wrong, and they left things out too, but there was no way of checking. *Blessed be those that mourn, for they shall be comforted.*

Nobody said when.

I check the clock, during dessert, canned pears with cinnamon, standard for lunch, and look for Moira in her place, two tables over. She's gone already. I put my hand up, I am excused. We don't do this too often, and always at different times of day.

In the washroom I go to the second-last stall, as usual.

Are you there? I whisper.

Large as life and twice as ugly, Moira whispers back.

What have you heard? I ask her.

Nothing much. I've got to get out of here, I'm going bats.

I feel panic. No, no, Moira, I say, don't try it. Not on your own.

I'll fake sick. They send an ambulance, I've seen it.

You'll only get as far as the hospital.

At least it'll be a change. I won't have to listen to that old bitch.

They'll find you out.

Not to worry, I'm good at it. When I was a kid in high school I cut out vitamin C, I got scurvy. In the early stages they can't diagnose it. Then you just start it again and you're fine. I'll hide my vitamin pills.

Moira, don't.

I couldn't stand the thought of her not being here, with me.

For me.

They send two guys with you, in the ambulance. Think about it. They must be starved for it, shit, they aren't even allowed to put their hands in their pockets, the possibilities are –

You in there. Time's up, said the voice of Aunt Elizabeth, from the doorway. I stood up, flushed the toilet. Two of Moira's fingers appeared, through the hole in the wall. It was only large enough for two fingers. I touched my own fingers to them, quickly, held on. Let go.

*

"And Leah said, God hath given me my hire, because I have given my maiden to my husband," says the Commander. He lets the book fall closed. It makes an exhausted sound, like a padded door shutting, by itself, at a distance: a puff of air. The sound suggests the softness of the thin oniony pages, how they would feel under the fingers. Soft and dry, like *papier poudre*, pink and powdery, from the time before, you'd get it in booklets for taking the shine off your nose, in those stores that sold candles and soap in the shapes of things: seashells, mushrooms. Like cigarette paper. Like petals.

The Commander sits with his eyes closed for a moment, as if tired. He works long hours. He has a lot of responsibilities.

Serena has begun to cry. I can hear her, behind my back. It isn't the first time. She always does this, the night of the Ceremony. She's trying not to make a noise. She's trying to preserve her dignity, in front of us. The upholstery and the rugs muffle her but we can hear her clearly despite that. The tension between her lack of control and her attempt to suppress it is horrible. It's like a fart in church. I feel, as always, the urge to laugh, but not because I think it's funny. The smell of her crying spreads over us and we pretend to ignore it.

The Commander opens his eyes, notices, frowns, ceases to notice. "Now we will have a moment of silent prayer," says the Commander. "We will ask for a blessing, and for success in all our ventures."

I bow my head and close my eyes. I listen to the held breath, the almost inaudible gasps, the shaking going on behind my back. How she must hate me, I think.

I pray silently: *Nolite te bastardes carborundorum*. I don't know what it means, but it sounds right, and it will have to do, because I don't know what else I can say to God. Not right now. Not, as they used to say, at this juncture. The scratched writing on my cupboard wall floats before me, left by an unknown woman, with the face of Moira. I saw her go out, to the ambulance, on a stretcher, carried by two Angels.

▷ **3** *the Beatitudes:* reference to Matthew 5:3–11 **19** *go bats* (sl): go mad **21** *fake sth.* (infml): pretend sth. **26** *scurvy:* disease caused by a lack of vitamin C **38–39** *And Leah said …:* reference to Genesis 30:18 **38** *hire:* reward **59** *venture:* project, activity **66** *at this juncture* (fml): at this time

What is it? I mouthed to the woman beside me; safe enough, a question like that, to all but a fanatic.

A fever, she formed with her lips. Appendicitis, they say.

I was having dinner, that evening, hamburger balls and hashed browns. My table was near the window, I could see out, as far as the front gates. I saw the ambulance come back, no siren this time. One of the Angels jumped out, talked with the guard. The guard went into the building; the ambulance stayed parked; the Angel stood with his back towards us, as they had been taught to do. Two of the Aunts came out of the building, with the guard. They went around to the back. They hauled Moira out, dragged her in through the gate and up the front steps, holding her under the armpits, one on each side. She was having trouble walking. I stopped eating, I couldn't eat; by this time all of us on my side of the table were staring out the window. The window was greenish, with that chickenwire mesh they used to put inside glass. Aunt Lydia said, Eat your dinner. She went over and pulled down the blind.

They took her into a room that used to be the Science Lab. It was a room where none of us ever went willingly. Afterwards she could not walk for a week, her feet would not fit into her shoes, they were too swollen. It was the feet they'd do, for a first offence. They used steel cables, frayed at the ends. After that the hands. They didn't care what they did to your feet and hands, even if it was permanent. Remember, said Aunt Lydia. For our purposes your feet and your hands are not essential.

Moira lay on her bed, an example. She shouldn't have tried it, not with the Angels, Alma said, from the next bed over. We had to carry her to classes. We stole extra paper packets of sugar for her, from the cafeteria at mealtimes, smuggled them to her, at night, handing them from bed to bed. Probably she didn't need the sugar but it was the only thing we could find to steal. To give.

I am still praying but what I am seeing is Moira's feet, the way they looked after they'd brought her back. Her feet did not look like feet at all. They looked like drowned feet, swollen and boneless, except for the color. They looked like lungs.

Oh God, I pray. *Nolite te bastardes carborundorum.*

Is this what you had in mind?

*

The Commander clears his throat. This is what he does to let us know that in his opinion it's time we stopped praying. "For the eyes of the Lord run to and fro throughout the whole earth, to know himself strong in the behalf of them whose heart is perfect towards him," he says.

It's the sign-off. He stands up. We are dismissed.

▷ **4–5** *hashed browns* (AE): fried potatoes and onions **21** *offence:* act of breaking a rule or law **22** *frayed:* coming apart **38** *clear your throat:* cough so that you can speak clearly or draw attention **39–41** *For the eyes … towards him:* reference to II Chronicles 16:9 **43** *be dismissed:* be told to leave

CHAPTER 16

The Ceremony goes as usual.

I lie on my back, fully clothed except for the healthy white cotton underdrawers. What I could see, if I were to open my eyes, would be the large white canopy of Serena Joy's outsized colonial-style four-poster bed, suspended like a sagging cloud above us, a cloud sprigged with tiny drops of silver rain, which, if you looked at them closely, would turn out to be four-petalled flowers. I would not see the carpet, which is white, or the sprigged curtains and skirted dressing table with its silver-backed brush and mirror set; only the canopy, which manages to suggest at one and the same time, by the gauziness of its fabric and its heavy downward curve, both ethereality and matter.

Or the sail of a ship. Big-bellied sails, they used to say, in poems. Bellying. Propelled forward by a swollen belly.

A mist of Lily of the Valley surrounds us, chilly, crisp almost. It's not warm in this room.

Above me, towards the head of the bed, Serena Joy is arranged, outspread. Her legs are apart, I lie between them, my head on her stomach, her pubic bone under the base of my skull, her thighs on either side of me. She too is fully clothed.

My arms are raised; she holds my hands, each of mine in each of hers. This is supposed to signify that we are one flesh, one being. What it really means is that she is in control, of the process and thus of the product. If any. The rings of her left hand cut into my fingers. It may or may not be revenge.

My red skirt is hitched up to my waist, though no higher. Below it the Commander is fucking. What he is fucking is the lower part of my body. I do not say making love, because this is not what he's doing. Copulating too would be inaccurate, because it would imply two people and only one is involved.

Nor does rape cover it: nothing is going on here that I haven't signed up for. There wasn't a lot of choice but there was some, and this is what I chose.

Therefore I lie still and picture the unseen canopy over my head. I remember Queen Victoria's advice to her daughter. *Close your eyes and think of England.* But this is not England. I wish he would hurry up.

Maybe I'm crazy and this is some new kind of therapy.

I wish it were true; then I could get better and this would go away.

Serena Joy grips my hands as if it is she, not I, who's being fucked, as if she finds it either pleasurable or painful, and the Commander fucks, with a regular two-four marching stroke, on and on like a tap dripping. He is preoccupied, like a man humming to himself in the shower without knowing he's humming; like a man who has other things on his mind. It's as if he's somewhere else, waiting for himself to come, drumming his fingers on the table while he waits. There's an impatience in his rhythm now. But isn't this everyone's wet dream, two women at once? They used to say that. Exciting, they used to say.

What's going on in this room, under Serena Joy's silvery canopy, is not exciting. It has nothing to do with passion or love or romance or any of those other notions we used to titillate ourselves with. It has nothing to do with sexual desire, at least for me, and certainly not for Serena. Arousal and orgasm are no longer thought necessary; they would be a symptom of frivolity merely, like jazz garters or beauty spots: superfluous distractions for the light-minded. Outdated. It seems odd that women once spent such time and energy reading about such things, thinking about them, worrying about them, writing about them. They are so obviously recreational.

This is not recreation, even for the Commander. This is serious business. The Commander, too, is doing his duty.

If I were to open my eyes a slit, I would be able to see him, his not-unpleasant face hanging over my torso, with a few strands of his silver hair falling perhaps over his forehead, intent on his inner journey, that place he is hurrying towards, which recedes as in a dream at the same speed with which he approaches it. I would see his open eyes.

If he were better looking would I enjoy this more?

At least he's an improvement on the previous one, who smelled like a church cloakroom in the rain; like your mouth when the dentist starts picking at your teeth; like a nostril. The Commander, instead,

▷ **3** *underdrawers:* underwear **4** *canopy:* cover that is fixed above a bed **6** *sprigged:* decorated with patterns of leaves or flowers **11** *gauziness:* lightness **11–12** *ethereality and matter:* the spiritual and the physical **15** *mist:* Nebel **51** *titillate sb.:* excite sb. **53** *arousal:* sexual excitement **54** *jazz garter:* Strumpfband

smells of mothballs, or is this odor some punitive form of aftershave? Why does he have to wear that stupid uniform? But would I like his white, tufted raw body any better?

Kissing is forbidden between us. This makes it bearable.

One detaches oneself. One describes.

He comes at last, with a stifled groan as of relief. Serena Joy, who has been holding her breath, expels it. The Commander, who has been propping himself on his elbows, away from our combined bodies, doesn't permit himself to sink down into us. He rests a moment, withdraws, recedes, rezippers. He nods, then turns and leaves the room, closing the door with exaggerated care behind him, as if both of us are his ailing mother. There's something hilarious about this, but I don't dare laugh.

Serena Joy lets go of my hands. "You can get up now," she says. "Get up and get out." She's supposed to have me rest, for ten minutes, with my feet on a pillow to improve the chances. This is meant to be a time of silent meditation for her, but she's not in the mood for that. There is loathing in her voice, as if the touch of my flesh sickens and contaminates her. I untangle myself from her body, stand up; the juice of the Commander runs down my legs. Before I turn away I see her straighten her blue skirt, clench her legs together; she continues lying on the bed, gazing up at the canopy above her, stiff and straight as an effigy.

Which of us is it worse for, her or me?

CHAPTER 17

This is what I do when I'm back in my room:

I take off my clothes and put on my nightgown.

I look for the pat of butter, in the toe of my right shoe, where I hid it after dinner. The cupboard was too warm, the butter is semi-liquid. Much of it has sunk into the paper napkin I wrapped it in. Now I'll have butter in my shoe. Not the first time, because whenever there is butter or even margarine, I save some in this way. I can get most of the butter off the shoe lining, with a washcloth or some toilet paper from the bathroom, tomorrow.

I rub the butter over my face, work it into the skin of my hands. There's no longer any hand lotion or face cream, not for us. Such things are considered vanities. We are containers, it's only the insides of our bodies that are important. The outside can become hard and wrinkled, for all they care, like the shell of a nut. This was a decree of the Wives, this absence of hand lotion. They don't want us to look attractive. For them, things are bad enough as it is.

The butter is a trick I learned at the Rachel and Leah Center. The Red Center, we called it, because there was so much red. My predecessor in this room, my friend with the freckles and the good laugh, must have done this too, this buttering. We all do it.

As long as we do this, butter our skin to keep it soft, we can believe that we will some day get out, that we will be touched again, in love or desire. We have ceremonies of our own, private ones.

The butter is greasy and it will go rancid and I will smell like an old cheese; but at least it's organic, as they used to say.

To such devices have we descended.

Buttered, I lie on my single bed, flat, like a piece of toast. I can't sleep. In the semi-dark I stare up at the blind plaster eye in the middle of the

▷ **1** *punitive* (fml): intended as a punishment **3** *tufted:* hairy **6** *stifle sth.* ['staɪfəl]: etwas unterdrücken, ersticken **10** *rezipper:* (here) den Reißverschluss wieder zumachen **12** *ailing* ['eɪlɪŋ]: ill • *hilarious:* extremely funny **18** *loathing* (n): strong feeling of hatred **23** *effigy:* statue of a saint or god **36** *vanity:* Eitelkeit **38** *decree:* official order

ceiling, which stares back down at me, even though it can't see. There's no breeze, my white curtains are like gauze bandages, hanging limp, glimmering in the aura cast by the searchlight that illuminates this house at night, or is there a moon?

I fold back the sheet, get carefully up, on silent bare feet, in my nightgown, go to the window, like a child, I want to see. The moon on the breast of the new-fallen snow. The sky is clear but hard to make out, because of the searchlight; but yes, in the obscured sky a moon does float, newly, a wishing moon, a sliver of ancient rock, a goddess, a wink. The moon is a stone and the sky is full of deadly hardware, but oh God, how beautiful anyway.

I want Luke here so badly. I want to be held and told my name. I want to be valued, in ways that I am not; I want to be more than valuable. I repeat my former name, remind myself of what I once could do, how others saw me.

I want to steal something.

In the hall the nightlight's on, the long space glows gently pink; I walk, one foot set carefully down, then the other, without creaking, along the runner, as if on a forest floor, sneaking, my heart quick, through the night house. I am out of place. This is entirely illegal.

Down past the fisheye on the hall wall, I can see my white shape, of tented body, hair down my back like a mane, my eyes gleaming. I like this. I am doing something, on my own. The active, is it a tense? Tensed. What I would like to steal is a knife, from the kitchen, but I'm not ready for that.

I reach the sitting room, door's ajar, slip in, leave the door a little open. A squeak of wood, but who's near enough to hear? I stand in the room, letting the pupils of my eyes dilate, like a cat's or owl's. Old perfume, cloth dust fill my nostrils. There's a slight mist of light, coming through the cracks around the closed drapes, from the searchlight outside, where two men doubtless patrol, I've seen them, from above, from behind my curtains, dark shapes, cutouts. Now I can see outlines, gleams: from the mirror, the bases of the lamps, the vases, the sofa looming like a cloud at dusk.

What should I take? Something that will not be missed. In the wood at midnight, a magic flower. A withered daffodil, not one from the dried arrangement. The daffodils will soon be thrown out, they're beginning to smell. Along with Serena's stale fumes, the stench of her knitting.

I grope, find an end table, feel. There's a clink, I must have knocked something. I find the daffodils, crisp at the edges where they've dried, limp towards the stems, use my fingers to pinch. I will press this, somewhere. Under the mattress. Leave it there, for the next woman, the one who comes after me, to find.

But there's someone in the room, behind me.

I hear the step, quiet as mine, the creaking of the same floorboard. The door closes behind me, with a little click, cutting the light. I freeze: white was a mistake. I'm snow in moonlight, even in the dark.

Then a whisper: "Don't scream. It's all right."

As if I'd scream, as if it's all right. I turn: a shape, that's all, dull glint of cheekbone, devoid of color.

He steps towards me. Nick.

"What are you doing in here?"

I don't answer. He too is illegal, here, with me, he can't give me away. Nor I him; for the moment we're mirrors. He puts his hand on my arm, pulls me against him, his mouth on mine, what else comes from such denial? Without a word. Both of us shaking, how I'd like to. In Serena's parlor, with the dried flowers, on the Chinese carpet, his thin body. A man entirely unknown. It would be like shouting, it would be like shooting someone. My hand goes down, how about that, I could unbutton, and then. But it's too dangerous, he knows it, we push each other away, not far. Too much trust, too much risk, too much already.

"I was coming to find you," he says, breathes, almost into my ear. I want to reach up, taste his skin, he makes me hungry. His fingers move, feeling my arm under the nightgown sleeve, as if his hand won't listen to reason. It's so good, to be touched by someone, to be felt so greedily, to feel so greedy. Luke, you'd know, you'd understand. It's you here, in another body.

Bullshit.

"Why?" I say. Is it so bad, for him, that he'd take the risk of coming to my room at night? I think of the hanged men, hooked on the Wall.

▷ **3** *limp:* loose **9** *sliver* ['slɪvər]: a small or thin piece of sth. **28** *dilate:* become wide **34** *loom:* appear as a large unclear shape **38** *stale:* old and unpleasant • *stench:* strong, unpleasant smell **68** *greedy:* wanting more of sth. than you really need

I can hardly stand up. I have to get away, back to the stairs, before I dissolve entirely. His hand's on my shoulder now, held still, heavy, pressing down on me like warm lead. Is this what I would die for? I'm a coward, I hate the thought of pain.

"He told me to," Nick says. "He wants to see you. In his office."

"What do you mean?" I say. The Commander, it must be. See me? What does he mean by *see*? Hasn't he had enough of me?

"Tomorrow," he says, just audible. In the dark parlor we move away from each other, slowly, as if pulled towards each other by a force, current, pulled apart also by hands equally strong.

I find the door, turn the knob, fingers on cool porcelain, open. It's all I can do.

▷ **2** *dissolve* [dɪ'zɑːlv]: melt, fall to pieces **3** *lead* [led]: Blei **4** *coward:* person who is not brave or does not have the courage to do sth. **8** *audible:* that can be heard clearly

VII

Night

CHAPTER 18

I lie in bed, still trembling. You can wet the rim of a glass and run your finger around the rim and it will make a sound. This is what I feel like: this sound of glass. I feel like the word *shatter*. I want to be with someone.

Lying in bed, with Luke, his hand on my rounded belly. The three of us, in bed, she kicking, turning over within me. Thunderstorm outside the window, that's why she's awake, they can hear, they sleep, they can be startled, even there in the soothing of the heart, like waves on the shore around them. A flash of lightning, quite close, Luke's eyes go white for an instant.

I'm not frightened. We're wide awake, the rain hits now, we will be slow and careful.

If I thought this would never happen again I would die.

But this is wrong, nobody dies from lack of sex. It's lack of love we die from. There's nobody here I can love, all the people I could love are dead or elsewhere. Who knows where they are or what their names are now? They might as well be nowhere, as I am for them. I too am a missing person.

From time to time I can see their faces, against the dark, flickering like the images of saints, in old foreign cathedrals, in the light of the drafty candles; candles you would light to pray by, kneeling, your forehead against the wooden railing, hoping for an answer. I can conjure them but they are mirages only, they don't last. Can I be blamed for wanting a real body, to put my arms around? Without it I too am disembodied. I can listen to my own heartbeat against the bedsprings, I can stroke myself, under the dry white sheets, in the dark, but I too am dry and white, hard, granular; it's like running my hand over a plateful of dried rice; it's like snow. There's something dead about it, something deserted. I am like a room where things

▷ **3** *shatter:* destroy completely **8** *startled:* surprised and slightly shocked or frightened • *soothing* (n): act of calming sth. **21** *drafty:* zugig **23** *conjure sth.* ['kɑːndʒər]: make sth. appear as a picture in your mind **25** *disembodied:* separate from the body

once happened and now nothing does, except the pollen of the weeds that grow up outside the window, blowing in as dust across the floor.

Here is what I believe.

I believe Luke is lying face down in a thicket, a tangle of bracken, the brown fronds from last year under the green ones just unrolled, or ground hemlock perhaps, although it's too early for the red berries. What is left of him: his hair, the bones, the plaid wool shirt, green and black, the leather belt, the workboots. I know exactly what he was wearing. I can see his clothes in my mind, bright as a lithograph or a full-color advertisement, from an ancient magazine, though not his face, not so well. His face is beginning to fade, possibly because it wasn't always the same: his face had different expressions, his clothes did not.

I pray that the hole, or two or three, there was more than one shot, they were close together, I pray that at least one hole is neatly, quickly, and finally through the skull, through the place where all the pictures were, so that there would have been only the one flash, of darkness or pain, dull I hope, like the word thud, only the one and then silence.

I believe this.

I also believe that Luke is sitting up, in a rectangle somewhere, gray cement, on a ledge or the edge of something, a bed or chair. God knows what he's wearing. God knows what they've put him in. God isn't the only one who knows, so maybe there could be some way of finding out. He hasn't shaved for a year, though they cut his hair short, whenever they feel like it, for lice they say. I'll have to revise that: if they cut the hair for lice, they'd cut the beard too. You'd think.

Anyway, they don't do it well, the hair is ragged, the back of his neck is nicked, that's hardly the worst, he looks ten years older, twenty, he's bent like an old man, his eyes are pouched, small purple veins have burst in his cheeks, there's a scar, no, a wound, it isn't yet healed, the color of tulips, near the stem end, down the left side of his face where the flesh split recently. The body is so easily damaged, so easily disposed of, water and chemicals is all it is, hardly more to it than a jellyfish, drying on sand.

He finds it painful to move his hands, painful to move. He doesn't know what he's accused of. A problem. There must be something, some accusation. Otherwise why are they keeping him, why isn't he already dead? He must know something they want to know. I can't imagine. I can't imagine he hasn't already said whatever it is. I would.

He is surrounded by a smell, his own, the smell of a cooped-up animal in a dirty cage. I imagine him resting, because I can't bear to imagine him at any other time, just as I can't imagine anything below his collar, above his cuffs. I don't want to think what they've done to his body. Does he have shoes? No, and the floor is cold and wet. Does he know I'm here, alive, that I'm thinking about him? I have to believe so. In reduced circumstances you have to believe all kinds of things. I believe in thought transference now, vibrations in the ether, that sort of junk. I never used to.

I also believe that they didn't catch him or catch up with him after all, that he made it, reached the bank, swam the river, crossed the border, dragged himself up on the far shore, an island, teeth chattering; found his way to a nearby farmhouse, was allowed in, with suspicion at first, but then when they understood who he was, they were friendly, not the sort who would turn him in, perhaps they were Quakers, they will smuggle him inland, from house to house, the woman made him some hot coffee and gave him a set of her husband's clothes. I picture the clothes. It comforts me to dress him warmly.

He made contact with the others, there must be a resistance, a government in exile. Someone must be out there, taking care of things. I believe in the resistance as I believe there can be no light without shadow; or rather, no shadow unless there is also light. There must be a resistance, or where do all the criminals come from, on the television?

Any day now there may be a message from him. It will come in the most unexpected way, from the least likely person, someone I never would have suspected. Under my plate, on the dinner tray? Slipped into my hand as I reach the tokens across the counter in All Flesh?

The message will say that I must have patience: sooner or later he will get me out, we will find her, wherever they've put her. She'll

▷ **4** *thicket:* group of bushes or small trees growing closely together **6** *ground hemlock:* Kanadische Eibe **7** *plaid* [plæd]: kariert **9** *lithograph:* print done from a metal plate **20** *rectangle:* Rechteck **21** *ledge:* Sims; Felsvorsprung **28** *nicked:* cut **29** *pouched:* having "bags" of skin under the eyes **34** *jellyfish:* Qualle **46** *reduced cirumstances:* (here) a difficult situation in which you do not have much **47** *thought transference:* Gedankenübertragung **65** *the least likely person:* die unwahrscheinlichste Person

remember us and we will be all three of us together. Meanwhile I must endure, keep myself safe for later. What has happened to me, what's happening to me now won't make any difference to him, he loves me anyway, he knows it isn't my fault. The message will say that also. It's this message, which may never arrive, that keeps me alive. I believe in the message.

The things I believe can't all be true, though one of them must be. But I believe in all of them, all three versions of Luke, at one and the same time. This contradictory way of believing seems to me, right now, the only way I can believe anything. Whatever the truth is, I will be ready for it.

This also is a belief of mine. This also may be untrue.

One of the gravestones in the cemetery near the earliest church has an anchor on it and an hourglass, and the words: *In Hope.*

In Hope. Why did they put that above a dead person? Was it the corpse hoping, or those still alive?

Does Luke hope?

VIII

Birth Day

CHAPTER 19

I'm dreaming that I am awake.

I dream that I get out of bed and walk across the room, not this room, and go out the door, not this door. I'm at home, one of my homes, and she's running to meet me, in her small green nightgown with the sunflower on the front, her feet bare, and I pick her up and feel her arms and legs go around me and I begin to cry, because I know then that I'm not awake. I'm back in this bed, trying to wake up, and I wake up and sit on the edge of the bed, and my mother comes in with a tray and asks me if I'm feeling better. When I was sick, as a child, she had to stay home from work. But I'm not awake this time either.

After these dreams I do awake, and I know I'm really awake because there is the wreath, on the ceiling, and my curtains hanging like drowned white hair. I feel drugged. I consider this: maybe they're drugging me. Maybe the life I think I'm living is a paranoid delusion.

Not a hope. I know where I am, and who, and what day it is. These are the tests, and I am sane. Sanity is a valuable possession; I hoard it the way people once hoarded money. I save it, so I will have enough, when the time comes.

Grayness comes through the curtains, hazy bright, not much sun today. I get out of bed, go to the window, kneel on the window seat, the hard little cushion, FAITH, and look out. There is nothing to be seen.

I wonder what has become of the other two cushions. There must have been three, once. HOPE and CHARITY, where have they been stowed? Serena Joy has tidy habits. She wouldn't throw away anything not quite worn out. One for Rita, one for Cora?

The bell goes, I'm up before it, ahead of time. I dress, not looking down.

I sit in the chair and think about the word *chair*. It can also mean the leader of a meeting. It can also mean a mode of execution. It is the first

▷ **17** *hoard sth.:* collect and keep sth. secretly

syllable in *charity*. It is the French word for flesh. None of these facts has any connection with the others.

These are the kinds of litanies I use, to compose myself.

In front of me is a tray, and on the tray are a glass of apple juice, a vitamin pill, a spoon, a plate with three slices of brown toast on it, a small dish containing honey, and another plate with an egg-cup on it, the kind that looks like a woman's torso, in a skirt. Under the skirt is the second egg, being kept warm. The egg-cup is white china with a blue stripe.

The first egg is white. I move the egg-cup a little, so it's now in the watery sunlight that comes through the window and falls, brightening, waning, brightening again, on the tray. The shell of the egg is smooth but also grained; small pebbles of calcium are defined by the sunlight, like craters on the moon. It's a barren landscape, yet perfect; it's the sort of desert the saints went into, so their minds would not be distracted by profusion. I think that this is what God must look like: an egg. The life of the moon may not be on the surface, but inside.

The egg is glowing now, as if it had an energy of its own. To look at the egg gives me intense pleasure.

The sun goes and the egg fades.

I pick the egg out of the cup and finger it for a moment. It's warm. Women used to carry such eggs between their breasts, to incubate them. That would have felt good.

The minimalist life. Pleasure is an egg. Blessings that can be counted, on the fingers of one hand. But possibly this is how I am expected to react. If I have an egg, what more can I want?

In reduced circumstances the desire to live attaches itself to strange objects. I would like a pet: a bird, say, or a cat. A familiar. Anything at all familiar. A rat would do, in a pinch, but there's no chance of that. This house is too clean.

I slice the top off the egg with the spoon, and eat the contents.

While I'm eating the second egg, I hear the siren, at a great distance at first, winding its way towards me among the large houses and clipped lawns, a thin sound like the hum of an insect; then nearing, opening out, like a flower of sound opening, into a trumpet. A proclamation, this siren. I put down my spoon, my heart speeds up, I go to the window again: will it be blue and not for me? But I see it turn the corner, come along the street, stop in front of the house, still blaring, and it's red. Joy to the world, rare enough these days. I leave the second egg half eaten, hurry to the closet for my cloak, and already I can hear feet on the stairs and the voices calling.

"Hurry," says Cora, "won't wait all day," and she helps me on with the cloak, she's actually smiling.

I almost run down the hall, the stairs are like skiing, the front door is wide, today I can go through it, and the Guardian stands there saluting. It's started to rain, a drizzle, and the gravid smell of earth and grass fills the air.

The red Birthmobile is parked in the driveway. Its back door is open and I clamber in. The carpet on the floor is red, red curtains are drawn over the windows. There are three women in here already, sitting on the benches that run the length of the van on either side. The Guardian closes and locks the double doors and climbs into the front, beside the driver; through the glassed-over wire grill we can see the backs of their heads. We start with a lurch, while overhead the siren screams: *Make way, make way!*

"Who is it?" I say to the woman next to me; into her ear, or where her ear must be under the white headdress. I almost have to shout, the noise is so loud.

"Ofwarren," she shouts back. Impulsively she grabs my hand, squeezes it, as we lurch around the corner; she turns to me and I see her face, there are tears running down her cheeks, but tears of what? Envy, disappointment? But no, she's laughing, she throws her arms around me, I've never seen her before, she hugs me, she has large breasts, under the red habit, she wipes her sleeve across her face. On this day we can do anything we want.

I revise that: within limits.

Across from us on the other bench, one woman is praying, eyes closed, hands up to her mouth. Or she may not be praying. She may be biting her thumbnails. Possibly she's trying to keep calm. The third woman is calm already. She sits with her arms folded, smiling a little. The siren goes on and on. That used to be the sound of death, for

▷ **3** *litany:* a series of prayers in which there are many repetitions of phrases, etc. **12** *wane:* become weaker **16** *profusion* (fml): a very large quantity of sth. **29** *in a pinch:* in a particularly difficult situation **39** *joy to the world:* reference to the religious song "Joy to the world, the Lord is come" **46** *gravid* (fml): pregnant **54** *lurch:* sudden movement **66** *revise sth.:* change what you have said about sth.

ambulances or fires. Possibly it will be the sound of death today also. We will soon know. What will Ofwarren give birth to? A baby, as we all hope? Or something else, an Unbaby, with a pinhead or a snout like a dog's, or two bodies, or a hole in its heart or no arms, or webbed hands and feet? There's no telling. They could tell once, with machines, but that is now outlawed. What would be the point of knowing, anyway? You can't have them taken out; whatever it is must be carried to term.

The chances are one in four, we learned that at the Center. The air got too full, once, of chemicals, rays, radiation, the water swarmed with toxic molecules, all of that takes years to clean up, and meanwhile they creep into your body, camp out in your fatty cells. Who knows, your very flesh may be polluted, dirty as an oily beach, sure death to shore birds and unborn babies. Maybe a vulture would die of eating you. Maybe you light up in the dark, like an old-fashioned watch. Deathwatch. That's a kind of beetle, it buries carrion.

I can't think of myself, my body, sometimes, without seeing the skeleton: how I must appear to an electron. A cradle of life, made of bones; and within, hazards, warped proteins, bad crystals jagged as glass. Women took medicines, pills, men sprayed trees, cows ate grass, all that souped-up piss flowed into the rivers. Not to mention the exploding atomic power plants, along the San Andreas fault, nobody's fault, during the earthquakes, and the mutant strain of syphilis no mold could touch. Some did it themselves, had themselves tied shut with catgut or scarred with chemicals. How could they, said Aunt Lydia, oh how could they have done such a thing? Jezebels! Scorning God's gifts! Wringing her hands.

It's a risk you're taking, said Aunt Lydia, but you are the shock troops, you will march out in advance, into dangerous territory. The greater the risk the greater the glory. She clasped her hands, radiant with our phony courage. We looked down at the tops of our desks. To go through all that and give birth to a shredder: it wasn't a fine thought. We didn't know exactly what would happen to the babies that didn't get passed, that were declared Unbabies. But we knew they were put somewhere, quickly, away.

There was no one cause, says Aunt Lydia. She stands at the front of the room, in her khaki dress, a pointer in her hand. Pulled down in front of the blackboard, where once there would have been a map, is a graph, showing the birth ratc pcr thousand, for years and years: a slippery slope, down past the zero line of replacement, and down and down.

Of course, some women believed there would be no future, they thought the world would explode. That was the excuse they used, says Aunt Lydia. They said there was no sense in breeding. Aunt Lydia's nostrils narrow: such wickedness. They were lazy women, she says. They were sluts.

On the top of my desk there are initials, carved into the wood, and dates. The initials are sometimes in two sets, joined by the word *loves*. *J.H. loves B.P. 1954. O.R. loves L.T.* These seem to me like the inscriptions I used to read about, carved on the stone walls of caves, or drawn with a mixture of soot and animal fat. They seem to me incredibly ancient. The desk top is of blonde wood; it slants down, and there is an armrest on the right side, to lean on when you were writing, on paper, with a pen. Inside the desk you could keep things: books, notebooks. These habits of former times appear to me now lavish, decadent almost; immoral, like the orgies of barbarian regimes. *M. loves G., 1972.* This carving, done with a pencil dug many times into the worn varnish of the desk, has the pathos of all vanished civilizations. It's like a handprint on stone. Whoever made that was once alive.

There are no dates after the mid-eighties. This must have been one of the schools that was closed down then, for lack of children.

They made mistakes, says Aunt Lydia. We don't intend to repeat them. Her voice is pious, condescending, the voice of those whose duty it is to tell us unpleasant things for our own good. I would like to strangle her. I shove this thought away almost as soon as I think it.

A thing is valued, she says, only if it is rare and hard to get. We want you to be valued, girls. She is rich in pauses, which she savors in her

▷ **3** *pinhead:* Stecknadelkopf **5** *there's no telling:* it is impossible to know what will happen **8** *carry sth. to term:* carry sth. (esp. a baby) to the end of pregnancy **14** *vulture:* Geier **16** *carrion:* the decaying flesh of dead animals **24** *mold:* (here) penicillin **25** *catgut:* Darmsaite • *scar sth.:* cause a permanent wound to sth. **27** *Jezebel:* evil woman (reference to I Kings 18:4–13 and II Kings 9:29–37) • *wring your hands:* hold your hands together and twist and squeeze them to show that you are anxious or upset **32** *shredder:* (hier) etwas für den Reißwolf **45** *slut* (sl): Schlampe **50** *soot:* black powder that is produced when wood or coal is burned **55** *lavish:* extravagant **63** *condescending:* herablassend **65** *strangle sb.:* jdn. erdrosseln **67** *savor sth.:* enjoy the feeling of sth.

mouth. Think of yourselves as pearls. We, sitting in our rows, eyes down, we make her salivate morally. We are hers to define, we must suffer her adjectives.

I think about pearls. Pearls are congealed oyster spit. This is what I will tell Moira, later; if I can.

All of us here will lick you into shape, says Aunt Lydia, with satisfied good cheer.

The van stops, the back doors are opened, the Guardian herds us out. At the front door stands another Guardian, with one of those snubby machine guns slung over his shoulder. We file towards the front door, in the drizzle, the Guardians saluting. The big Emerge van, the one with the machines and the mobile doctors, is parked farther along the circular drive. I see one of the doctors looking out the window of the van. I wonder what they do in there, waiting. Play cards, most likely, or read; some masculine pursuit. Most of the time they aren't needed at all; they're only allowed in if it can't be helped.

It used to be different, they used to be in charge. A shame it was, said Aunt Lydia. Shameful. What she'd just showed us was a film, made in an olden-days hospital: a pregnant woman, wired up to a machine, electrodes coming out of her every which way so that she looked like a broken robot, an intravenous drip feeding into her arm. Some man with a searchlight looking up between her legs, where she'd been shaved, a mere beardless girl, a trayful of bright sterilized knives, everyone with masks on. A co-operative patient. Once they drugged women, induced labor, cut them open, sewed them up. No more. No anaesthetics, even. Aunt Elizabeth said it was better for the baby, but also: *I will greatly multiply thy sorrow and thy conception; in sorrow thou shalt bring forth children.* At lunch we got that, brown bread and lettuce sandwiches.

As I'm going up the steps, wide steps with a stone urn on either side, Ofwarren's Commander must be higher status than ours, I hear another siren. It's the blue Birthmobile, for Wives. That will be Serena Joy, arriving in state. No benches for them, they get real seats, upholstery. They face front and are not curtained off. They know where they're going.

Probably Serena Joy has been here before, to this house, for tea. Probably Ofwarren, formerly that whiny bitch Janine, was paraded out in front of her, her and the other Wives, so they could see her belly, feel it perhaps, and congratulate the Wife. A strong girl, good musclcs. No Agent Orange in her family, we checked the records, you can never be too careful. And perhaps one of the kinder ones: Would you like a cookie, dear?

Oh no, you'll spoil her, too much sugar is bad for them.

Surely one won't hurt, just this once, Mildred.

And sucky Janine: Oh yes, can I Ma'am, please?

Such a, so well behaved, not surly like some of them, do their job and that's that. More like a daughter to you, as you might say. One of the family. Comfortable matronly chuckles. That's all dear, you can go back to your room.

And after she's gone: Little whores, all of them, but still, you can't be choosy. You take what they hand out, right, girls? That from the Commander's Wife.

Oh, but you've been so *lucky*. Some of them, why, they aren't even clean. And won't give you a smile, mope in their rooms, don't wash their hair, the *smell*. I have to get the Marthas to do it, almost have to hold her down in the bathtub, you practically have to bribe her to get her to take a bath even, you have to threaten her.

I had to take stern measures with mine, and now she doesn't eat her dinner properly; and as for the other thing, not a nibble, and we've been so regular. But yours, she's a credit to you. And any day now, oh, you must be so excited, she's big as a house, I bet you can hardly wait.

More tea? Modestly changing the subject.

I know the sort of thing that goes on.

And Janine, up in her room, what does she do? Sits with the taste of sugar still in her mouth, licking her lips. Stares out the window. Breathes in and out. Caresses her swollen breasts. Thinks of nothing.

▷ **2** *salivate:* seibern **6** *lick sb. into shape:* force sb. to become strong, organized and successful **9** *snubby:* (here) with a short barrel (= Lauf) **15** *pursuit* [pər'suːt]: (here) hobby, way to spend time **25** *induce labor:* make a woman start giving birth to her baby by giving her special drugs **27–28** *I will greatly multiply … children:* reference to Genesis 3:16 **40** *Agent Orange:* chemical used by the US army in the Vietnam War which had a disastrous effect on many babies born later • *the records:* (here) sb.'s past **46** *surly* ['sɜːrli]: bad-tempered and rude **48** *matronly* ['meɪtrənli]: (of a woman) no longer young or attractive • *chuckle:* quiet laughter **54** *mope:* spend your time doing nothing and feeling sorry for yourself **56** *bribe sb.:* give sb. money to make them do sth. **58** *take stern measures:* be very strict

CHAPTER 20

The central staircase is wider than ours, with a curved banister on either side. From above I can hear the chanting of the women who are already there. We go up the stairs, single file, being careful not to step on the trailing hems of each other's dresses. To the left, the double doors to the dining room are folded back, and inside I can see the long table, covered with a white cloth and spread with a buffet: ham, cheese, oranges – they have oranges! – and fresh-baked breads and cakes. As for us, we'll get milk and sandwiches, on a tray, later. But they have a coffee urn, and bottles of wine, for why shouldn't the Wives get a little drunk on such a triumphant day? First they'll wait for the results, then they'll pig out. They're gathered in the sitting room on the other side of the stairway now, cheering on this Commander's Wife, the Wife of Warren. A small thin woman, she lies on the floor, in a white cotton nightgown, her graying hair spreading like mildew over the rug; they massage her tiny belly, just as if she's really about to give birth herself.

The Commander, of course, is nowhere in sight. He's gone wherever men go on such occasions, some hideout. Probably he's figuring out when his promotion is likely to be announced, if all goes well. He's sure to get one, now.

Ofwarren is in the master bedroom, a good name for it; where this Commander and his Wife nightly bed down. She's sitting on their king-sized bed, propped with pillows: Janine, inflated but reduced, shorn of her former name. She's wearing a white cotton shift, which is hiked up over her thighs; her long broom-colored hair is pulled back and tied behind her head, to keep it out of the way. Her eyes are squeezed closed, and this way I can almost like her. After all, she's one of us; what did she ever want but to lead her life as agreeably as possible? What else did any of us want? It's the *possible* that's the catch. She's not doing badly, under the circumstances.

Two women I don't know stand on either side of her, gripping her hands, or she theirs. A third lifts the nightgown, pours baby oil onto her mound of stomach, rubs downwards. At her feet stands Aunt Elizabeth, in her khaki dress with the military breast pockets; she was the one who taught Gyn Ed. All I can see of her is the side of her head, her profile, but I know it's her, that jutting nose and handsome chin, severe. At her side stands the Birthing Stool, with its double seat, the back one raised like a throne behind the other. They won't put Janine on it before it's time. The blankets stand ready, the small tub for bathing, the bowl of ice for Janine to suck.

The rest of the women sit cross-legged on the rug; there's a crowd of them, everyone in this district is supposed to be here. There must be twenty-five, thirty. Not every Commander has a Handmaid: some of their Wives have children. *From each*, says the slogan, *according to her ability; to each according to his needs.* We recited that, three times, after dessert. It was from the Bible, or so they said. St. Paul again, in Acts.

You are a transitional generation, said Aunt Lydia. It is the hardest for you. We know the sacrifices you are being expected to make. It is hard when men revile you. For the ones who come after you, it will be easier. They will accept their duties with willing hearts.

She did not say: Because they will have no memories, of any other way.

She said: Because they won't want things they can't have.

Once a week we had movies, after lunch and before our nap. We sat on the floor of the Domestic Science room, on our little gray mats, and waited while Aunt Helena and Aunt Lydia struggled with the projection equipment. If we were lucky they wouldn't get the film threaded upside-down. What it reminded me of was geography classes, at my own high school thousands of years before, where they showed movies of the rest of the world; women in long skirts or cheap printed cotton dresses, carrying bundles of sticks, or baskets, or plastic buckets of water, from some river or other, with babies slung

▷ **4** *trail:* (here) move behind on the floor • *hem:* Saum **11** *pig out* (infml): eat too much food **15** *mildew* ['mɪldu:]: Mehltau, Schimmel **18** *hideout:* place where you go when you do not want anyone to find you **24** *be shorn of sth.* (fml): have sth. important taken away from you **30** *catch:* hidden difficulty **35** *Gyn Ed:* (here) gynaecological education **36** *jutting:* sticking out **44–45** *From each … needs:* adapted from Karl Marx's "From each according to his abilities, to each according to his needs", which is taken from earlier revolutionary writing; cf. also Acts 4:35 (*Acts:* Apostelgeschichte) **48** *transitional:* in-between, of a time of change **50** *revile sb.:* criticize sb. in a way that shows how much you dislike him/her

on them in shawls or net slings, looking squint-eyed or afraid out of the screen at us, knowing something was being done to them by a machine with one glass eye but not knowing what. Those movies were comforting and faintly boring. They made me feel sleepy, even when men came onto the screen, with naked muscles, hacking away at hard dirt with primitive hoes and shovels, hauling rocks. I preferred movies with dancing in them, singing, ceremonial masks, carved artifacts for making music: feathers, brass buttons, conch shells, drums. I liked watching these people when they were happy, not when they were miserable, starving, emaciated, straining themselves to death over some simple thing, the digging of a well, the irrigation of land, problems the civilized nations had long ago solved. I thought someone should just give them the technology and let them get on with it.

Aunt Lydia didn't show these kinds of movies.

Sometimes the movie she showed would be an old porno film, from the seventies or eighties. Women kneeling, sucking penises or guns, women tied up or chained or with dog collars around their necks, women hanging from trees, or upsidedown, naked, with their legs held apart, women being raped, beaten up, killed. Once we had to watch a woman being slowly cut into pieces, her fingers and breasts snipped off with garden shears, her stomach slit open and her intestines pulled out.

Consider the alternatives, said Aunt Lydia. You see what things used to be like? That was what they thought of women, then. Her voice trembled with indignation.

Moira said later that it wasn't real, it was done with models; but it was hard to tell.

Sometimes, though, the movie would be what Aunt Lydia called an Unwoman documentary. Imagine, said Aunt Lydia, wasting their time like that, when they should have been doing something useful. Back then, the Unwomen were always wasting time. They were encouraged to do it. The government gave them money to do that very thing. Mind you, some of their ideas were sound enough, she went on, with the smug authority in her voice of one who is in a position to judge. We would have to condone some of their ideas, even today. Only some, mind you, she said coyly, raising her index finger, waggling it at us. But they were Godless, and that can make all the difference, don't you agree?

I sit on my mat, hands folded, and Aunt Lydia steps to the side, away from the screen, and the lights go out, and I wonder whether I can, in the dark, lean far over to the right without being seen, and whisper, to the woman next to me. What will I whisper? I will say, Have you seen Moira. Because nobody has, she wasn't at breakfast. But the room, although dim, isn't dark enough, so I switch my mind into the holding pattern that passes for attention. They don't play the soundtrack, on movies like these, though they do on the porno films. They want us to hear the screams and grunts and shrieks of what is supposed to be either extreme pain or extreme pleasure or both at once, but they don't want us to hear what the Unwomen are saying.

First come the title and some names, blacked out on the film with a crayon so we can't read them, and then I see my mother. My young mother, younger than I remember her, as young as she must have been once before I was born. She's wearing the kind of outfit Aunt Lydia told us was typical of Unwomen in those days, overall jeans with a green and mauve plaid shirt underneath and sneakers on her feet; the sort of thing Moira once wore, the sort of thing I can remember wearing, long ago, myself. Her hair is tucked into a mauve kerchief tied behind her head. Her face is very young, very serious, even pretty. I've forgotten my mother was once as pretty and as earnest as that. She's in a group of other women, dressed in the same fashion; she's holding a stick, no, it's part of a banner, the handle. The camera pans up and we see the writing, in paint on what must have been a bedsheet: TAKE BACK THE NIGHT. This hasn't been blacked out, even though we aren't supposed to be reading. The women around me breathe in, there's a stirring in the room, like wind over grass. Is this an oversight, have we gotten away with something? Or is this a thing we're intended to see, to remind us of the old days of no safety?

Behind this sign there are other signs, and the camera notices them briefly: FREEDOM TO CHOOSE. EVERY BABY A WANTED BABY. RECAPTURE OUR BODIES. DO YOU BELIEVE A WOMAN'S PLACE IS ON THE KITCHEN TABLE? Under the last sign there's a line drawing of woman's body, lying on a table, blood dripping out of it.

▷ **6** *hoe:* Hacke • *haul sth.:* carry sth. away **10** *emaciated:* very thin and weak **34** *sound* (adj): good but not excellent **35** *smug:* feeling too pleased with yourself or about sth. you have done **36** *condone sth.:* accept sth. that is morally wrong **46** *holding pattern:* Warteschleife; Stillstand

Now my mother is moving forward, she's smiling, laughing, they all move forward, and now they're raising their fists in the air. The camera moves to the sky, where hundreds of balloons rise, trailing their strings: red balloons, with a circle painted on them, a circle with a stem like the stem of an apple, the stem is a cross. Back on the earth, my mother is part of the crowd now, and I can't see her anymore.

I had you when I was thirty-seven, my mother said. It was a risk, you could have been deformed or something. You were a wanted child, all right, and did I get shit from some quarters! My oldest buddy Tricia Foreman accused me of being pronatalist, the bitch. Jealousy, I put that down to. Some of the others were okay though. But when I was six months' pregnant, a lot of them started sending me these articles about how the birth defect rate went zooming up after thirty-five. Just what I needed. And stuff about how hard it was to be a single parent. Fuck that shit, I told them, I've started this and I'm going to finish it. At the hospital they wrote down "Aged Primipara" on the chart, I caught them in the act. That's what they call you when it's your first baby over thirty, over *thirty* for godsake. Garbage, I told them, biologically I'm twenty-two, I could run rings around you any day. I could have triplets and walk out of here while you were still trying to get up off the bed.

When she said that she'd jut out her chin. I remember her like that, her chin jutted out, a drink in front of her on the kitchen table; not young and earnest and pretty the way she was in the movie, but wiry, spunky, the kind of old woman who won't let anyone butt in front of her in a supermarket line. She liked to come over to my house and have a drink while Luke and I were fixing dinner and tell us what was wrong with her life, which always turned into what was wrong with ours. Her hair was gray by that time, of course. She wouldn't dye it. Why pretend, she'd say. Anyway what do I need it for, I don't want a man around, what use are they except for ten seconds' worth of half babies. A man is just a woman's strategy for making other women. Not that your father wasn't a nice guy and all, but he wasn't up to fatherhood. Not that I expected it of him. Just do the job, then you can bugger off, I said, I make a decent salary, I can afford daycare. So he went to the coast and sent Christmas cards. He had beautiful blue eyes though. But there's something missing in them, even the nice ones. It's like they're permanently absent-minded, like they can't quite remember who they are. They look at the sky too much. They lose touch with their feet. They aren't a patch on a woman except they're better at fixing cars and playing football, just what we need for the improvement of the human race, right?

That was the way she talked, even in front of Luke. He didn't mind, he teased her by pretending to be macho, he'd tell her women were incapable of abstract thought and she'd have another drink and grin at him.

Chauvinist pig, she'd say.

Isn't she quaint, Luke would say to me, and my mother would look sly, furtive almost.

I'm entitled, she'd say. I'm old enough, I've paid my dues, it's time for me to be quaint. You're still wet behind the ears. Piglet, I should have said.

As for you, she'd say to me, you're just a backlash. Flash in the pan. History will absolve me.

But she wouldn't say things like that until after the third drink.

You young people don't appreciate things, she'd say. You don't know what we had to go through, just to get you where you are. Look at him, slicing up the carrots. Don't you know how many women's lives, how many women's *bodies*, the tanks had to roll over just to get that far?

Cooking's my hobby, Luke would say. I enjoy it.

Hobby, schmobby, my mother would say. You don't have to make excuses to me. Once upon a time you wouldn't have been allowed to have such a hobby, they'd have called you queer.

Now, Mother, I would say. Let's not get into an argument about nothing.

▷ **16** *primipara* [praɪ'mɪpərə]: woman who is pregnant with her first child **19** *run rings around sb.:* jdn. in die Tasche stecken **20** *triplets:* three children born at the same time to the same mother **25** *spunky* (infml): brave and determined, full of energy • *butt in front of sb.:* force your way in front of sb. **35** *bugger off* (sl): go away **40** *they aren't a patch on sth.* (infml): they aren't as good as sth. **49** *sly:* verschlagen • *furtive:* verstohlen, heimlich **50** *I've paid my dues:* I've done what I owe (society), I've done what I had to do **53** *backlash:* strong negative reaction • *flash in the pan:* an event that lasts only for a short time and is not likely to be repeated or to last **62** *hobby, schmobby:* rhyme that indicates that you do not think much of sth. **64** *queer* (derog sl): homosexual

Nothing, she'd say bitterly. You call it nothing. You don't understand, do you. You don't understand at all what I'm talking about.

Sometimes she would cry. I was so lonely, she'd say. You have no idea how lonely I was. And I had friends, I was a lucky one, but I was lonely anyway.

I admired my mother in some ways, although things between us were never easy. She expected too much from me, I felt. She expected me to vindicate her life for her, and the choices she'd made. I didn't want to live my life on her terms. I didn't want to be the model offspring, the incarnation of her ideas. We used to fight about that. I am not your justification for existence, I said to her once.

I want her back. I want everything back, the way it was. But there is no point to it, this wanting.

CHAPTER 21

It's hot in here, and too noisy. The women's voices rise around me, a soft chant that is still too loud for me, after the days and days of silence. In the corner of the room there's a bloodstained sheet, bundled and tossed there, from when the waters broke. I hadn't noticed it before.

The room smells too, the air is close, they should open a window. The smell is of our own flesh, an organic smell, sweat and a tinge of iron, from the blood on the sheet, and another smell, more animal, that's coming, it must be, from Janine: a smell of dens, of inhabited caves, the smell of the plaid blanket on the bed when the cat gave birth on it, once, before she was spayed. Smell of matrix.

"Breathe, breathe," we chant, as we have been taught. "Hold, hold. Expel, expel, expel." We chant to the count of five. Five in, hold for five, out for five. Janine, her eyes closed, tries to slow her breathing. Aunt Elizabeth feels for the contractions.

Now Janine is restless, she wants to walk. The two women help her off the bed, support her on either side while she paces. A contraction hits her, she doubles over. One of the women kneels and rubs her back. We are all good at this, we've had lessons. I recognize Ofglen, my shopping partner, sitting two away from me. The soft chanting envelops us like a membrane.

A Martha arrives, with a tray: a jug of fruit juice, the kind you make from powder, grape it looks like, and a stack of paper cups. She sets it on the rug in front of the chanting women. Ofglen, not missing a beat, pours, and the paper cups pass down the line.

I receive a cup, lean to the side to pass it, and the woman next to me says, low in my ear, "Are you looking for anyone?"

"Moira," I say, just as low. "Dark hair, freckles."

▷ **8** *vindicate sth.:* prove that you were right to do sth. **17** *the waters break:* the liquid in a pregnant woman's womb passes out of her body just before the baby is born **22** *den:* hidden home of a wild animal **24** *spay sth.:* remove the ovaries of sth. (a female animal) to prevent it from breeding • *matrix:* (here) the living tissue in which an embryo grows **34** *membrane:* a thin layer of skin that connects or covers parts inside the body

"No," the woman says. I don't know this woman, she wasn't at the Center with me, though I've seen her, shopping.

"But I'll watch for you."

"Are you?" I say.

"Alma," she says. "What's your real name?"

I want to tell her there was an Alma with me at the Center. I want to tell her my name, but Aunt Elizabeth raises her head, staring around the room, she must have heard a break in the chant, so there's no more time. Sometimes you can find things out, on Birth Days. But there would be no point in asking about Luke. He wouldn't be where any of these women would be likely to see him.

The chanting goes on, it begins to catch me. It's hard work, you're supposed to concentrate. Identify with your body, said Aunt Elizabeth. Already I can feel slight pains, in my belly, and my breasts are heavy. Janine screams, a weak scream, partway between a scream and a groan.

"She's going into transition," says Aunt Elizabeth.

One of the helpers wipes Janine's forehead with a damp cloth. Janine is sweating now, her hair is escaping in wisps from the elastic band, bits of it stick to her forehead and neck. Her flesh is damp, saturated, lustrous.

"Pant! pant! pant!" we chant.

"I want to go outside," says Janine. "I want to go for a walk. I feel fine. I have to go to the can."

We all know that she's in transition, she doesn't know what she's doing. Which of these statements is true? Probably the last one. Aunt Elizabeth signals, two women stand beside the portable toilet, Janine is lowered gently onto it. There's another smell, added to the others in the room. Janine groans again, her head bent over so all we can see is her hair. Crouching like that, she's like a doll, an old one that's been pillaged and discarded, in some corner, akimbo.

Janine is up again and walking. "I want to sit down," she says. How long have we been here? Minutes or hours. I'm sweating now, my dress under my arms is drenched, I taste salt on my upper lip, the false pains clench at me, the others feel it too, I can tell by the way they sway. Janine is sucking on an ice cube. Then, after that, inches away or miles, "No," she screams, "Oh no, oh no oh no." It's her second baby, she had another child, once, I know that from the Center, when she used to cry about it at night, like the rest of us only more noisily.

So she ought to be able to remember this, what it's like, what's coming. But who can remember pain, once it's over? All that remains of it is a shadow, not in the mind even, in the flesh. Pain marks you, but too deep to see. Out of sight, out of mind.

Someone has spiked the grape juice. Someone has pinched a bottle, from downstairs. It won't be the first time at such a gathering; but they'll turn a blind eye. We too need our orgies.

"Dim the lights" says Aunt Elizabeth. "Tell her it's time."

Someone stands, moves to the wall, the light in the room fades to twilight, our voices dwindle to a chorus of creaks, of husky whispers, like grasshoppers in a field at night. Two leave the room, two others lead Janine to the Birthing Stool, where she sits on the lower of the two seats. She's calmer now, air sucks evenly into her lungs, we lean forward, tensed, the muscles in our backs and bellies hurt from the strain. It's coming, it's coming, like a bugle, a call to arms, like a wall falling, we can feel it like a heavy stone moving down, pulled down inside us, we think we will burst. We grip each other's hands, we are no longer single.

The Commander's Wife hurries in, in her ridiculous white cotton nightgown, her spindly legs sticking out beneath it. Two of the Wives in their blue dresses and veils hold her by the arms, as if she needs it; she has a tight little smile on her face, like a hostess at a party she'd rather not be giving. She must know what we think of her. She scrambles onto the Birthing Stool, sits on the seat behind and above Janine, so that Janine is framed by her: her skinny legs come down on either side, like the arms of an eccentric chair. Oddly enough, she's wearing white cotton socks, and bedroom slippers, blue ones made of fuzzy material, like toilet-seat covers. But we pay no attention to the Wife, we hardly even see her, our eyes are on Janine. In the dim light, in her white gown, she glows like a moon in cloud.

She's grunting now, with the effort. "Push, push, push," we whisper. "Relax. Pant. Push, push, push." We're with her, we're the same as her, we're drunk. Aunt Elizabeth kneels, with an outspread

▷ **21** *saturated:* completely wet • *lustrous:* soft and shining **22** *pant:* breathe quickly with short breaths **24** *can* (AE sl): toilet **31** *pillage sth.:* etwas plündern • *discard sth.:* throw sth. away • *akimbo:* with your hands on your hips and your ellbows pointing outwards **44** *spike sth.:* add alcohol to sth. **54** *bugle* ['bju:gəl]: Jagdhorn **65** *oddly:* strangely

towel to catch the baby, here's the crowning, the glory, the head, purple and smeared with yoghurt, another push and it slithers out, slick with fluid and blood, into our waiting. Oh praise.

We hold our breath as Aunt Elizabeth inspects it: a girl, poor thing, but so far so good, at least there's nothing wrong with it, that can be seen, hands, feet, eyes, we silently count, everything is in place. Aunt Elizabeth, holding the baby, looks up at us and smiles. We smile too, we are one smile, tears run down our cheeks, we are so happy.

Our happiness is part memory. What I remember is Luke with me in the hospital, standing beside my head, holding my hand, in the green gown and white mask they gave him. Oh, he said, Oh Jesus, breath coming out in wonder. That night he couldn't go to sleep at all, he said, he was so high.

Aunt Elizabeth is gently washing the baby off, it isn't crying much, it stops. As quietly as possible, so as not to startle it, we rise, crowd around Janine, squeezing her, patting her. She's crying too. The two Wives in blue help the third Wife, the Wife of the household, down from the Birthing Stool and over to the bed, where they lay her down and tuck her in. The baby, washed now and quiet, is placed ceremoniously in her arms. The Wives from downstairs are crowding in now, pushing among us, pushing us aside. They talk too loud, some of them are still carrying their plates, their coffee cups, their wine glasses, some of them are still chewing, they cluster around the bed, the mother and child, cooing and congratulating. Envy radiates from them, I can smell it, faint wisps of acid, mingled with their perfume. The Commander's Wife looks down at the baby as if it's a bouquet of flowers: something she's won, a tribute.

The Wives are here to bear witness to the naming. It's the Wives who do the naming, around here.

"Angela," says the Commander's Wife.

"Angela, Angela," the Wives repeat, twittering. "What a sweet name! Oh, she's perfect! Oh, she's wonderful!"

We stand between Janine and the bed, so she won't have to see this. Someone gives her a drink of grape juice, I hope there's wine in it, she's still having the pains, for the afterbirth, she's crying helplessly, burnt-out miserable tears. Nevertheless we are jubilant, it's a victory, for all of us. We've done it.

She'll be allowed to nurse the baby, for a few months, they believe in mother's milk. After that she'll be transferred, to see if she can do it again, with someone else who needs a turn. But she'll never be sent to the Colonies, she'll never be declared Unwoman. That is her reward.

The Birthmobile is waiting outside, to deliver us back to our own households. The doctors are still in their van; their faces appear at the window, white blobs, like the faces of sick children confined to the house. One of them opens the door and comes towards us.

"Was it all right?" he asks, anxious.

"Yes," I say. By now I'm wrung out, exhausted. My breasts are painful, they're leaking a little. Fake milk, it happens this way with some of us. We sit on our benches, facing one another, as we are transported; we're without emotion now, almost without feeling, we might be bundles of red cloth. We ache. Each of us holds in her lap a phantom, a ghost baby. What confronts us, now the excitement's over, is our own failure. Mother, I think. Wherever you may be. Can you hear me? You wanted a women's culture. Well, now there is one. It isn't what you meant, but it exists. Be thankful for small mercies.

▷ **24** *coo:* make a soft, low sound **48** *wrung out* (infml): totally tired **56** *be thankful for small mercies:* be thankful even if it is less than you expected

CHAPTER 22

By the time the Birthmobile arrives in front of the house it's late afternoon. The sun is coming weakly through the clouds, the smell of wet grass warming up is in the air. I've been at the Birth all day; you lose track of time. Cora will have done the shopping today, I'm excused from all duties. I go up the stairs, lifting my feet heavily from one step to the next, holding onto the banister. I feel as if I've been awake for days and running hard, my chest hurts; my muscles cramp as if they're out of sugar. For once I welcome solitude.

I lie on the bed. I would like to rest, go to sleep, but I'm too tired, at the same time too excited, my eyes won't close. I look up at the ceiling, tracing the foliage of the wreath. Today it makes me think of a hat, the large-brimmed hats women used to wear at some period during the old days: hats like enormous haloes, festooned with fruit and flowers, and the feathers of exotic birds; hats like an idea of paradise, floating just above the head, a thought solidified.

In a minute the wreath will start to color and I will begin seeing things. That's how tired I am: as when you'd driven all night, into the dawn, for some reason, I won't think about that now, keeping each other awake with stories and taking turns at the wheel, and as the sun would begin to come up you'd see things at the sides of your eyes: purple animals, in the bushes beside the road, the vague outlines of men, which would disappear when you looked at them straight.

I'm too tired to go on with this story. I'm too tired to think about where I am. Here is a different story, a better one. This is the story of what happened to Moira.

Part of it I can fill in myself, part of it I heard from Alma, who heard it from Dolores, who heard it from Janine. Janine heard it from Aunt Lydia. There can be alliances even in such places, even under such circumstances. This is something you can depend upon: there will always be alliances, of one kind or another.

Aunt Lydia called Janine into her office.

Blessed be the fruit, Janine, Aunt Lydia would have said, without looking up from her desk, where she was writing something. For every rule there is always an exception: this too can be depended upon. The Aunts are allowed to read and write.

May the Lord open, Janine would have replied, tonelessly, in her transparent voice, her voice of raw egg white.

I feel I can rely on you, Janine, Aunt Lydia would have said, raising her eyes from the page at last and fixing Janine with that look of hers, through the spectacles, a look that managed to be both menacing and beseeching, all at once. Help me, that look said, we are all in this together. You are a reliable girl, she went on, not like some of the others.

She thought all Janine's snivelling and repentance meant something, she thought Janine had been broken, she thought Janine was a true believer. But by that time Janine was like a puppy that's been kicked too often, by too many people, at random: she'd roll over for anyone, she'd tell anything, just for a moment of approbation.

So Janine would have said: I hope so, Aunt Lydia. I hope I have become worthy of your trust. Or some such thing.

Janine, said Aunt Lydia, something terrible has happened.

Janine looked down at the floor. Whatever it was, she knew she would not be blamed for it, she was blameless. But what use had that been to her in the past, to be blameless? So at the same time she felt guilty, and as if she was about to be punished.

Do you know about it, Janine? said Aunt Lydia softly.

No, Aunt Lydia, said Janine. She knew at this moment it was necessary to look up, to look Aunt Lydia straight in the eyes. After a moment she managed it.

Because if you do I will be very disappointed in you, said Aunt Lydia.

As the Lord is my witness, said Janine with a show of fervor.

Aunt Lydia allowed herself one of her pauses. She fiddled with her pen. Moira is no longer with us, she said at last.

Oh, said Janine. She was neutral about this. Moira wasn't a friend of hers. Is she dead? she asked after a moment.

▷ **8** *solitude:* being alone **13** *halo* ['heɪləʊ]: Heiligenschein • *festooned:* decorated **38** *rely on sb.:* trust sb., depend on sb. **40** *menacing* (adj): threatening **41** *beseeching:* show that you want sth. very much **44** *repentance:* act of showing that you are sorry for sth. bad or wrong you have done **48** *approbation* (fml): approval or agreement **62** *fervor:* very strong feelings

Then Aunt Lydia told her the story. Moira had raised her hand to go to the washroom, during Exercises. She had gone. Aunt Elizabeth was on washroom duty. Aunt Elizabeth stayed outside the washroom door, as usual; Moira went in. After a moment Moira called to Aunt Elizabeth: the toilet was overflowing, could Aunt Elizabeth come and fix it? It was true that the toilets sometimes overflowed. Unknown persons stuffed wads of toilet paper down them to make them do this very thing. The Aunts had been working on some foolproof way of preventing this, but funds were short and right now they had to make do with what was at hand, and they hadn't figured out a way of locking up the toilet paper. Possibly they should keep it outside the door on a table and hand each person a sheet or several sheets as she went in. But that was for the future. It takes a while to get the wrinkles out, of anything new.

Aunt Elizabeth, suspecting no harm, went into the washroom. Aunt Lydia had to admit it was a little foolish of her. On the other hand, she'd gone in to fix a toilet on several previous occasions without mishap.

Moira was not lying, water was running over the floor, and several pieces of disintegrating fecal matter. It was not pleasant and Aunt Elizabeth was annoyed. Moira stood politely aside, and Aunt Elizabeth hurried into the cubicle Moira had indicated, and bent over the back of the toilet. She intended to lift off the porcelain lid and fiddle with the arrangement of bulb and plug inside. She had both hands on the lid when she felt something hard and sharp and possibly metallic jab into her ribs from behind. Don't move, said Moira, or I'll stick it all the way in, I know where, I'll puncture your lung.

They found out afterwards that she'd dismantled the inside of one of the toilets and taken out the long thin pointed lever, the part that attaches to the handle at one end and the chain at the other. It isn't too hard to do if you know how, and Moira had mechanical ability, she used to fix her own car, the minor things. Soon after this the toilets were fitted with chains to hold the tops on, and when they overflowed it took a long time to get them open. We had several floods that way.

Aunt Elizabeth couldn't see what was poking into her back, Aunt Lydia said. She was a brave woman ...

Oh yes, said Janine.

... but not foolhardy, said Aunt Lydia, frowning a little. Janine had been overenthusiastic, which sometimes has the force of a denial.

She did as Moira said, Aunt Lydia continued. Moira got hold of her cattle prod and her whistle, ordering Aunt Elizabeth to unclip them from her belt. Then she hurried Aunt Elizabeth down the stairs to the basement. They were on the second floor, not the third, so there were only two flights of stairs to be negotiated. Classes were in session so there was nobody in the halls. They did see another Aunt, but she was at the far end of the corridor and not looking their way. Aunt Elizabeth could have screamed at this point but she knew Moira meant what she said; Moira had a bad reputation.

Oh yes, said Janine.

Moira took Aunt Elizabeth along the corridor of empty lockers, past the door to the gymnasium, and into the furnace room. She told Aunt Elizabeth to take off all her clothes ...

Oh, said Janine weakly, as if to protest this sacrilege.

... and Moira took off her own clothes and put on those of Aunt Elizabeth, which did not fit her exactly but well enough. She was not overly cruel to Aunt Elizabeth, she allowed her to put on her own red dress. The veil she tore into strips, and tied Aunt Elizabeth up with them, in behind the furnace. She stuffed some of the cloth into her mouth and tied it in place with another strip. She tied a strip around Aunt Elizabeth's neck and tied the other end to her feet, behind. She is a cunning and dangerous woman, said Aunt Lydia.

Janine said: May I sit down? As if it had all been too much for her. She had something to trade at last, for a token at least.

Yes, Janine, said Aunt Lydia, surprised, but knowing she could not refuse at this point. She was asking for Janine's attention, her co-operation. She indicated the chair in the corner. Janine drew it forward.

I could kill you, you know, said Moira, when Aunt Elizabeth was safely stowed out of sight behind the furnace. I could injure you badly so you would never feel good in your body again. I could zap you with this, or stick this thing into your eye. Just remember I didn't, if it ever comes to that.

▷ **8** *foolproof:* so well designed that it cannot go wrong **13** *the wrinkles:* (here) the problems **18** *mishap* ['mɪshæp]: small accident **28** *dismantle sth.:* take sth. apart **38** *foolhardy:* taking unnecessary risks **44** *negotiate sth.:* (here) successfully get past sth. difficult **51** *furnace:* boiler **61** *cunning* (adj): using tricks to get what you want **70** *zap sb.* (infml): strike sb. with sth. electric

Aunt Lydia didn't repeat any of this part to Janine, but I expect Moira said something like it. In any case she didn't kill or mutilate Aunt Elizabeth, who a few days later, after she'd recovered from her seven hours behind the furnace and presumably from the interrogation – for the possibility of collusion would not have been ruled out, by the Aunts or by anyone else – was back in operation at the Center.

Moira stood up straight and looked firmly ahead. She drew her shoulders back, pulled up her spine, and compressed her lips. This was not our usual posture. Usually we walked with heads bent down, our eyes on our hands or the ground. Moira didn't look much like Aunt Elizabeth, even with the brown wimple in place, but her stiff-backed posture was apparently enough to convince the Angels on guard, who never looked at any of us very closely, even and perhaps especially the Aunts; because Moira marched straight out the front door, with the bearing of a person who knew where she was going; was saluted, presented Aunt Elizabeth's pass, which they didn't bother to check, because who would affront an Aunt in that way? And disappeared.

Oh, said Janine. Who can tell what she felt? Maybe she wanted to cheer. If so, she kept it well hidden.

So, Janine, said Aunt Lydia. Here is what I want you to do.

Janine opened her eyes wide and tried to look innocent and attentive.

I want you to keep your ears open. Maybe one of the others was involved.

Yes, Aunt Lydia, said Janine.

And come and tell me about it, won't you, dear? If you hear anything.

Yes, Aunt Lydia, said Janine. She knew she would not have to kneel down any more, at the front of the classroom, and listen to all of us shouting at her that it was her fault. Now it would be someone else for a while. She was, temporarily, off the hook.

The fact that she told Dolores all about this encounter in Aunt Lydia's office meant nothing. It didn't mean she wouldn't testify against us, any of us, if she had the occasion. We knew that. By this time we were treating her the way people used to treat those with no legs who sold pencils on street corners. We avoided her when we could, were charitable to her when it couldn't be helped. She was a danger to us, we knew that.

Dolores probably patted her on the back and said she was a good sport to tell us. Where did this exchange take place? In the gymnasium, when we were getting ready for bed. Dolores had the bed next to Janine's.

The story passed among us that night, in the semi-darkness, under our breath, from bed to bed.

Moira was out there somewhere. She was at large, or dead. What would she do? The thought of what she would do expanded till it filled the room. At any moment there might be a shattering explosion, the glass of the windows would fall inwards, the doors would swing open ... Moira had power now, she'd been set loose, she'd set herself loose. She was now a loose woman.

I think we found this frightening.

Moira was like an elevator with open sides. She made us dizzy. Already we were losing the taste for freedom, already we were finding these walls secure. In the upper reaches of the atmosphere you'd come apart, you'd vaporize, there would be no pressure holding you together.

Nevertheless Moira was our fantasy. We hugged her to us, she was with us in secret, a giggle; she was lava beneath the crust of daily life. In the light of Moira, the Aunts were less fearsome and more absurd. Their power had a flaw to it. They could be shanghaied in toilets. The audacity was what we liked.

We expected her to be dragged in at any minute, as she had been before. We could not imagine what they might do to her this time. It would be very bad, whatever it was.

But nothing happened. Moira didn't reappear. She hasn't yet.

▷ **2** *mutilate sb.:* damage sb.'s body very severely **5** *collusion:* secret agreement to do sth. illegal **5–6** *rule sth. out:* exclude sth. from being a possibility **18** *affront sb.:* insult sb. **33** *off the hook:* free from some sort of punishment **35** *testify:* make a statement that sth. has happened or that sth. is true **39** *charitable:* kind **41–42** *be a good sport* (infml): be pleasant and helpful in a difficult situation **47** *at large:* not captured, free **62** *flaw:* (here) weakness • *shanghai sb.* (old-fashioned): trick or force sb. into sth. they do not really want to do **63** *audacity:* brave but rude or shocking behavior

CHAPTER 23

This is a reconstruction. All of it is a reconstruction. It's a reconstruction now, in my head, as I lie flat on my single bed rehearsing what I should or shouldn't have said, what I should or shouldn't have done, how I should have played it. If I ever get out of here –

Let's stop there. I intend to get out of here. It can't last forever. Others have thought such things, in bad times before this, and they were always right, they did get out one way or another, and it didn't last forever. Although for them it may have lasted all the forever they had. When I get out of here, if I'm ever able to set this down, in any form, even in the form of one voice to another, it will be a reconstruction then too, at yet another remove. It's impossible to say a thing exactly the way it was, because what you say can never be exact, you always have to leave something out, there are too many parts, sides, crosscurrents, nuances; too many gestures, which could mean this or that, too many shapes which can never be fully described, too many flavors, in the air or on the tongue, half-colors, too many. But if you happen to be a man, sometime in the future, and you've made it this far, please remember: you will never be subjected to the temptation of feeling you must forgive, a man, as a woman. It's difficult to resist, believe me. But remember that forgiveness too is a power. To beg for it is a power, and to withhold or bestow it is a power, perhaps the greatest.

Maybe none of this is about control. Maybe it isn't really about who can own whom, who can do what to whom and get away with it, even as far as death. Maybe it isn't about who can sit and who has to kneel or stand or lie down, legs spread open. Maybe it's about who can do what to whom and be forgiven for it. Never tell me it amounts to the same thing.

I want you to kiss me, said the Commander.

Well, of course something came before that. Such requests never come flying out of the blue.

I went to sleep after all, and dreamed I was wearing earrings, and one of them was broken; nothing beyond that, just the brain going through its back files, and I was wakened by Cora with the dinner tray, and time was back on track.

"It a good baby?" says Cora as she's setting down the tray. She must know already, they have a kind of word-of-mouth telegraph, from household to household, news gets around; but it gives her pleasure to hear about it, as if my words will make it more real.

"It's fine," I say. "A keeper. A girl."

Cora smiles at me, a smile which includes. These are the moments that must make what she is doing seem worthwhile to her.

"That's good," she says. Her voice is almost wistful, and I think: of course. She would have liked to have been there. It's like a party she couldn't go to.

"Maybe we have one, soon," she says, shyly. By we she means me. It's up to me to repay the team, justify my food and keep, like a queen ant with eggs. Rita may disapprove of me, but Cora does not. Instead she depends on me. She hopes, and I am the vehicle for her hope.

Her hope is of the simplest kind. She wants a Birth Day, here, with guests and food and presents, she wants a little child to spoil in the kitchen, to iron clothes for, to slip cookies into when no one's watching. I am to provide these joys for her. I would rather have the disapproval, I feel more worthy of it.

The dinner is beef stew. I have some trouble finishing it, because halfway through it I remember what the day has erased right out of my head. It's true what they say, it's a trance state, giving birth or being there, you lose track of the rest of your life, you focus only on that one instant. But now it comes back to me, and I know I'm not prepared.

The clock in the hall downstairs strikes nine. I press my hands against the sides of my thighs, breathe in, set out along the hall and softly down the stairs. Serena Joy may still be at the house where the Birth took place; that's lucky, he couldn't have foreseen it. On these days the Wives hang around for hours, helping to open the presents, gossiping, getting drunk. Something has to be done to dispel their

▷ **11** *at yet another remove:* still further away **14** *crosscurrents:* set of ideas, beliefs that are different from those most people hold **21** *withhold sth.* (fml): refuse to give sth. • *bestow sth.* [bɪ'stəʊ] (fml): give sth. **43** *wistful:* wehmütig, sehnsüchtig **48** *ant:* Ameise **56** *erase sth.:* remove sth. **58** *lose track of sth.:* no longer be aware of what is happening **65** *dispel sth.:* make sth. go away

envy. I follow the downstairs corridor back, past the door that leads into the kitchen, along to the next door, his. I stand outside it, feeling like a child who's been summoned, at school, to the principal's office. What have I done wrong?

My presence here is illegal. It's forbidden for us to be alone with the Commanders. We are for breeding purposes: we aren't concubines, geisha girls, courtesans. On the contrary: everything possible has been done to remove us from that category. There is supposed to be nothing entertaining about us, no room is to be permitted for the flowering of secret lusts; no special favors are to be wheedled, by them or us, there are to be no toeholds for love. We are two-legged wombs, that's all: sacred vessels, ambulatory chalices.

So why does he want to see me, at night, alone?

If I'm caught, it's to Serena's tender mercies I'll be delivered. He isn't supposed to meddle in such household discipline, that's women's business. After that, reclassification. I could become an Unwoman.

But to refuse to see him could be worse. There's no doubt about who holds the real power.

But there must be something he wants, from me. To want is to have a weakness. It's this weakness, whatever it is, that entices me. It's like a small crack in a wall, before now impenetrable. If I press my eye to it, this weakness of his, I may be able to see my way clear.

I want to know what he wants.

I raise my hand, knock, on the door of this forbidden room where I have never been, where women do not go. Not even Serena Joy comes here, and the cleaning is done by Guardians. What secrets, what male totems are kept in here?

I'm told to enter. I open the door, step in.

What is on the other side is normal life. I should say: what is on the other side looks like normal life. There is a desk, of course, with a Computalk on it, and a black leather chair behind it. There's a potted plant on the desk, a pen-holder set, papers. There's an oriental rug on the floor, and a fireplace without a fire in it. There's a small sofa, covered in brown plush, a television set, an end table, a couple of chairs.

But all around the walls there are bookcases. They're filled with books. Books and books and books, right out in plain view, no locks, no boxes. No wonder we can't come in here. It's an oasis of the forbidden. I try not to stare.

The Commander is standing in front of the fireless fireplace, back to it, one elbow on the carved wooden overmantel, other hand in his pocket. It's such a studied pose, something of the country squire, some old come-on from a glossy men's mag. He probably decided ahead of time that he'd be standing like that when I came in. When I knocked he probably rushed over to the fireplace and propped himself up. He should have a black patch, over one eye, a cravat with horseshoes on it.

It's all very well for me to think these things, quick as staccato, a jittering of the brain. An inner jeering. But it's panic. The fact is I'm terrified.

I don't say anything.

"Close the door behind you," he says, pleasantly enough. I do it, and turn back.

"Hello," he says.

It's the old form of greeting. I haven't heard it for a long time, for years. Under the circumstances it seems out of place, comical even, a flip backward in time, a stunt. I can think of nothing appropriate to say in return.

I think I will cry.

He must have noticed this, because he looks at me, puzzled, gives a little frown I choose to interpret as concern, though it may merely be irritation. "Here," he says. "You can sit down." He pulls a chair out for me, sets it in front of his desk. Then he goes around behind the desk and sits down, slowly and it seems to me elaborately. What this act tells me is that he hasn't brought me here to touch me in any way, against my will. He smiles. The smile is not sinister or predatory. It's merely a smile, a formal kind of smile, friendly but a little distant, as if I'm a kitten in a window. One he's looking at but doesn't intend to buy.

▷ **10** *wheedle:* persuade sb. to give you sth. **12** *ambulatory:* walking **21** *entice sb.:* persuade sb. to do sth. **43** *country squire:* englischer Gutsherr **44** *come-on:* (here) sexuelle Anmache **47** *cravat:* Halstuch **50** *jeering* (n): special kind of laughter which shows that you do not respect sb. **65** *elaborately:* in a way that seems carefully prepared and organized **67** *predatory* ['predətɔːri]: using weaker people for sexual advantage

I sit up straight on the chair, my hands folded on my lap. I feel as if my feet in their flat red shoes aren't quite touching the floor. But of course they are.

"You must find this strange," he says.

I simply look at him. The understatement of the year, was a phrase my mother uses. Used.

I feel like cotton candy: sugar and air. Squeeze me and I'd turn into a small sickly damp wad of weeping pinky-red.

"I guess it is a little strange," he says, as if I've answered.

I think I should have a hat on, tied with a bow under my chin.

"I want ..." he says.

I try not to lean forward. Yes? Yes yes? What, then? What does he want? But I won't give it away, this eagerness of mine. It's a bargaining session, things are about to be exchanged. She who does not hesitate is lost. I'm not giving anything away: selling only.

"I would like – " he says. "This will sound silly." And he does look embarrassed, *sheepish* was the word, the way men used to look once. He's old enough to remember how to look that way, and to remember also how appealing women once found it. The young ones don't know those tricks. They've never had to use them.

"I'd like you to play a game of Scrabble with me," he says.

I hold myself absolutely rigid. I keep my face unmoving. So that's what's in the forbidden room! Scrabble! I want to laugh, shriek with laughter, fall off my chair. This was once the game of old women, old men, in the summers or in retirement villas, to be played when there was nothing good on television. Or of adolescents, once, long long ago. My mother had a set, kept at the back of the hall cupboard, with the Christmas tree decorations in their cardboard boxes. Once she tried to interest me in it, when I was thirteen and miserable and at loose ends.

Now of course it's something different. Now it's forbidden, for us. Now it's dangerous. Now it's indecent. Now it's something he can't do with his Wife. Now it's desirable. Now he's compromised himself. It's as if he's offered me drugs.

"All right," I say, as if indifferent. I can in fact hardly speak.

He doesn't say why he wants to play Scrabble with me. I don't ask him. He merely takes a box out from one of the drawers in his desk and opens it up. There are the plasticized wooden counters I remember, the board divided into squares, the little holders for setting the letters in. He dumps the counters out on the top of his desk and begins to turn them over. After a moment I join in.

"You know how to play?" he says.

I nod.

We play two games. *Larynx*, I spell. *Valance. Quince. Zygote.* I hold the glossy counters with their smooth edges, finger the letters. The feeling is voluptuous. This is freedom, an eyeblink of it. *Limp*, I spell. *Gorge.* What a luxury. The counters are like candies, made of peppermint, cool like that. Humbugs, those were called. I would like to put them into my mouth. They would taste also of lime. The letter *C*. Crisp, slightly acid on the tongue, delicious.

I win the first game, I let him win the second: I still haven't discovered what the terms are, what I will be able to ask for, in exchange.

Finally he tells me it's time for me to go home. Those are the words he uses: *go home*. He means to my room. He asks me if I will be all right, as if the stairway is a dark street. I say yes. We open his study door, just a crack, and listen for noises in the hall.

This is like being on a date. This is like sneaking into the dorm after hours.

This is conspiracy.

"Thank you," he says. "For the game." Then he says, "I want you to kiss me."

I think about how I could take the back of the toilet apart, the toilet in my own bathroom, on a bath night, quickly and quietly, so Cora outside on the chair would not hear me. I could get the sharp lever out and hide it in my sleeve, and smuggle it into the Commander's study, the next time, because after a request like that there's always a next time, whether you say yes or no. I think about how I could approach the Commander, to kiss him, here alone, and take off his jacket, as if to allow or invite something further, some approach to true love, and put my arms around him and slip the lever out from the sleeve and drive the sharp end into him suddenly, between his ribs. I think about the blood coming out of him, hot as soup, sexual, over my hands.

▷ **14** *bargain:* discuss prices and conditions **29–30** *be at loose ends:* not know what to do with yourself **32** *indecent:* offensive, immoral **57** *sneak:* go quietly

In fact I don't think about anything of the kind. I put it in only afterwards. Maybe I should have thought about that, at the time, but I didn't. As I said, this is a reconstruction.

"All right," I say. I go to him and place my lips, closed, against his. I smell the shaving lotion, the usual kind, the hint of mothballs, familiar enough to me. But he's like someone I've only just met.

He draws away, looks down at me. There's the smile again, the sheepish one. Such candor. "Not like that," he says. "As if you meant it."

He was so sad.

That is a reconstruction, too.

▷ **8** *candor:* quality of saying what you think openly and frankly

IX

Night

CHAPTER 24

I go back, along the dimmed hall and up the muffled stairs, stealthily to my room. There I sit in the chair, with the lights off, in my red dress, hooked and buttoned. You can think clearly only with your clothes on.

What I need is perspective. The illusion of depth, created by a frame, the arrangement of shapes on a flat surface. Perspective is necessary. Otherwise there are only two dimensions. Otherwise you live with your face squashed against a wall, everything a huge foreground, of details, close-ups, hairs, the weave of the bedsheet, the molecules of the face. Your own skin like a map, a diagram of futility, crisscrossed with tiny roads that lead nowhere. Otherwise you live in the moment. Which is not where I want to be.

But that's where I am, there's no escaping it. Time's a trap, I'm caught in it. I must forget about my secret name and all ways back. My name is Offred now, and here is where I live.

Live in the present, make the most of it, it's all you've got. Time to take stock.

I am thirty-three years old. I have brown hair. I stand five seven without shoes. I have trouble remembering what I used to look like. I have viable ovaries. I have one more chance.

But something has changed, now, tonight. Circumstances have altered.

I can ask for something. Possibly not much; but something.

Men are sex machines, said Aunt Lydia, and not much more. They only want one thing. You must learn to manipulate them, for your own good. Lead them around by the nose; that is a metaphor. It's nature's way. It's God's device. It's the way things are.

Aunt Lydia did not actually say this, but it was implicit in everything she did say. It hovered over her head, like the golden mottoes over the saints, of the darker ages. Like them too, she was angular and without flesh.

▷ **1** *stealthily:* quietly **10** *futility:* senselessness, hopelessness **17** *take stock:* consider the situation in which you find yourself **18** *five seven = five feet seven inches:* ca. 1,74 m **20** *viable ovaries:* funktionierende Eierstöcke **29** *hover* ['hʌvər]: stay in the air

But how to fit the Commander into this, as he exists in his study, with his word games and his desire, for what? To be played with, to be gently kissed, as if I meant it.

I know I need to take it seriously, this desire of his. It could be important, it could be a passport, it could be my downfall. I need to be earnest about it, I need to ponder it. But no matter what I do, sitting here in the dark, with the searchlights illuminating the oblong of my window, from outside, through the curtains gauzy as a bridal dress, as ectoplasm, one of my hands holding the other, rocking back and forth a little, no matter what I do there's something hilarious about it.

He wanted me to play Scrabble with him, and kiss him as if I meant it.

This is one of the most bizarre things that's happened to me, ever.

Context is all.

I remember a television program I saw once; a rerun, made years before. I must have been seven or eight, too young to understand it. It was the sort of thing my mother liked to watch: historical, educational. She tried to explain it to me afterwards, to tell me that the things in it had really happened, but to me it was only a story. I thought someone had made it up. I suppose all children think that, about any history before their own. If it's only a story, it becomes less frightening.

The program was a documentary, about one of those wars. They interviewed people and showed clips from films of the time, black and white, and still photos. I don't remember much about it, but I remember the quality of the pictures, the way everything in them seemed to be coated with a mixture of sunlight and dust, and how dark the shadows were under people's eyebrows and along their cheekbones.

The interviews with people still alive then were in color. The one I remember best was with a woman who had been the mistress of a man who had supervised one of the camps where they put the Jews, before they killed them. In ovens, my mother said; but there weren't any pictures of the ovens, so I got some confused notion that these deaths had taken place in kitchens. There is something especially terrifying to a child in that idea. Ovens mean cooking, and cooking comes before eating. I thought these people had been eaten. Which in a way I suppose they had been.

From what they said, the man had been cruel and brutal. The mistress – my mother explained *mistress*, she did not believe in mystification, I had a pop-up book of sexual organs by the time I was four – the mistress had once been very beautiful. There was a black-and-white shot of her and another woman, in the two-piece bathing suits and platform shoes and picture hats of the time; they were wearing cat's-eye sunglasses and sitting in deck chairs by a swimming pool. The swimming pool was beside their house, which was near the camp with the ovens. The woman said she didn't notice much that she found unusual. She denied knowing about the ovens.

At the time of the interview, forty or fifty years later, she was dying of emphysema. She coughed a lot, and she was very thin, almost emaciated; but she still took pride in her appearance. (Look at that, said my mother, half grudgingly, half admiringly. She still takes pride in her appearance.) She was carefully made up, heavy mascara on her eyelashes, rouge on the bones of her cheeks, over which the skin was stretched like a rubber glove pulled tight. She was wearing pearls.

He was not a monster, she said. People say he was a monster, but he was not one.

What could she have been thinking about? Not much, I guess; not back then, not at the time. She was thinking about how not to think. The times were abnormal. She took pride in her appearance. She did not believe he was a monster. He was not a monster, to her. Probably he had some endearing trait: he whistled, off key, in the shower, he had a yen for truffles, he called his dog Liebchen and made it sit up for little pieces of raw steak. How easy it is to invent a humanity, for anyone at all. What an available temptation. A big child, she would have said to herself. Her heart would have melted, she'd have smoothed the hair back from his forehead, kissed him on the ear, and not just to get something out of him either. The instinct to soothe, to make it better. There there, she'd say, as he woke from a nightmare. Things are so hard for you. All this she would have believed, because otherwise how could she have kept on living? She was very ordinary,

▷ **6** *ponder sth.:* think carefully about sth. **8** *bridal dress:* Brautkleid **9** *ectoplasm:* substance believed by spiritualists to flow from a medium in trance **15** *rerun* (n): Wiederholung **27** *be coated with sth.:* covered with a layer of sth. **50** *emphysema* [ˌemfɪ'siːmə]: a disease of the lungs **62** *endearing:* loveable • *off key:* out of tune **63** *have a yen for sth.:* have a strong desire or liking for sth.

under that beauty. She believed in decency, she was nice to the Jewish maid, or nice enough, nicer than she needed to be.

Several days after this interview with her was filmed, she killed herself. It said that, right on television.

Nobody asked her whether or not she had loved him.

What I remember now, most of all, is the makeup.

I stand up, in the dark, start to unbutton. Then I hear something, inside my body. I've broken, something has cracked, that must be it. Noise is coming up, coming out, of the broken place, in my face. Without warning: I wasn't thinking about here or there or anything. If I let the noise get out into the air it will be laughter, too loud, too much of it, someone is bound to hear, and then there will be hurrying footsteps and commands and who knows? Judgement: emotion inappropriate to the occasion. The wandering womb, they used to think. Hysteria. And then a needle, a pill. It could be fatal.

I cram both hands over my mouth as if I'm about to be sick, drop to my knees, the laughter boiling like lava in my throat. I crawl into the cupboard, draw up my knees, I'll choke on it. My ribs hurt with holding back, I shake, I heave, seismic, volcanic, I'll burst. Red all over the cupboard, mirth rhymes with birth, oh to die of laughter.

I stifle it in the folds of the hanging cloak, clench my eyes, from which tears are squeezing. Try to compose myself.

After a while it passes, like an epileptic fit. Here I am in the closet. *Nolite te bastardes carborundorum*. I can't see it in the dark but I trace the tiny scratched writing with the ends of my fingers, as if it's a code in Braille. It sounds in my head now less like a prayer, more like a command; but to do what? Useless to me in any case, an ancient hieroglyph to which the key's been lost. Why did she write it, why did she bother? There's no way out of here.

I lie on the floor, breathing too fast, then slower, evening out my breathing, as in the exercises, for giving birth. All I can hear now is the sound of my own heart, opening and closing, opening and closing, opening.

▷ **1** *decency:* honest, polite behavior that follows moral standards and shows respect **19** *heave:* rise up and down with strong movement **20** *mirth:* happiness **26** *Braille* [breɪəl]: a system of printing for blind people **30** *even sth. out:* (here) make sth. regular and normal again

X

Soul Scrolls

CHAPTER 25

What I heard first the next morning was a scream and a crash. Cora, dropping the breakfast tray. It woke me up. I was still half in the cupboard, head on the bundled cloak. I must have pulled it off the hanger, and gone to sleep there; for a moment I couldn't remember where I was. Cora was kneeling beside me, I felt her hand touch my back. She screamed again when I moved.

What's wrong? I said. I rolled over, pushed myself up.

Oh, she said. I thought.

She thought what?

Like ... she said.

The eggs had broken on the floor, there was orange juice and shattered glass.

I'll have to bring another one, she said. Such a waste. What was you doing on the floor like that? She was pulling at me, to get me up, respectably onto my feet.

I didn't want to tell her I'd never been to bed at all. There would be no way of explaining that. I told her I must have fainted. That was almost as bad, because she seized on it.

It's one of the early signs, she said, pleased. That, and throwing up. She should have known there hadn't been time enough; but she was very hopeful.

No, it's not that, I said. I was sitting in the chair. I'm sure it isn't that. I was just dizzy. I was just standing here and things went dark.

It must have been the strain, she said, of yesterday and all. Takes it out of you.

She meant the Birth, and I said it did. By this time I was sitting in the chair, and she was kneeling on the floor, picking up the pieces of broken glass and egg, gathering them onto the tray. She blotted some of the orange juice with the paper napkin.

▷ **p. 153** *scroll:* long roll of paper for writing on **13** *waste:* Verschwendung **17** *faint:* lose consciousness **18** *seize on sth.* [siːz]: suddenly show a lot of interest in sth. **23** *be dizzy:* feel as if you are going to faint **24–25** *take a lot out of sb.:* make sb. very tired

I'll have to bring a cloth, she said. They'll want to know why the extra eggs. Unless you could do without. She looked up at me sideways, slyly, and I saw that it would be better if we could both pretend I'd eaten my breakfast after all. If she said she'd found me lying on the floor, there would be too many questions. She'd have to account for the broken glass in any case; but Rita would get surly if she had to cook a second breakfast.

I'll do without, I said. I'm not that hungry. This was good, it fit in with the dizziness. But I could manage the toast, I said. I didn't want to go without breakfast altogether.

It's been on the floor, she said.

I don't mind, I said. I sat there eating the piece of brown toast while she went into the bathroom and flushed the handful of egg, which could not be salvaged, down the toilet. Then she came back.

I'll say I dropped the tray on the way out, she said. It pleased me that she was willing to lie for me, even in such a small thing, even for her own advantage. It was a link between us.

I smiled at her. I hope nobody heard you, I said.

It did give me a turn, she said, as she stood in the doorway with the tray. At first I thought it was just your clothes, like. Then I said to myself, what're they doing there on the floor? I thought maybe you'd ...

Run off, I said.

Well, but, she said. But it was you.

Yes, I said. It was.

And it was, and she went out with the tray and came back with a cloth for the rest of the orange juice, and Rita that afternoon made a grumpy remark about some folks being all thumbs. Too much on their minds, don't look where they're going, she said, and we continued on from there as if nothing had happened.

That was in May. Spring has now been undergone. The tulips have had their moment and are done, shedding their petals one by one, like teeth. One day I came upon Serena Joy, kneeling on a cushion in the garden, her cane beside her on the grass. She was snipping off the seed pods with a pair of shears. I watched her sideways as I went past, with my basket of oranges and lamb chops. She was aiming, positioning the blades of the shears, then cutting with a convulsive jerk of the hands. Was it the arthritis, creeping up? Or some blitzkrieg, some kamikaze, committed on the swelling genitalia of the flowers?

The fruiting body. To cut off the seed pods is supposed to make the bulb store energy.

Saint Serena, on her knees, doing penance.

I often amused myself this way, with small mean-minded bitter jokes about her; but not for long. It doesn't do to linger, watching Serena Joy, from behind.

What I coveted was the shears.

Well. Then we had the irises, rising beautiful and cool on their tall stalks, like blown glass, like pastel water momentarily frozen in a splash, light blue, light mauve, and the darker ones, velvet and purple, black cat's-ears in the sun, indigo shadow, and the bleeding hearts, so female in shape it was a surprise they'd not long since been rooted out. There is something subversive about this garden of Serena's, a sense of buried things bursting upwards, wordlessly, into the light, as if to point, to say: Whatever is silenced will clamor to be heard, though silently. A Tennyson garden, heavy with scent, languid; the return of the word *swoon*. Light pours down upon it from the sun, true, but also heat rises, from the flowers themselves, you can feel it: like holding your hand an inch above an arm, a shoulder. It breathes, in the warmth, breathing itself in. To walk through it in these days, of peonies, of pinks and carnations, makes my head swim.

The willow is in full plumage and is no help, with its insinuating whispers. *Rendezvous*, it says, *terraces*; the sibilants run up my spine, a shiver as if in fever. The summer dress rustles against the flesh of my thighs, the grass grows underfoot, at the edges of my eyes there are movements, in the branches; feathers, flittings, grace notes, tree into bird, metamorphosis run wild. Goddesses are possible now and the air suffuses with desire. Even the bricks of the house are softening,

▷ **6** *account for sth.:* give an explanation for sth. **19** *give sb. a turn* (old-fashioned): give sb. a shock **27** *grumpy:* bad-tempered • *be all thumbs:* ungeschickt sein **34** *seed pods:* the part of a plant that contains the seed **36** *convulsive jerk:* sudden and quick movement **41** *do penance:* Buße tun **42** *mean-minded:* nasty **53** *clamor:* demand loudly **54** *Tennyson garden:* garden typical of those described in the poems of Alfred, Lord Tennyson (1809–1892) • *languid:* inactive, without energy **55** *swoon* (old-fashioned): faint **60** *be in full plumage:* (here) be full of leaves • *insinuating:* andeutungsvoll **61** *sibilant:* sound made up of the consonant 's' **64** *flitting* (n): (here) light and quick movement • *grace note:* ornamental musical note **66** *suffuse with sth.:* be spread all over with sth.

becoming tactile; if I leaned against them they'd be warm and yielding. It's amazing what denial can do. Did the sight of my ankle make him lightheaded, faint, at the checkpoint yesterday, when I dropped my pass and let him pick it up for me? No handkerchief, no fan, I use what's handy.

Winter is not so dangerous. I need hardness, cold, rigidity; not this heaviness, as if I'm a melon on a stem, this liquid ripeness.

The Commander and I have an arrangement. It's not the first such arrangement in history, though the shape it's taken is not the usual one.

I visit the Commander two or three nights a week, always after dinner, but only when I get the signal. The signal is Nick. If he's polishing the car when I set out for the shopping, or when I come back, and if his hat is on askew or not on at all, then I go. If he isn't there or if he has his hat on straight, then I stay in my room in the ordinary way. On Ceremony nights, of course, none of this applies.

The difficulty is the Wife, as always. After dinner she goes to their bedroom, from where she could conceivably hear me as I sneak along the hall, although I take care to be very quiet. Or she stays in the sitting room, knitting away at her endless Angel scarves, turning out more and more yards of intricate and useless wool people: her form of procreation, it must be. The sitting-room door is usually left ajar when she's in there, and I don't dare to go past it. When I've had the signal but can't make it, down the stairs or along the hall past the sitting room, the Commander understands. He knows my situation, none better. He knows all the rules.

Sometimes, however, Serena Joy is out, visiting another Commander's Wife, a sick one; that's the only place she could conceivably go, by herself, in the evenings. She takes food, a cake or pie or loaf of bread baked by Rita, or a jar of jelly, made from the mint leaves that grow in her garden. They get sick a lot, these Wives of the Commanders. It adds interest to their lives. As for us, the Handmaids and even the Marthas, we avoid illness. The Marthas don't want to be forced to retire, because who knows where they go? You don't see that many old women around any more. And as for us, any real illness, anything lingering, weakening, a loss of flesh or appetite, a fall of hair, a failure of the glands, would be terminal. I remember Cora, earlier in the spring, staggering around even though she had the flu, holding onto the doorframes when she thought no one was looking, being careful not to cough. A slight cold, she said when Serena asked her.

Serena herself sometimes takes a few days off, tucked up in bed. Then she's the one to get the company, the Wives rustling up the stairs, clucking and cheerful; she gets the cakes and pies, the jelly, the bouquets of flowers from their gardens.

They take turns. There is some sort of list, invisible, unspoken. Each is careful not to hog more than her share of the attention.

On the nights when Serena is due to be out, I'm sure to be summoned.

The first time, I was confused. His needs were obscure to me, and what I could perceive of them seemed to me ridiculous, laughable, like a fetish for lace-up shoes.

Also, there had been a letdown of sorts. What had I been expecting, behind that closed door, the first time? Something unspeakable, down on all fours perhaps, perversions, whips, mutilations? At the very least some minor sexual manipulation, some bygone peccadillo now denied him, prohibited by law and punishable by amputation. To be asked to play Scrabble, instead, as if we were an old married couple, or two children, seemed kinky in the extreme, a violation too in its own way. As a request it was opaque.

So when I left the room, it still wasn't clear to me what he wanted, or why, or whether I could fulfil any of it for him. If there's to be a bargain, the terms of exchange must be set forth. This was something he certainly had not done. I thought he might be toying, some cat-and-a-mouse routine, but now I think that his motives and desires weren't obvious even to him. They had not yet reached the level of words.

The second evening began in the same way as the first. I went to the door, which was closed, knocked on it, was told to come in. Then followed the same two games, with the smooth beige counters. *Prolix*, *quartz*, *quandary*, *sylph*, *rhythm*, all the old tricks with consonants I could dream up or remember. My tongue felt thick with

▷ **1** *tactile:* pleasant to touch **14** *askew* [ə'skjuː]: not straight **21** *intricate:* (here) complex **22** *procreation:* Fortpflanzung **37** *glands:* Drüsen **46** *hog sth.:* take too much of sth. so that others cannot get any **52** *letdown:* disappointment **55** *peccadillo:* kleine Sünde **59** *opaque* [oʊ'peɪk]: not clear **63** *toy:* play carelessly

the effort of spelling. It was like using a language I'd once known but had nearly forgotten, a language having to do with customs that had long before passed out of the world: café au lait at an outdoor table, with a brioche, absinthe in a tall glass, or shrimp in a cornucopia of newspaper; things I'd once read about but had never seen. It was like trying to walk without crutches, like those phony scenes in old TV movies. *You can do it. I know you can.* That was the way my mind lurched and stumbled, among the sharp *r*'s and *t*'s, sliding over the ovoid vowels as if on pebbles.

The Commander was patient when I hesitated, or asked him for a correct spelling. We can always look it up in the dictionary, he said. He said we. The first time, I realized, he'd let me win.

That night I was expecting everything to be the same, including the good-night kiss. But when we'd finished the second game, he sat back in his chair. He placed his elbows on the arms of the chair, the tips of his fingers together, and looked at me.

I have a little present for you, he said.

He smiled a little. Then he pulled open the top drawer of his desk and took something out. He held it a moment, casually enough, between thumb and finger, as if deciding whether or not to give it to me. Although it was upside-down from where I was sitting, I recognized it. They were once common enough. It was a magazine, a women's magazine it looked like from the picture, a model on glossy paper, hair blown, neck scarfed, mouth lipsticked; the fall fashions. I thought such magazines had all been destroyed, but here was one, left over, in a Commander's private study, where you'd least expect to find such a thing. He looked down at the model, who was right-side-up to him; he was still smiling, that wistful smile of his. It was a look you'd give to an almost extinct animal, at the zoo.

Staring at the magazine, as he dangled it before me like fishbait, I wanted it. I wanted it with a force that made the ends of my fingers ache. At the same time I saw this longing of mine as trivial and absurd, because I'd taken such magazines lightly enough once. I'd read them in dentists' offices, and sometimes on planes; I'd bought them to take to hotel rooms, a device to fill in empty time while I was waiting for Luke. After I'd leafed through them I would throw them away, for they were infinitely discardable, and a day or two later I wouldn't be able to remember what had been in them.

Though I remembered now. What was in them was promise. They dealt in transformations; they suggested an endless series of possibilities, extending like the reflections in two mirrors set facing one another, stretching on, replica after replica, to the vanishing point. They suggested one adventure after another, one wardrobe after another, one improvement after another, one man after another. They suggested rejuvenation, pain overcome and transcended, endless love. The real promise in them was immortality.

This was what he was holding, without knowing it. He riffled the pages. I felt myself leaning forward.

It's an old one, he said, a curio of sorts. From the seventies, I think. *A Vogue*. This like a wine connoisseur dropping a name. I thought you might like to look at it.

I hung back. He might be testing me, to see how deep my indoctrination had really gone. It's not permitted, I said.

In here, it is, he said quietly. I saw the point. Having broken the main taboo, why should I hesitate over another one, something minor? Or another, or another; who could tell where it might stop? Behind this particular door, taboo dissolved.

I took the magazine from him and turned it the right way round. There they were again, the images of my childhood: bold, striding, confident, their arms flung out as if to claim space, their legs apart, feet planted squarely on the earth. There was something Renaissance about the pose, but it was princes I thought of, not coiffed and ringleted maidens. Those candid eyes, shadowed with makeup, yes, but like the eyes of cats, fixed for the pounce. No quailing, no clinging there, not in those capes and rough tweeds, those boots that came to the knee. Pirates, these women, with their ladylike briefcases for the loot and their horsy, acquisitive teeth.

I felt the Commander watching me as I turned the pages. I knew I was doing something I shouldn't have been doing, and that he found

▷ **4** *brioche* (French): type of sweet bread • *absinthe* (French): type of alcoholic drink • *cornucopia:* Füllhorn **6** *crutches:* Krücken **8** *lurch:* make a sudden, unsteady movement **9** *ovoid* (fml): egg-shaped **37** *discardable:* that can be thrown away **47** *riffle sth.:* turn over sth. (esp. pages) quickly **49** *curio:* small object that is rare or unusual, often sth. that people collect **64** *pounce:* attack • *quail:* feel frightened **67** *loot:* Beute

pleasure in seeing me do it. I should have felt evil; by Aunt Lydia's lights, I was evil. But I didn't feel evil. Instead I felt like an old Edwardian seaside postcard: *naughty*. What was he going to give me next? A girdle?

Why do you have this? I asked him.

Some of us, he said, retain an appreciation for the old things.

But these were supposed to have been burned, I said. There were house-to-house searches, bonfires ...

What's dangerous in the hands of the multitudes, he said, with what may or may not have been irony, is safe enough for those whose motives are ...

Beyond reproach, I said.

He nodded gravely. Impossible to tell whether or not he meant it.

But why show it to me? I said, and then felt stupid. What could he possibly say? That he was amusing himself, at my expense? For he must have known how painful it was to me, to be reminded of the former time.

I wasn't prepared for what he actually did say. Who else could I show it to? he said, and there it was again, that sadness.

Should I go further? I thought. I didn't want to push him, too far, too fast. I knew I was dispensable. Nevertheless I said, too softly, How about your Wife?

He seemed to think about that. No, he said. She wouldn't understand. Anyway, she won't talk to me much any more. We don't seem to have much in common, these days.

So there it was, out in the open: his wife didn't understand him.

That's what I was there for, then. The same old thing. It was too banal to be true.

On the third night I asked him for some hand lotion. I didn't want to sound begging, but I wanted what I could get.

Some what? he said, courteous as ever. He was across the desk from me. He didn't touch me much, except for that one obligatory kiss. No pawing, no heavy breathing, none of that; it would have been out of place, somehow, for him as well as for me.

Hand lotion, I said. Or face lotion. Our skin gets very dry. For some reason I said *our* instead of *my*. I would have liked to ask also for some bath oil, in those little colored globules you used to be able to get, that were so much like magic to me when they existed in the round glass bowl in my mother's bathroom at home. But I thought he wouldn't know what they were. Anyway, they probably weren't made any more.

Dry? the Commander said, as if he'd never thought about that before. What do you do about it?

We use butter, I said. When we can get it. Or margarine. A lot of the time it's margarine.

Butter, he said, musing. That's very clever. Butter. He laughed.

I could have slapped him.

I think I could get some of that, he said, as if indulging a child's wish for bubble gum. But she might smell it on you. I wondered if this fear of his came from past experience. Long past: lipstick on the collar, perfume on the cuffs, a scene, late at night, in some kitchen or bedroom. A man devoid of such experience wouldn't think of that. Unless he's craftier than he looks.

I'd be careful, I said. Besides, she's never that close to me.

Sometimes she is, he said.

I looked down. I'd forgotten about that. I could feel myself blushing. I won't use it on those nights, I said.

On the fourth evening he gave me the hand lotion, in an unlabelled plastic bottle. It wasn't very good quality; it smelled faintly of vegetable oil. No Lily of the Valley for me.

It may have been something they made up for use in hospitals, on bedsores. But I thanked him anyway.

The trouble is, I said, I don't have anywhere to keep it.

In your room, he said, as if it were obvious.

They'd find it, I said. Someone would find it.

Why? he asked, as if he really didn't know. Maybe he didn't. It wasn't the first time he gave evidence of being truly ignorant of the real conditions under which we lived.

▷ **1–2** *by sb.'s lights:* according to sb.'s standards **3** *Edwardian seaside postcard:* postcards showing slightly frivolous pictures of young women, esp. popular at the beginning of the 20th century (during the reign of the British king, Edward VII, 1901–1910) • *naughty:* ungezogen **4** *girdle:* Hüfthalter **12** *beyond reproach:* that cannot be criticized **31** *courteous:* polite **33** *paw sb.:* touch sb. (in a rough sexual way) **46** *muse:* think carefully **48** *indulge sb./sth.:* be generous in allowing sb./sth. to have their/its way **51** *cuff:* Hemdenmanschette **52** *devoid of sth.:* lacking in sth. **53** *crafty* (derog): clever and calculating **62** *bedsore:* a painful and infected place on sb.'s body caused by lying in bed for a long time

They look, I said. They look in all our rooms.

What for? he said. I think I lost control then, a little. Razor blades, I said. Books, writing, black-market stuff. All the things we aren't supposed to have. Jesus Christ, you ought to know. My voice was angrier than I'd intended, but he didn't even wince.

Then you'll have to keep it here, he said.

So that's what I did.

He watched me smoothing it over my hands and then my face with that same air of looking in through the bars. I wanted to turn my back on him – it was as if he were in the bathroom with me – but I didn't dare.

For him, I must remember, I am only a whim.

CHAPTER 26

When the night for the Ceremony came round again, two or three weeks later, I found that things were changed. There was an awkwardness now that there hadn't been before. Before, I'd treated it as a job, an unpleasant job to be gone through as fast as possible so it could be over with. Steel yourself, my mother used to say, before examinations I didn't want to take or swims in cold water. I never thought much at the time about what the phrase meant, but it had something to do with metal, with armor, and that's what I would do, I would steel myself. I would pretend not to be present, not in the flesh.

This state of absence, of existing apart from the body, had been true of the Commander too, I knew now. Probably he thought about other things the whole time he was with me; with us, for of course Serena Joy was there on those evenings also. He might have been thinking about what he did during the day, or about playing golf, or about what he'd had for dinner. The sexual act, although he performed it in a perfunctory way, must have been largely unconscious, for him, like scratching himself.

But that night, the first since the beginning of whatever this new arrangement was between us – I had no name for it – I felt shy of him. I felt, for one thing, that he was actually looking at me, and I didn't like it. The lights were on, as usual, since Serena Joy always avoided anything that would have created an aura of romance or eroticism, however slight: overhead lights, harsh despite the canopy. It was like being on an operating table, in the full glare; like being on a stage. I was conscious that my legs were hairy, in the straggly way of legs that have once been shaved but have grown back; I was conscious of my armpits too, although of course he couldn't see them. I felt uncouth. This act of copulation, fertilization perhaps, which should have been no more to me than a bee is to a flower, had become for me

▷ **15** *awkwardness* ['ɔːkwərdnəs]: feeling of embarrassment **17** *steel yourself:* be strong **20** *armor:* Rüstung **29** *perfunctory* (fml): done as a duty or habit without any real interest or feeling **36** *harsh:* cruel, unkind **40** *uncouth* [ʌn'kuːθ]: unattractive, uncultured

indecorous, an embarrassing breach of propriety, which it hadn't been before.

He was no longer a thing to me. That was the problem. I realized it that night, and the realization has stayed with me. It complicates.

Serena Joy had changed for me, too. Once I'd merely hated her, for her part in what was being done to me; and because she hated me too and resented my presence, and because she would be the one to raise my child, should I be able to have one after all. But now, although I still hated her, no more so than when she was gripping my hands so hard that her rings bit my flesh, pulling my hands back as well, which she must have done on purpose to make me as uncomfortable as she could, the hatred was no longer pure and simple. Partly I was jealous of her; but how could I be jealous of a woman so obviously dried-up and unhappy? You can only be jealous of someone who has something you think you ought to have yourself. Nevertheless I was jealous.

But I also felt guilty about her. I felt I was an intruder, in a territory that ought to have been hers. Now that I was seeing the Commander on the sly, if only to play his games and listen to him talk, our functions were no longer as separate as they should have been in theory. I was taking something away from her, although she didn't know it. I was filching. Never mind that it was something she apparently didn't want or had no use for, had rejected even; still, it was hers, and if I took it away, this mysterious "it" I couldn't quite define – for the Commander wasn't in love with me, I refused to believe he felt anything for me as extreme as that – what would be left for her?

Why should I care? I told myself. She's nothing to me, she dislikes me, she'd have me out of the house in a minute, or worse, if she could think up any excuse at all. If she were to find out, for instance. He wouldn't be able to intervene, to save me; the transgressions of women in the household, whether Martha or Handmaid, are supposed to be under the jurisdiction of the Wives alone. She was a malicious and vengeful woman, I knew that. Nevertheless I couldn't shake it, that small compunction towards her.

Also: I now had power over her, of a kind, although she didn't know it. And I enjoyed that. Why pretend? I enjoyed it a lot.

But the Commander could give me away so easily, by a look, by a gesture, some tiny slip that would reveal to anyone watching that there was something between us now. He almost did it the night of the

Ceremony. He reached his hand up as if to touch my face; I moved my head to the side, to warn him away, hoping Serena Joy hadn't noticed, and he withdrew his hand again, withdrew into himself and his single-minded journey.

Don't do that again, I said to him the next time we were alone.

Do what? he said.

Try to touch me like that, when we're ... when she's there.

Did I? he said.

You could get me transferred, I said. To the Colonies. You know that. Or worse. I thought he should continue to act, in public, as if I were a large vase or a window: part of the background, inanimate or transparent.

I'm sorry, he said. I didn't mean to. But I find it ...

What? I said, when he didn't go on.

Impersonal, he said.

How long did it take you to find that out? I said. You can see from the way I was speaking to him that we were already on different terms.

For the generations that come after, Aunt Lydia said, it will be so much better. The women will live in harmony together, all in one family; you will be like daughters to them, and when the population level is up to scratch again we'll no longer have to transfer you from one house to another because there will be enough to go round. There can be bonds of real affection, she said, blinking at us ingratiatingly, under such conditions. Women united for a common end! Helping one another in their daily chores as they walk the path of life together, each performing her appointed task. Why expect one woman to carry out all the functions necessary to the serene running of a household? It isn't reasonable or humane. Your daughters will have greater freedom. We are working towards the goal of a little garden for each one, each one of you – the clasped hands again, the breathy voice – and that's just one *for instance*. The raised finger, wagging at us. But

▷ **1** *indecorous* [ɪn'dekərəs]: violating good manners • *breach of propriety* [prə'praɪəti]: failure to behave in a morally acceptable way **19** *on the sly* (derog): secretly **22** *filch* (infml): steal **30** *transgression* (fml): mistake, immoral or illegal act **33** *malicious:* hateful and wanting to hurt or harm • *vengeful:* having a desire to punish sb. **38** *slip:* small mistake that reveals a secret **60** *up to scratch:* satisfactory, as good as it should be **62** *ingratiating:* trying too hard to please

we can't be greedy pigs and demand too much before it's ready, now can we?

The fact is that I'm his mistress. Men at the top have always had mistresses, why should things be any different now? The arrangements aren't quite the same, granted. The mistress used to be kept in a minor house or apartment of her own, and now they've amalgamated things. But underneath it's the same. More or less. *Outside woman*, they used to be called, in some countries. I am the outside woman. It's my job to provide what is otherwise lacking. Even the Scrabble. It's an absurd as well as an ignominious position.

Sometimes I think she knows. Sometimes I think they're in collusion. Sometimes I think she put him up to it, and is laughing at me; as I laugh, from time to time and with irony, at myself. Let her take the weight, she can say to herself. Maybe she's withdrawn from him, almost completely; maybe that's her version of freedom.

But even so, and stupidly enough, I'm happier than I was before. It's something to do, for one thing. Something to fill the time, at night, instead of sitting alone in my room. It's something else to think about. I don't love the Commander or anything like it, but he's of interest to me, he occupies space, he is more than a shadow.

And I for him. To him I'm no longer merely a usable body. To him I'm not just a boat with no cargo, a chalice with no wine in it, an oven – to be crude – minus the bun. To him I am not merely empty.

CHAPTER 27

I walk with Ofglen along the summer street. It's warm, humid; this would have been sundress-and-sandals weather, once. In each of our baskets are strawberries – the strawberries are in season now, so we'll eat them and eat them until we're sick of them – and some wrapped fish. We got the fish at Loaves and Fishes, with its wooden sign, a fish with a smile and eyelashes. It doesn't sell loaves though. Most households bake their own, though you can get dried-up rolls and wizened doughnuts at Daily Bread, if you run short. Loaves and Fishes is hardly ever open. Why bother opening when there's nothing to sell? The sea fisheries were defunct several years ago; the few fish they have now are from fish farms, and taste muddy. The news says the coastal areas are being "rested." Sole, I remember, and haddock, swordfish, scallops, tuna; lobsters, stuffed and baked, salmon, pink and fat, grilled in steaks. Could they all be extinct, like the whales? I've heard that rumor, passed on to me in soundless words, the lips hardly moving, as we stood in line outside, waiting for the store to open, lured by the picture of succulent white fillets in the window. They put the picture in the window when they have something, take it away when they don't. Sign language.

Ofglen and I walk slowly today; we are hot in our long dresses, wet under the arms, tired. At least in this heat we don't wear gloves. There used to be an ice-cream store, somewhere in this block. I can't remember the name. Things can change so quickly, buildings can be torn down or turned into something else, it's hard to keep them straight in your mind the way they used to be. You could get double scoops, and if you wanted they would put chocolate sprinkles on the top. These had the name of a man. Johnnies? Jackies? I can't remember.

We would go there, when she was little, and I'd hold her up so she could see through the glass side of the counter, where the vats of ice

▷ **6–7** *amalgamate sth.:* join sth. together **10** *ignominious* (fml): that makes you feel ashamed **23** *oven minus the bun:* reference to the expression "have a bun in the oven" (= be pregnant) • *crude:* offensive, rude **31** *wizened* ['wɪzənd]: verschrumpelt **33** *defunct:* no longer working **37** *extinct:* no longer in existence **40** *lured:* persuaded, tricked **52** *vat:* large container

cream were on display, colored so delicately, pale orange, pale green, pale pink, and I'd read the names to her so she could choose. She wouldn't choose by the name, though, but by the color. Her dresses and overalls were those colors too. Ice cream pastels.

Jimmies, that was the name.

Ofglen and I are more comfortable with one another now, we're used to each other. Siamese twins. We don't bother much with the formalities any more when we greet each other; we smile and move off, in tandem, travelling smoothly along our daily track. Now and again we vary the route; there's nothing against it, as long as we stay within the barriers. A rat in a maze is free to go anywhere, as long as it stays inside the maze.

We've been to the stores already, and the church; now we're at the Wall. Nothing on it today, they don't leave the bodies hanging as long in summer as they do in winter, because of the flies and the smell. This was once the land of air sprays, Pine and Floral, and people retain the taste; especially the Commanders, who preach purity in all things.

"You have everything on your list?" Ofglen says to me now, though she knows I do. Our lists are never long. She's given up some of her passivity lately, some of her melancholy. Often she speaks to me first.

"Yes," I say.

"Let's go around," she says. She means down, towards the river. We haven't been that way for a while.

"Fine," I say. I don't turn at once, though, but remain standing where I am, taking a last look at the Wall. There are the red bricks, there are the searchlights, there's the barbed wire, there are the hooks. Somehow the Wall is even more foreboding when it's empty like this. When there's someone hanging on it at least you know the worst. But vacant, it is also potential, like a storm approaching. When I can see the bodies, the actual bodies, when I can guess from the sizes and shapes that none of them is Luke, I can believe also that he is still alive.

I don't know why I expect him to appear on this wall. There are hundreds of other places they could have killed him. But I can't shake the idea that he's in there, at this moment, behind the blank red bricks.

I try to imagine which building he's in. I can remember where the buildings are, inside the Wall; we used to be able to walk freely there, when it was a university. We still go in there once in a while, for Women's Salvagings. Most of the buildings are red brick too; some have arched doorways, a Romanesque effect, from the nineteenth century. We aren't allowed inside the buildings any more; but who would want to go in? Those buildings belong to the Eyes.

Maybe he's in the Library. Somewhere in the vaults. The stacks.

The Library is like a temple. There's a long flight of white steps, leading to the rank of doors. Then, inside, another white staircase going up. To either side of it, on the wall, there are angels. Also there are men fighting, or about to fight, looking clean and noble, not dirty and blood-stained and smelly the way they must have looked. Victory is on one side of the inner doorway, leading them on, and Death is on the other. It's a mural in honour of some war or other. The men on the side of Death are still alive. They're going to Heaven. Death is a beautiful woman, with wings and one breast almost bare; or is that Victory? I can't remember.

They won't have destroyed that.

We turn our backs to the Wall, head left. Here there are several empty storefronts, their glass windows scrawled with soap. I try to remember what was sold in them, once. Cosmetics? Jewellery? Most of the stores carrying things for men are still open; it's just the ones dealing in what they call vanities that have been shut down.

At the corner is the store known as Soul Scrolls. It's a franchise: there are Soul Scrolls in every city center, in every suburb, or so they say. It must make a lot of profit.

The window of Soul Scrolls is shatterproof. Behind it are print-out machines, row on row of them; these machines are known as Holy Rollers, but only among us, it's a disrespectful nickname. What the machines print is prayers, roll upon roll, prayers going out endlessly. They're ordered by Compuphone, I've overheard the Commander's Wife doing it. Ordering prayers from Soul Scrolls is supposed to be a sign of piety and faithfulness to the regime, so of course the Commanders' Wives do it a lot. It helps their husbands' careers.

There are five different prayers: for health, wealth, a death, a birth, a sin. You pick the one you want, punch in the number, then punch

▷ **11** *maze:* labyrinth **27** *foreboding:* dangerous, threatening **39** *arched:* curved **42** *vault:* Kellergewölbe, Gruft • *stacks:* part of a library where books that are not often needed are stored **49** *mural:* wall painting **58** *vanity:* (here) things to make you look attractive

in your own number so your account will be debited, and punch in the number of times you want the prayer repeated.

The machines talk as they print out the prayers; if you like, you can go inside and listen to them, the toneless metallic voices repeating the same thing over and over. Once the prayers have been printed out and said, the paper rolls back through another slot and is recycled into fresh paper again. There are no people inside the building: the machines run by themselves. You can't hear the voices from outside; only a murmur, a hum, like a devout crowd, on its knees. Each machine has an eye painted in gold on the side, flanked by two small golden wings.

I try to remember what this place sold when it was a store, before it was turned into Soul Scrolls. I think it was lingerie. Pink and silver boxes, colored pantyhose, brassieres with lace, silk scarves? Something lost.

Ofglen and I stand outside Soul Scrolls, looking through the shatterproof windows, watching the prayers well out from the machines and disappear again through the slot, back to the realm of the unsaid. Now I shift my gaze. What I see is not the machines, but Ofglen, reflected in the glass of the window. She's looking straight at me.

We can see into each other's eyes. This is the first time I've ever seen Ofglen's eyes, directly, steadily, not aslant. Her face is oval, pink, plump but not fat, her eyes roundish.

She holds my stare in the glass, level, unwavering. Now it's hard to look away. There's a shock in this seeing; it's like seeing somebody naked, for the first time. There is risk, suddenly, in the air between us, where there was none before. Even this meeting of eyes holds danger. Though there's nobody near.

At last Ofglen speaks. "Do you think God listens," she says, "to these machines?" She is whispering: our habit at the Center.

In the past this would have been a trivial enough remark, a kind of scholarly speculation. Right now it's treason.

I could scream. I could run away. I could turn from her silently, to show her I won't tolerate this kind of talk in my presence. Subversion, sedition, blasphemy, heresy, all rolled into one.

I steel myself. "No," I say.

She lets out her breath, in a long sigh of relief. We have crossed the invisible line together. "Neither do I," she says.

"Though I suppose it's faith, of a kind," I say. "Like Tibetan prayer wheels."

"What are those?" she asks.

"I only read about them," I say. "They were moved around by the wind. They're all gone now."

"Like everything," she says. Only now do we stop looking at one another.

"Is it safe here?" I whisper.

"I figure it's the safest place," she says. "We look like we're praying, is all."

"What about them?"

"Them?" she says, still whispering. "You're always safest out of doors, no mikes, and why would they put one here? They'd think nobody would dare. But we've stayed long enough. There's no sense in being late getting back." We turn away together. "Keep your head down as we walk," she says, "and lean just a little towards me. That way I can hear you better. Don't talk when there's anyone coming."

We walk, heads bent as usual. I'm so excited I can hardly breathe, but I keep a steady pace. Now more than ever I must avoid drawing attention to myself.

"I thought you were a true believer," Ofglen says.

"I thought you were," I say.

"You were always so stinking pious."

"So were you," I reply. I want to laugh, shout, hug her.

"You can join us," she says.

"Us?" I say. There is an *us* then, there's a *we*. I knew it.

"You didn't think I was the only one," she says.

I didn't think that. It occurs to me that she may be a spy, a plant, set to trap me; such is the soil in which we grow. But I can't believe it; hope is rising in me, like sap in a tree. Blood in a wound. We have made an opening.

I want to ask her if she's seen Moira, if anyone can find out what's happened, to Luke, to my child, my mother even, but there's not

▷ **9** *devout:* having strong religious faith **33** *treason:* Hochverrat **36** *sedition:* Volksverhetzung, Aufwiegelung • *heresy:* Ketzerei **70** *sap:* liquid (in a tree) that carries food to all parts of the tree

much time; too soon we're approaching the corner of the main street, the one before the first barrier. There will be too many people.

"Don't say a word," Ofglen warns me, though she doesn't need to. "In any way."

"Of course I won't," I say. Who could I tell?

We walk the main street in silence, past Lilies, past All Flesh. There are more people on the sidewalks this afternoon than usual: the warm weather must have brought them out. Women, in green, blue, red, stripes; men too, some in uniform, some only in civilian suits. The sun is free, it is still there to be enjoyed. Though no one bathes in it any more, not in public.

There are more cars too, Whirlwinds with their chauffeurs and their cushioned occupants, lesser cars driven by lesser men.

Something is happening: there's a commotion, a flurry among the shoals of cars. Some are pulling over to the side, as if to get out of the way. I look up quickly: it's a black van, with the white-winged eye on the side. It doesn't have the siren on, but the other cars avoid it anyway. It cruises slowly along the street, as if looking for something: shark on the prowl.

I freeze, cold travels through me, down to my feet. There must have been microphones, they've heard us after all.

Ofglen, under cover of her sleeve, grips my elbow. "Keep moving," she whispers. "Pretend not to see."

But I can't help seeing. Right in front of us the van pulls up. Two Eyes, in gray suits, leap from the opening double doors at the back. They grab a man who is walking along, a man with a briefcase, an ordinary-looking man, slam him back against the black side of the van. He's there a moment, splayed out against the metal as if stuck to it; then one of the Eyes moves in on him, does something sharp and brutal that doubles him over, into a limp cloth bundle. They pick him up and heave him into the back of the van like a sack of mail. Then they are inside also and the doors are closed and the van moves on.

It's over, in seconds, and the traffic on the street resumes as if nothing has happened.

What I feel is relief. It wasn't me.

CHAPTER 28

I don't feel like a nap this afternoon, there's still too much adrenalin. I sit on the window seat, looking out through the semi-sheer of the curtains. White nightgown. The window is as open as it goes, there's a breeze, hot in the sunlight, and the white cloth blows across my face. From the outside I must look like a cocoon, a spook, face enshrouded like this, only the outlines visible, of nose, bandaged mouth, blind eyes. But I like the sensation, the soft cloth brushing my skin. It's like being in a cloud.

They've given me a small electric fan, which helps in this humidity. It whirs on the floor, in the corner, its blades encased in grillwork. If I were Moira, I'd know how to take it apart, reduce it to its cutting edges. I have no screwdriver, but if I were Moira I could do it without a screwdriver. I'm not Moira.

What would she tell me, about the Commander, if she were here? Probably she'd disapprove. She disapproved of Luke, back then. Not of Luke but of the fact that he was married. She said I was poaching, on another woman's ground. I said Luke wasn't a fish or a piece of dirt either, he was a human being and could make his own decisions. She said I was rationalizing. I said I was in love. She said that was no excuse. Moira was always more logical than I am.

I said she didn't have that problem herself any more, since she'd decided to prefer women, and as far as I could see she had no scruples about stealing them or borrowing them when she felt like it. She said it was different, because the balance of power was equal between women so sex was an even-steven transaction. I said "even-steven" was a sexist phrase, if she was going to be like that, and anyway that argument was outdated. She said I had trivialized the issue and if I thought it was outdated I was living with my head in the sand.

We said all this in my kitchen, drinking coffee, sitting at my kitchen table, in those low, intense voices we used for such arguments when

▷ **14** *flurry:* sudden period of activity and excitement **15** *shoal:* group (usu. of fish) **19** *shark:* Hai • *on the prowl:* looking for sth., hunting **40** *cocoon:* Kokon **51** *poach:* illegally hunt animals or fish on sb. else's property **60** *even-steven* (rhyming slang): (here) between equals

we were in our early twenties; a carry-over from college. The kitchen was in a run-down apartment in a clapboard house near the river, the kind with three storeys and a rickety outside back staircase. I had the second floor, which meant I got noise from both above and below, two unwanted stereo disc players thumping late into the night. Students, I knew. I was still on my first job, which didn't pay much: I worked a computer in an insurance company. So the hotels, with Luke, didn't mean only love or even only sex to me. They also meant time off from the cockroaches, the dripping sink, the linoleum that was peeling off the floor in patches, even from my own attempts to brighten things up by sticking posters on the wall and hanging prisms in the windows. I had plants, too; though they always got spider mites or died from being unwatered. I would go off with Luke, and neglect them.

I said there was more than one way of living with your head in the sand and that if Moira thought she could create Utopia by shutting herself up in a women-only enclave she was sadly mistaken. Men were not just going to go away, I said. You couldn't just ignore them.

That's like saying you should go out and catch syphilis merely because it exists, Moira said.

Are you calling Luke a social disease? I said.

Moira laughed. Listen to us, she said. Shit. We sound like your mother.

We both laughed then, and when she left we hugged each other as usual. There was a time when we didn't hug, after she'd told me about being gay; but then she said I didn't turn her on, reassuring me, and we'd gone back to it. We could fight and wrangle and name-call, but it didn't change anything underneath. She was still my oldest friend.

Is.

I got a better apartment after that, where I lived for the two years it took Luke to pry himself loose. I paid for it myself, with my new job. It was in a library, not the big one with Death and Victory, a smaller one.

I worked transferring books to computer discs, to cut down on storage space and replacement costs, they said. Discers, we called ourselves. We called the library a discotheque, which was a joke of ours. After the books were transferred they were supposed to go to the shredder, but sometimes I took them home with me. I liked the feel of them, and the look. Luke said I had the mind of an antiquarian. He liked that, he liked old things himself.

It's strange, now, to think about having a job. *Job*. It's a funny word. It's a job for a man. Do a jobbie, they'd say to children, when they were being toilet-trained. Or of dogs: he did a job on the carpet. You were supposed to hit them with rolled-up newspapers, my mother said. I can remember when there were newspapers, though I never had a dog, only cats.

The Book of Job.

All those women having jobs: hard to imagine, now, but thousands of them had jobs, millions. It was considered the normal thing. Now it's like remembering the paper money, when they still had that. My mother kept some of it, pasted into her scrapbook along with the early photos. It was obsolete by then, you couldn't buy anything with it. Pieces of paper, thickish, greasy to the touch, green-colored, with pictures on each side, some old man in a wig and on the other side a pyramid with an eye above it. It said *In God We Trust*. My mother said people used to have signs beside their cash registers, for a joke: *In God We Trust, All Others Pay Cash*. That would be blasphemy now.

You had to take those pieces of paper with you when you went shopping, though by the time I was nine or ten most people used plastic cards. Not for the groceries though, that came later. It seems so primitive, totemistic even, like cowrie shells. I must have used that kind of money myself, a little, before everything went on the Compubank.

I guess that's how they were able to do it, in the way they did, all at once, without anyone knowing beforehand. If there had still been portable money, it would have been more difficult.

It was after the catastrophe, when they shot the President and machine-gunned the Congress and the army declared a state of emergency. They blamed it on the Islamic fanatics, at the time.

Keep calm, they said on television. Everything is under control.

▷ **2** *clapboard:* Schindel **9** *cockroach:* Kakerlake **31** *pry sth. loose:* separate sth. (from sth. else) with force **47** *the Book of Job:* das Buch Hiob **62** *cowrie shell:* small shiny shell that was formerly used as money in parts of Africa and Asia

I was stunned. Everyone was, I know that. It was hard to believe. The entire government, gone like that. How did they get in, how did it happen?

That was when they suspended the Constitution. They said it would be temporary. There wasn't even any rioting in the streets. People stayed home at night, watching television, looking for some direction. There wasn't even an enemy you could put your finger on.

Look out, said Moira to me, over the phone. Here it comes.

Here what comes? I said.

You wait, she said. They've been building up to this. It's you and me up against the wall, baby. She was quoting an expression of my mother's, but she wasn't intending to be funny.

Things continued in that state of suspended animation for weeks, although some things did happen. Newspapers were censored and some were closed down, for security reasons they said. The roadblocks began to appear, and Identipasses.

Everyone approved of that, since it was obvious you couldn't be too careful. They said that new elections would be held, but that it would take some time to prepare for them. The thing to do, they said, was to continue on as usual.

The Pornomarts were shut, though, and there were no longer any Feels on Wheels vans and Bun-Dle Buggies circling the Square. But I wasn't sad to see them go. We all knew what a nuisance they'd been.

It's high time somebody did something, said the woman behind the counter, at the store where I usually bought my cigarettes. It was on the corner, a newsstand chain: papers, candy, cigarettes. The woman was older, with gray hair; my mother's generation.

Did they just close them, or what? I asked.

She shrugged. Who knows, who cares, she said. Maybe they just moved them off somewhere else. Trying to get rid of it altogether is like trying to stamp out mice, you know? She punched my Compunumber into the till, barely looking at it: I was a regular, by then. People were complaining, she said.

The next morning, on my way to the library for the day, I stopped by the same store for another pack, because I'd run out. I was smoking more those days, it was the tension, you could feel it, like a subterranean hum, although things seemed so quiet. I was drinking more coffee too, and having trouble sleeping. Everyone was a little jumpy. There was a lot more music on the radio than usual, and fewer words.

It was after we'd been married, for years it seemed; she was three or four, in daycare.

We'd all got up in the usual way and had breakfast, granola, I remember, and Luke had driven her off to school, in the little outfit I'd bought her just a couple of weeks before, striped overalls and a blue T-shirt. What month was this? It must have been September. There was a School Pool that was supposed to pick them up, but for some reason I'd wanted Luke to do it, I was getting worried even about the School Pool. No children walked to school any more, there had been too many disappearances.

When I got to the corner store, the usual woman wasn't there. Instead there was a man, a young man, he couldn't have been more than twenty.

She sick? I said as I handed him my card.

Who? he said, aggressively I thought.

The woman who's usually here, I said.

How would I know, he said. He was punching my number in, studying each number, punching with one finger. He obviously hadn't done it before. I drummed my fingers on the counter, impatient for a cigarette, wondering if anyone had ever told him something could be done about those pimples on his neck. I remember quite clearly what he looked like: tall, slightly stooped, dark hair cut short, brown eyes that seemed to focus two inches behind the bridge of my nose, and that acne. I suppose I remember him so clearly because of what he said next.

Sorry, he said. This number's not valid.

That's ridiculous, I said. It must be, I've got thousands in my account. I just got the statement two days ago. Try it again.

It's not valid, he repeated obstinately. See that red light? Means it's not valid.

You must have made a mistake, I said. Try it again.

▷ **4** *suspend sth.*: officially stop sth. from being used **37** *subterranean:* under the ground • *hum:* low continuous noise **39** *jumpy* (infml): nervous and anxious esp. because you think that sth. bad is going to happen **43** *granola* (AE): cereal made of toasted grain, nuts, etc.

He shrugged and gave me a fed-up smile, but he did try the number again. This time I watched his fingers, on each number, and checked the numbers that came up in the window. It was my number all right, but there was the red light again.

See? he said again, still with that smile, as if he knew some private joke he wasn't going to tell me.

I'll phone them from the office, I said. The system had fouled up before, but a few phone calls usually straightened it out. Still, I was angry, as if I'd been unjustly accused of something I didn't even know about. As if I'd made the mistake myself.

You do that, he said indifferently. I left the cigarettes on the counter, since I hadn't paid for them. I figured I could borrow some at work.

I did phone from the office, but all I got was a recording. The lines were overloaded, the recording said. Could I please phone back?

The lines stayed overloaded all morning, as far as I could tell. I phoned back several times, but no luck. Even that wasn't too unusual.

About two o'clock, after lunch, the director came in to the discing room.

I have something to tell you, he said. He looked terrible; his hair was untidy, his eyes were pink and wobbling, as though he'd been drinking.

We all looked up, turned off our machines. There must have been eight or ten of us in the room.

I'm sorry, he said, but it's the law. I really am sorry.

For what? somebody said.

I have to let you go, he said. It's the law, I have to. I have to let you all go. He said this almost gently, as if we were wild animals, frogs he'd caught, in a jar, as if he were being humane.

We're being fired? I said. I stood up. But why?

Not fired, he said. Let go. You can't work here any more, it's the law. He ran his hands through his hair and I thought, He's gone crazy. The strain has been too much for him and he's blown his wiring.

You can't just *do* that, said the woman who sat next to me.

This sounded false, improbable, like something you would say on television.

It isn't me, he said. You don't understand. Please go, now.

His voice was rising. I don't want any trouble. If there's trouble the books might be lost, things will get broken ... He looked over his shoulder. They're outside, he said, in my office. If you don't go now they'll come in themselves. They gave me ten minutes. By now he sounded crazier than ever.

He's loopy, someone said out loud; which we must all have thought.

But I could see out into the corridor, and there were two men standing there, in uniforms, with machine guns. This was too theatrical to be true, yet here they were: sudden apparitions, like Martians. There was a dreamlike quality to them; they were too vivid, too at odds with their surroundings.

Just leave the machines, he said while we were getting our things together, filing out. As if we could have taken them.

We stood in a cluster, on the steps outside the library. We didn't know what to say to one another. Since none of us understood what had happened, there was nothing much we could say. We looked at one another's faces and saw dismay, and a certain shame, as if we'd been caught doing something we shouldn't.

It's outrageous, one woman said, but without belief. What was it about this that made us feel we deserved it?

When I got back to the house nobody was there. Luke was still at work, my daughter was at school. I felt tired, bone-tired, but when I sat down I got up again, I couldn't seem to sit still. I wandered through the house, from room to room. I remember touching things, not even that consciously, just placing my fingers on them; things like the toaster, the sugar bowl, the ashtray in the living room. After a while I picked up the cat and carried her around with me. I wanted Luke to come home. I thought I should do something, take steps; but I didn't know what steps I could take.

I tried phoning the bank again, but I only got the same recording. I poured myself a glass of milk – I told myself I was too jittery for another coffee – and went into the living room and sat down on the sofa and put the glass of milk on the coffee table, carefully, without

▷ **44** *loopy* (sl): crazy **58** *outrageous:* very shocking and unacceptable **70** *jittery* (infml): anxious and nervous

drinking any of it. I held the cat up against my chest so I could feel her purring against my throat.

After a while I phoned my mother at her apartment, but there was no answer. She'd settled down more by then, she'd stopped moving every few years; she lived across the river, in Boston. I waited a while and phoned Moira. She wasn't there either, but when I tried half an hour later she was in. In between those phone calls I just sat on the sofa. What I thought about was my daughter's school lunches. I thought maybe I'd been giving her too many peanut-butter sandwiches.

I've been fired, I told Moira when I got her on the phone. She said she would come over. By that time she was working for a women's collective, the publishing division. They put out books on birth control and rape and things like that, though there wasn't as much demand for those things as there used to be.

I'll come over, she said. She must have been able to tell from my voice that this was what I wanted.

She got there after some time. So, she said. She threw off her jacket, sprawled into the oversized chair. Tell me. First we'll have a drink.

She got up and went to the kitchen and poured us a couple of Scotches, and came back and sat down and I tried to tell her what had happened to me. When I'd finished, she said, Tried getting anything on your Compucard today?

Yes, I said. I told her about that too.

They've frozen them, she said. Mine too. The collective's too. Any account with an F on it instead of an M. All they needed to do is push a few buttons. We're cut off.

But I've got over two thousand dollars in the bank, I said, as if my own account was the only one that mattered.

Women can't hold property any more, she said. It's a new law. Turned on the TV today?

No, I said.

It's on there, she said. All over the place. She was not stunned, the way I was. In some strange way she was gleeful, as if this was what she'd been expecting for some time and now she'd been proven right. She even looked more energetic, more determined. Luke can use your Compucount for you, she said. They'll transfer your number to him, or that's what they say. Husband or male next of kin.

But what about you? I said. She didn't have anyone.

I'll go underground, she said. Some of the gays can take over our numbers and buy us things we need.

But why? I said. Why did they?

Ours is not to reason why, said Moira. They had to do it that way, the Compucounts and the jobs both at once. Can you picture the airports, otherwise? They don't want us going anywhere, you can bet on that.

I went to pick my daughter up from school. I drove with exaggerated care. By the time Luke got home I was sitting at the kitchen table. She was drawing with little felt pens at her own little table in the corner, where her paintings were taped up next to the refrigerator.

Luke knelt beside me and put his arms around me. I heard, he said, on the car radio, driving home. Don't worry, I'm sure it's temporary.

Did they say why? I said.

He didn't answer that. We'll get through it, he said, hugging me.

You don't know what it's like, I said. I feel as if somebody cut off my feet. I wasn't crying. Also, I couldn't put my arms around him.

It's only a job, he said, trying to soothe me.

I guess you get all my money, I said. And I'm not even dead. I was trying for a joke, but it came out sounding macabre.

Hush, he said. He was still kneeling on the floor. You know I'll always take care of you.

I thought, already he's starting to patronize me. Then I thought, already you're starting to get paranoid.

I know, I said. I love you.

Later, after she was in bed and we were having supper, and I wasn't feeling so shaky, I told him about the afternoon. I described the director coming in, blurting out his announcement. It would have been funny if it wasn't so awful, I said. I thought he was drunk. Maybe he was. The army was there, and everything.

Then I remembered something I'd seen and hadn't noticed, at the time. It wasn't the army. It was some other army.

*

▷ **35** *gleeful:* happy because of sth. bad that has happened **58** *soothe sb.:* make sb. who is anxious feel calmer

There were marches, of course, a lot of women and some men. But they were smaller than you might have thought. I guess people were scared. And when it was known that the police, or the army, or whoever they were, would open fire almost as soon as any of the marches even started, the marches stopped. A few things were blown up, post offices, subway stations. But you couldn't even be sure who was doing it. It could have been the army, to justify the computer searches and the other ones, the door-to-doors.

I didn't go on any of the marches. Luke said it would be futile and I had to think about them, my family, him and her. I did think about my family. I started doing more housework, more baking. I tried not to cry at mealtimes. By this time I'd started to cry, without warning, and to sit beside the bedroom window, staring out. I didn't know many of the neighbors, and when we met, outside on the street, we were careful to exchange nothing more than the ordinary greetings. Nobody wanted to be reported, for disloyalty.

Remembering this, I remember also my mother, years before. I must have been fourteen, fifteen, that age when daughters are most embarrassed by their mothers. I remember her coming back to one of our many apartments, with a group of other women, part of her ever-changing circle of friends. They'd been in a march that day; it was during the time of the porn riots, or was it the abortion riots, they were close together. There were a lot of bombings then: clinics, video stores; it was hard to keep track.

My mother had a bruise on her face, and a little blood. You can't stick your hand through a glass window without getting cut, is what she said about it. Fucking pigs.

Fucking bleeders, one of her friends said. They called the other side *bleeders*, after the signs they carried: *Let them bleed*. So it must have been the abortion riots.

I went into my bedroom, to be out of their way. They were talking too much, and too loudly. They ignored me, and I resented them. My mother and her rowdy friends. I didn't see why she had to dress that way, in overalls, as if she were young; or to swear so much.

You're such a prude, she would say to me, in a tone of voice that was on the whole pleased. She liked being more outrageous than I was, more rebellious. Adolescents are always such prudes.

Part of my disapproval was that, I'm sure: perfunctory, routine. But also I wanted from her a life more ceremonious, less subject to makeshift and decampment.

You were a wanted child, God knows, she would say at other moments, lingering over the photo albums in which she had me framed; these albums were thick with babies, but my replicas thinned out as I grew older, as if the population of my duplicates had been hit by some plague. She would say this a little regretfully, as though I hadn't turned out entirely as she'd expected. No mother is ever, completely, a child's idea of what a mother should be, and I suppose it works the other way around as well. But despite everything, we didn't do badly by one another, we did as well as most.

I wish she were here, so I could tell her I finally know this.

Someone has come out of the house. I hear the distant closing of a door, around at the side, footsteps on the walk. It's Nick, I can see him now; he's stepped off the path, onto the lawn, to breathe in the humid air which stinks of flowers, of pulpy growth, of pollen thrown into the wind in handfuls, like oyster spawn into the sea. All this prodigal breeding. He stretches in the sun, I feel the ripple of muscles go along him, like a cat's back arching. He's in his shirt sleeves, bare arms sticking shamelessly out from the rolled cloth. Where does the tan end? I haven't spoken to him since that one night, dreamscape in the moon-filled sitting room. He's only my flag, my semaphore. Body language.

Right now his cap's on sideways. Therefore I am sent for.

What does he get for it, his role as page boy? How does he feel, pimping in this ambiguous way for the Commander? Does it fill him with disgust, or make him want more of me, want me more? Because he has no idea what really goes on in there, among the books. Acts of perversion, for all he knows. The Commander and me, covering each

▷ **9** *futile:* having no purpose because there is no chance of success **32** *resent sb./sth.* [rɪ'zent]: feel bitter or angry about sb./sth. **40** *makeshift:* Notbehelf • *decampment:* act of leaving a place suddenly, often secretly **55** *spawn:* Laich • *prodigal:* (here) wasteful **60** *semaphore:* a system for sending signals in which you hold your arms or flags in a particular position to represent different letters of the alphabet **64** *pimp* (v): get customers for a prostitute

other with ink, licking it off, or making love on stacks of forbidden newsprint. Well, he wouldn't be far off at that.

But depend on it, there's something in it for him. Everyone's on the take, one way or another. Extra cigarettes? Extra freedoms, not allowed to the general run? Anyway, what can he prove? It's his word against the Commander's, unless he wants to head a posse. Kick in the door, and what did I tell you? Caught in the act, sinfully Scrabbling. Quick, eat those words.

Maybe he just likes the satisfaction of knowing something secret. Of having something on me, as they used to say. It's the kind of power you can use only once.

I would like to think better of him.

That night, after I'd lost my job, Luke wanted me to make love. Why didn't I want to? Desperation alone should have driven me. But I still felt numbed. I could hardly even feel his hands on me.

What's the matter? he said.

I don't know, I said.

We still have ... he said. But he didn't go on to say what we still had. It occurred to me that he shouldn't be saying we, since nothing that I knew of had been taken away from him.

We still have each other, I said. It was true. Then why did I sound, even to myself, so indifferent?

He kissed me then, as if now I'd said that, things could get back to normal. But something had shifted, some balance. I felt shrunken, so that when he put his arms around me, gathering me up, I was small as a doll. I felt love going forward without me.

He doesn't mind this, I thought. He doesn't mind it at all. Maybe he even likes it. We are not each other's, any more. Instead, I am his.

Unworthy, unjust, untrue. But that is what happened.

So Luke: what I want to ask you now, what I need to know is, Was I right? Because we never talked about it. By the time I could have done that, I was afraid to. I couldn't afford to lose you.

CHAPTER 29

I'm sitting in the Commander's office, across from him at his desk, in the client position, as if I'm a bank customer negotiating a hefty loan. But apart from my placement in the room, little of that formality remains between us. I no longer sit stiff-necked, straight-backed, feet regimented side by side on the floor, eyes at the salute. Instead my body's lax, cozy even. My red shoes are off, my legs tucked up underneath me on the chair, surrounded by a buttress of red skirt, true, but tucked nonetheless, as at a campfire, of earlier and more picnic days. If there were a fire in the fireplace, its light would be twinkling on the polished surfaces, glimmering warmly on flesh. I add the firelight in.

As for the Commander, he's casual to a fault tonight. Jacket off, elbows on the table. All he needs is a toothpick in the corner of his mouth to be an ad for rural democracy, as in an etching. Flyspecked, some old burned book.

The squares on the board in front of me are filling up: I'm making my penultimate play of the night. *Zilch*, I spell, a convenient one-vowel word with an expensive Z.

"Is that a word?" says the Commander.

"We could look it up," I say. "It's archaic."

"I'll give it to you," he says. He smiles. The Commander likes it when I distinguish myself, show precocity, like an attentive pet, prick-eared and eager to perform. His approbation laps me like a warm bath. I sense in him none of the animosity I used to sense in men, even in Luke sometimes. He's not saying *bitch* in his head. In fact he is positively daddyish. He likes to think I am being entertained; and I am, I am.

Deftly he adds up our final scores on his pocket computer. "You ran away with it," he says. I suspect him of cheating, to flatter me, to

▷ **5** *general run:* (here) general public **6** *head a posse* ['pɑːsi]: lead a group of people to catch a criminal **34–35** *negotiate a hefty loan:* arrange to borrow a large sum of money **39** *buttress:* Stützpfeiler **44** *to a fault:* to a perfect degree **46** *etching:* Radierung, Kupferstich • *flyspecked:* marked by flies **49** *penultimate:* last but one **54** *precocity:* a cleverness not expected in a young person **60** *deft:* skillful and quick

put me in a good mood. But why? It remains a question. What does he have to gain from this sort of pampering? There must be something.

He leans back, fingertips together, a gesture familiar to me now. We have built up a repertoire of such gestures, such familiarities, between us. He's looking at me, not unbenevolently, but with curiosity, as if I am a puzzle to be solved.

"What would you like to read tonight?" he says. This too has become routine. So far I've been through a *Mademoiselle* magazine, an old *Esquire* from the eighties, a *Ms.*, a magazine I can remember vaguely as having been around my mother's various apartments while I was growing up, and a *Reader's Digest*. He even has novels. I've read a Raymond Chandler, and right now I'm halfway through *Hard Times*, by Charles Dickens. On these occasions I read quickly, voraciously, almost skimming, trying to get as much into my head as possible before the next long starvation. If it were eating it would be the gluttony of the famished, if it were sex it would be a swift furtive stand-up in an alley somewhere.

While I read, the Commander sits and watches me doing it, without speaking but also without taking his eyes off me. This watching is a curiously sexual act, and I feel undressed while he does it. I wish he would turn his back, stroll around the room, read something himself. Then perhaps I could relax more, take my time. As it is, this illicit reading of mine seems a kind of performance.

"I think I'd rather just talk," I say. I'm surprised to hear myself saying it.

He smiles again. He doesn't appear surprised. Possibly he's been expecting this, or something like it. "Oh?" he says.

"What would you like to talk about?" I falter. "Anything, I guess. Well, you, for instance."

"Me?" He continues to smile. "Oh, there's not much to say about me. I'm just an ordinary kind of guy."

The falsity of this, and even the falsity of the diction – *guy?* – pulls me up short. Ordinary guys do not become Commanders. "You must be good at something," I say. I know I'm prompting him, playing up to him, drawing him out, and I dislike myself for it, it's nauseating, in fact. But we are fencing. Either he talks or I will. I know it, I can feel speech backing up inside me, it's so long since I've really talked with anyone. The terse whispered exchange with Ofglen, on our walk today, hardly counts; but it was a tease, a preliminary. Having felt the relief of even that much speaking, I want more.

And if I talk to him I'll say something wrong, give something away. I can feel it coming, a betrayal of myself. I don't want him to know too much.

"Oh, I was in market research, to begin with," he says diffidently. "After that I sort of branched out."

It strikes me that, although I know he's a Commander, I don't know what he's a Commander of. What does he control, what is his field, as they used to say? They don't have specific titles.

"Oh," I say, trying to sound as if I understand.

"You might say I'm a sort of scientist," he says. "Within limits, of course."

After that he doesn't say anything for a while, and neither do I. We are outwaiting each other.

I'm the one to break first. "Well, maybe you could tell me something I've been wondering about."

He shows interest. "What might that be?"

I'm heading into danger, but I can't stop myself. "It's a phrase I remember from somewhere." Best not to say where.

"I think it's in Latin, and I thought maybe ..." I know he has a Latin dictionary. He has dictionaries of several kinds, on the top shelf to the left of the fireplace.

"Tell me," he says. Distanced, but more alert, or am I imagining it?

"*Nolite te bastardes carborundorum*," I say.

"What?" he says.

I haven't pronounced it properly. I don't know how. "I could spell it," I say. "Write it down."

He hesitates at this novel idea. Possibly he doesn't remember I can. I've never held a pen or a pencil, in this room, not even to add up the scores. Women can't add, he said once, jokingly.

When I asked him what he meant, he said, For them, one and one and one and one don't make four.

What do they make? I said, expecting five or three.

Just one and one and one and one, he said.

▷ **29** *falter:* stocken **36** *draw sb. out:* jdn. aus der Reserve locken **37** *fence* (v): fechten

But now he says, "All right," and thrusts his roller-tip pen across the desk at me almost defiantly, as if taking a dare. I look around for something to write on and he hands me the score pad, a desk-top notepad with a little smile-button face printed at the top of the page. They still make those things.

I print the phrase carefully, copying it down from inside my head, from inside my closet. *Nolite te bastardes carborundorum.* Here, in this context, it's neither prayer nor command, but a sad graffiti, scrawled once, abandoned. The pen between my fingers is sensuous, alive almost, I can feel its power, the power of the words it contains. Pen Is Envy, Aunt Lydia would say, quoting another Center motto, warning us away from such objects. And they were right, it is envy. Just holding it is envy. I envy the Commander his pen. It's one more thing I would like to steal.

The Commander takes the smile-button page from me and looks at it. Then he begins to laugh, and is he blushing? "That's not real Latin," he says. "That's just a joke."

"A joke?" I say, bewildered now. It can't be only a joke. Have I risked this, made a grab at knowledge, for a mere joke?"What sort of a joke?"

"You know how schoolboys are," he says. His laughter is nostalgic, I see now, the laughter of indulgence towards his former self. He gets up, crosses to the bookshelves, takes down a book from his trove; not the dictionary though. It's an old book, a textbook it looks like, dog-eared and inky. Before showing it to me he thumbs through it, contemplative, reminiscent; then, "Here," he says, laying it open on the desk in front of me.

What I see first is a picture: the Venus de Milo, in a black-and-white photo, with a moustache and a black brassiere and armpit hair drawn clumsily on her. On the opposite page is the Coliseum in Rome, labelled in English, and below a conjugation: *sum es est, sumus estis sunt*. "There," he says, pointing, and in the margin I see it, written in the same ink as the hair on the Venus. *Nolite te bastardes carborundorum.*

"It's sort of hard to explain why it's funny unless you know Latin," he says. "We used to write all kinds of things like that. I don't know where we got them, from older boys perhaps." Forgetful of me and of himself, he's turning the pages. "Look at this," he says. The picture is called *The Sabine Women*, and in the margin is scrawled: *pim pis pit, pimus pistis pants.* “There was another one,” he says. “*Cim, cis, cit* ...” He stops, returning to the present, embarrassed. Again he smiles; this time you could call it a grin. I imagine freckles on him, a cowlick. Right now I almost like him.

“But what did it mean?” I say.

“Which?” he says. “Oh. It meant, ‘Don’t let the bastards grind you down.’ I guess we thought we were pretty smart, back then.”

I force a smile, but it’s all before me now. I can see why she wrote that, on the wall of the cupboard, but I also see that she must have learned it, here, in this room. Where else? She was never a schoolboy. With him, during some previous period of boyhood reminiscence, of confidences exchanged. I have not been the first then. To enter his silence, play children’s word games with him.

“What happened to her?” I say.

He hardly misses a beat. “Did you know her somehow?”

“Somehow,” I say.

“She hanged herself,” he says; thoughtfully, not sadly. “That’s why we had the light fixture removed. In your room.” He pauses. “Serena found out,” he says, as if this explains it. And it does.

If your dog dies, get another.

“What with?” I say.

He doesn’t want to give me any ideas. “Does it matter?” he says. Torn bedsheet, I figure. I’ve considered the possibilities.

“I suppose it was Cora who found her,” I say. That’s why she screamed.

“Yes,” he says. “Poor girl.” He means Cora.

“Maybe I shouldn’t come here any more,” I say.

“I thought you were enjoying it,” he says lightly, watching me, however, with intent bright eyes. If I didn’t know better I would think it was fear. “I wish you would.”

“You want my life to be bearable to me,” I say. It comes out not as a question but as a flat statement; flat and without dimension. If my life is bearable, maybe what they’re doing is all right after all.

“Yes,” he says. “I do. I would prefer it.”

▷ **2** *take a dare:* show courage to go against the rules **24** *trove:* Vorrat **43** *cowlick:* a tuft of turned-up hair on the forehead **70** *bearable:* acceptable

"Well then," I say. Things have changed. I have something on him, now. What I have on him is the possibility of my own death. What I have on him is his guilt. At last.

"What would you like?" he says, still with that lightness, as if it's a money transaction merely, and a minor one at that: candy, cigarettes.

"Besides hand lotion, you mean," I say.

"Besides hand lotion," he agrees.

"I would like ..." I say. "I would like to know." It sounds indecisive, stupid even, I say it without thinking.

"Know what?" he says.

"Whatever there is to know," I say; but that's too flippant. "What's going on."

XI

Night

CHAPTER 30

Night falls. Or has fallen. Why is it that night falls, instead of rising, like the dawn? Yet if you look east, at sunset, you can see night rising, not falling; darkness lifting into the sky, up from the horizon, like a black sun behind cloudcover. Like smoke from an unseen fire, a line of fire just below the horizon, brushfire or a burning city. Maybe night falls because it's heavy, a thick curtain pulled up over the eyes. Wool blanket. I wish I could see in the dark, better than I do.

Night has fallen, then. I feel it pressing down on me like a stone. No breeze. I sit by the partly open window, curtains tucked back because there's no one out there, no need for modesty, in my night-gown, long-sleeved even in summer, to keep us from the temptations of our own flesh, to keep us from hugging ourselves, bare-armed. Nothing moves in the searchlight moonlight. The scent from the garden rises like heat from a body, there must be night-blooming flowers, it's so strong. I can almost see it, red radiation, wavering upwards like the shimmer above highway tarmac at noon.

Down there on the lawn, someone emerges from the spill of darkness under the willow, steps across the light, his long shadow attached sharply to his heels. Is it Nick, or is it someone else, some-one of no importance? He stops, looks up at this window, and I can see the white oblong of his face. Nick. We look at each other. I have no rose to toss, he has no lute. But it's the same kind of hunger.

Which I can't indulge. I pull the left-hand curtain so that it falls between us, across my face, and after a moment he walks on, into the invisibility around the corner.

What the Commander said is true. One and one and one and one doesn't equal four. Each one remains unique, there is no way of joining them together. They cannot be exchanged, one for the other. They cannot replace each other. Nick for Luke or Luke for Nick. *Should* does not apply.

You can't help what you feel, Moira said once, but you can help how you behave.

▷ **22** *lute:* Laute

Which is all very well.

Context is all; or is it ripeness? One or the other.

The night before we left the house, that last time, I was walking through the rooms. Nothing was packed up, because we weren't taking much with us and we couldn't afford even then to give the least appearance of leaving. So I was just walking through, here and there, looking at things, at the arrangement we had made together, for our life. I had some idea that I would be able to remember, afterwards, what it had looked like.

Luke was in the living room. He put his arms around me. We were both feeling miserable. How were we to know we were happy, even then? Because we at least had that: arms, around.

The cat, is what he said.

Cat? I said, against the wool of his sweater.

We can't just leave her here.

I hadn't thought about the cat. Neither of us had. Our decision had been sudden, and then there had been the planning to do. I must have thought she was coming with us. But she couldn't, you don't take a cat on a day trip across the border.

Why not outside? I said. We could just leave her.

She'd hang around and mew at the door. Someone would notice we were gone.

We could give her away, I said. One of the neighbors. Even as I said this, I saw how foolish that would be.

I'll take care of it, Luke said. And because he said *it* instead of *her*, I knew he meant *kill*. That is what you have to do before you kill, I thought. You have to create an it, where none was before. You do that first, in your head, and then you make it real. So that's how they do it, I thought. I seemed never to have known that before.

Luke found the cat, who was hiding under our bed. They always know. He went into the garage with her. I don't know what he did and I never asked him. I sat in the living room, hands folded in my lap. I should have gone out with him, taken that small responsibility. I should at least have asked him about it afterwards, so he didn't have to carry it alone; because that little sacrifice, that snuffing out of love, was done for my sake as well.

That's one of the things they do. They force you to kill, within yourself.

Useless, as it turned out. I wonder who told them. It could have been a neighbor, watching our car pull out from the driveway in the morning, acting on a hunch, tipping them off for a gold star on someone's list. It could even have been the man who got us the passports; why not get paid twice? Like them, even, to plant the passport forgers themselves, a net for the unwary. The Eyes of God run over all the earth.

Because they were ready for us, and waiting. The moment of betrayal is the worst, the moment when you know beyond any doubt that you've been betrayed: that some other human being has wished you that much evil.

It was like being in an elevator cut loose at the top. Falling, falling, and not knowing when you will hit.

I try to conjure, to raise my own spirits, from wherever they are. I need to remember what they look like. I try to hold them still behind my eyes, their faces, like pictures in an album. But they won't stay still for me, they move, there's a smile and it's gone, their features curl and bend as if the paper's burning, blackness eats them. A glimpse, a pale shimmer on the air; a glow, aurora, dance of electrons, then a face again, faces. But they fade, though I stretch out my arms towards them, they slip away from me, ghosts at daybreak. Back to wherever they are. Stay with me, I want to say. But they won't.

It's my fault. I am forgetting too much.

Tonight I will say my prayers.

No longer kneeling at the foot of the bed, knees on the hard wood of the gym floor, Aunt Elizabeth standing by the double doors, arms folded, cattle prod hung on her belt, while Aunt Lydia strides along the rows of kneeling nightgowned women, hitting our backs or feet or bums or arms lightly, just a flick, a tap, with her wooden pointer if we slouch or slacken. She wanted our heads bowed just right, our toes together and pointed, our elbows at the proper angle. Part of her interest in this was aesthetic: she liked the look of the thing. She wanted us to look like something Anglo-Saxon, carved on a tomb; or

▷ **41** *on a hunch:* auf Verdacht **44** *forger:* person who makes illegal copies of documents

Christmas-card angels, regimented in our robes of purity. But she knew too the spiritual value of bodily rigidity, of muscle strain: a little pain cleans out the mind, she'd say.

What we prayed for was emptiness, so we would be worthy to be filled: with grace, with love, with self-denial, semen and babies.

Oh God, King of the universe, thank you for not creating me a man.

Oh God, obliterate me. Make me fruitful. Mortify my flesh, that I may be multiplied. Let me be fulfilled ...

Some of them would get carried away with this. The ecstasy of abasement. Some of them would moan and cry.

There is no point in making a spectacle of yourself, Janine, said Aunt Lydia.

I pray where I am, sitting by the window, looking out through the curtain at the empty garden. I don't even close my eyes. Out there or inside my head, it's an equal darkness. Or light.

My God. Who Art in the Kingdom of Heaven, which is within.

I wish you would tell me Your Name, the real one I mean. But *You* will do as well as anything.

I wish I knew what You were up to. But whatever it is, help me to get through it, please. Though maybe it's not Your doing; I don't believe for an instant that what's going on out there is what You meant.

I have enough daily bread, so I won't waste time on that. It isn't the main problem. The problem is getting it down without choking on it.

Now we come to forgiveness. Don't worry about forgiving me right now. There are more important things. For instance: keep the others safe, if they are safe. Don't let them suffer too much. If they have to die, let it be fast. You might even provide a Heaven for them. We need You for that. Hell we can make for ourselves.

I suppose I should say I forgive whoever did this, and whatever they're doing now. I'll try, but it isn't easy.

Temptation comes next. At the Center, temptation was anything much more than eating and sleeping. Knowing was a temptation. What you don't know won't tempt you, Aunt Lydia used to say.

Maybe I don't really want to know what's going on. Maybe I'd rather not know. Maybe I couldn't bear to know. The Fall was a fall from innocence to knowledge.

I think about the chandelier too much, though it's gone now. But you could use a hook, in the closet. I've considered the possibilities. All you'd have to do, after attaching yourself, would be to lean your weight forward and not fight.

Deliver us from evil.

Then there's Kingdom, power, and glory. It takes a lot to believe in those right now. But I'll try it anyway. In Hope, as they say on the gravestones.

You must feel pretty ripped off. I guess it's not the first time.

If I were You I'd be fed up. I'd really be sick of it. I guess that's the difference between us.

I feel very unreal, talking to You like this. I feel as if I'm talking to a wall. I wish You'd answer. I feel so alone.

All alone by the telephone. Except I can't use the telephone. And if I could, who could I call?

Oh God. It's no joke. Oh God oh God. How can I keep on living?

▷ **8** *obliterate sb./sth.:* jdn./etwas auslöschen • *mortify sth.:* etwas kasteien **11** *abasement:* Erniedrigung **17** *Who Art in Heaven, which is within:* reference to the Lord's Prayer (= Vaterunser); cf. also Luke 17:21 **25** *choke on sth.:* sich an etwas verschlucken **47** *rip sb. off* (infml): cheat sb.

XII

Jezebel's

Every night when I go to bed I think, In the morning I will wake up in my own house and things will be back the way they were.

It hasn't happened this morning, either.

I put on my clothes, summer clothes, it's still summer; it seems to have stopped at summer. July, its breathless days and sauna nights, hard to sleep. I make a point of keeping track. I should scratch marks on the wall, one for each day of the week, and run a line through them when I have seven. But what would be the use, this isn't a jail sentence; there's no time here that can be done and finished with. Anyway, all I have to do is ask, to find out what day it is. Yesterday was July the Fourth, which used to be Independence Day, before they abolished it. September First will be Labor Day, they still have that. Though it didn't used to have anything to do with mothers.

But I tell time by the moon. Lunar, not solar.

I bend over to do up my red shoes; lighter weight these days, with discreet slits cut in them, though nothing so daring as sandals. It's an effort to stoop; despite the exercises, I can feel my body gradually seizing up, refusing. Being a woman this way is how I used to imagine it would be to be very old. I feel I even walk like that: crouched over, my spine constricting to a question mark, my bones leached of calcium and porous as limestone. When I was younger, imagining age, I would think, Maybe you appreciate things more when you don't have much time left. I forgot to include the loss of energy. Some days I do appreciate things more, eggs, flowers, but then I decide I'm only having an attack of sentimentality, my brain going pastel Technicolor, like the beautiful-sunset greeting cards they used to make so many of in California. High-gloss hearts.

The danger is grayout.

*

▷ **6** *keep track (of sth.):* stay aware (of sth.) **12** *Labor Day:* Tag der Arbeit (in the USA: first Monday in September); (here also) child labor, i.e. the pains in childbirth **18** *seize up* [siːz]: no longer function properly **20** *leached of sth:.* drained of sth. **21** *limestone:* Kalkstein **28** *grayout* (cf. blackout): living in gray monotony

I'd like to have Luke here, in this bedroom while I'm getting dressed, so I could have a fight with him. Absurd, but that's what I want. An argument, about who should put the dishes in the dishwasher, whose turn it is to sort the laundry, clean the toilet; something daily and unimportant in the big scheme of things. We could even have a fight about that, about *unimportant, important*. What a luxury it would be. Not that we did it much. These days I script whole fights, in my head, and the reconciliations afterwards too.

I sit in my chair, the wreath on the ceiling floating above my head, like a frozen halo, a zero. A hole in space where a star exploded. A ring, on water, where a stone's been thrown. All things white and circular. I wait for the day to unroll, for the earth to turn, according to the round face of the implacable clock. The geometrical days, which go around and around, smoothly and oiled. Sweat already on my upper lip, I wait, for the arrival of the inevitable egg, which will be lukewarm like the room and will have a green film on the yolk and will taste faintly of sulphur.

Today, later, with Ofglen, on our shopping walk:

We go to the church, as usual, and look at the graves. Then to the Wall. Only two hanging on it today: one Catholic, not a priest though, placarded with an upside-down cross, and some other sect I don't recognize. The body is marked only with a J, in red. It doesn't mean Jewish, those would be yellow stars. Anyway there haven't been many of them. Because they were declared Sons of Jacob and therefore special, they were given a choice. They could convert, or emigrate to Israel. A lot of them emigrated, if you can believe the news. I saw a boatload of them, on the TV, leaning over the railings in their black coats and hats and their long beards, trying to look as Jewish as possible, in costumes fished up from the past, the women with shawls over their heads, smiling and waving, a little stiffly it's true, as if they were posing; and another shot, of the richer ones, lining up for the planes. Ofglen says some other people got out that way, by pretending to be Jewish, but it wasn't easy because of the tests they gave you and they've tightened up on that now.

You don't get hanged only for being a Jew though. You get hanged for being a noisy Jew who won't make the choice. Or for pretending to convert. That's been on the TV too: raids at night, secret hoards of

Jewish things dragged out from under beds, Torahs, talliths, Mogen Davids. And the owners of them, sullen-faced, unrepentant, pushed by the Eyes against the walls of their bedrooms, while the sorrowful voice of the announcer tells us voice-over about their perfidy and ungratefulness.

So the J isn't for Jew. What could it be? Jehovah's Witness? Jesuit? Whatever it meant, he's just as dead.

After this ritual viewing we continue on our way, heading as usual for some open space we can cross, so we can talk. If you can call it talking, these clipped whispers, projected through the funnels of our white wings. It's more like a telegram, a verbal semaphore. Amputated speech.

We can never stand long in any one place. We don't want to be picked up for loitering.

Today we turn in the opposite direction from Soul Scrolls, to where there's an open park of sorts, with a large old building on it; ornate late Victorian, with stained glass. It used to be called Memorial Hall, though I never knew what it was a memorial for. Dead people of some kind.

Moira told me once that it used to be where the undergraduates ate, in the earlier days of the university. If a woman went in there, they'd throw buns at her, she said.

Why? I said. Moira became, over the years, increasingly versed in such anecdotes. I didn't much like it, this grudgeholding against the past.

To make her go out, said Moira.

Maybe it was more like throwing peanuts at elephants, I said.

Moira laughed; she could always do that. Exotic monsters, she said.

*

▷ **5** *the big scheme of things:* der große Plan der Dinge **13** *implacable:* unerbittlich **24** *Sons of Jacob:* God changed Jacob's name to Israel, as he was the father of the Jewish people **38** *Torah:* (in Judaism) the first five books of the Bible, usu. kept on a scroll • *tallith:* white shawl worn over the head by Jewish men during prayer **38–39** *Mogen David:* Star of David **39** *sullen:* mürrisch **41** *perfidy:* betrayal, treacherous behaviour **51** *loiter:* stand in a public place doing nothing **54** *ornate:* highly decorated **54–55** *Memorial Hall:* usu. quite grand-looking building on American campuses commemorating dead ex-students (esp. those who died in wars) **61** *hold a grudge:* einen Groll haben

We stand looking at this building, which is in shape more or less like a church, a cathedral. Ofglen says, "I hear that's where the Eyes hold their banquets."

"Who told you?" I say. There's no one near, we can speak more freely, but out of habit we keep our voices low.

"The grapevine," she says. She pauses, looks sideways at me, I can sense the blur of white as her wings move. "There's a password," she says.

"A password?" I ask. "What for?"

"So you can tell," she says. "Who is and who isn't."

Although I can't see what use it is for me to know, I ask, "What is it then?"

"Mayday," she says. "I tried it on you once."

"Mayday," I repeat. I remember that day. *M'aidez.*

"Don't use it unless you have to," say Ofglen. "It isn't good for us to know about too many of the others, in the network. In case you get caught."

I find it hard to believe in these whisperings, these revelations, though I always do at the time. Afterwards though they seem improbable, childish even, like something you'd do for fun; like a girls' club, like secrets at school. Or like the spy novels I used to read, on weekends, when I should have been finishing my homework, or like late-night television. Passwords, things that cannot be told, people with secret identities, dark linkages: this does not seem as if it ought to be the true shape of the world. But that is my own illusion, a hangover from a version of reality I learned in the former time.

And networks. *Networking*, one of my mother's old phrases, musty slang of yesteryear. Even in her sixties she still did something she called that, though as far as I could see all it meant was having lunch with some other woman.

I leave Ofglen at the corner. "I'll see you later," she says. She glides away along the sidewalk and I go up the walk towards the house. There's Nick, hat askew; today he doesn't even look at me. He must have been waiting around for me though, to deliver his silent message, because as soon as he knows I've seen him he gives the Whirlwind one last swipe with the chamois and walks briskly off towards the garage door.

I walk along the gravel, between the slabs of overgreen lawn. Serena Joy is sitting under the willow tree, in her chair, cane propped at her elbow. Her dress is crisp cool cotton. For her it's blue, watercolor, not this red of mine that sucks in heat and blazes with it at the same time. Her profile's towards me, she's knitting. How can she bear to touch the wool, in this heat? But possibly her skin's gone numb; possibly she feels nothing, like one formerly scalded.

I lower my eyes to the path, glide by her, hoping to be invisible, knowing I'll be ignored. But not this time.

"Offred," she says.

I pause, uncertain.

"Yes, you."

I turn towards her my blinkered sight.

"Come over here. I want you."

I walk over the grass and stand before her, looking down.

"You can sit," she says. "Here, take the cushion. I need you to hold this wool." She's got a cigarette, the ashtray's on the lawn beside her, and a cup of something, tea or coffee. "It's too damn close in there. You need a little air," she says. I sit, putting down my basket, strawberries again, chicken again, and I note the swear word: something new. She fits the skein of wool over my two outstretched hands, starts winding. I am leashed, it looks like, manacled; cobwebbed, that's closer. The wool is gray and has absorbed moisture from the air, it's like a wetted baby blanket and smells faintly of damp sheep. At least my hands will get lanolined.

Serena winds, the cigarette held in the corner of her mouth smoldering, sending out tempting smoke. She winds slowly and with difficulty because of her gradually crippling hands, but with determination. Perhaps the knitting, for her, involves a kind of willpower; maybe it even hurts. Maybe it's been medically prescribed: ten rows a day of plain, ten of purl. Though she must do more than that. I see those evergreen trees and geometric boys and girls in a different light: evidence of her stubbornness, and not altogether despicable.

*

▷ **24** *linkage* ['lɪŋkɪdʒ]: link **28** *musty:* (here) old and no longer used **44** *scalded:* burned by hot liquid **58** *skein* [skeɪn]: a long piece of wool **59** *leashed:* held on a strip of leather like a dog • *manacled* ['mænəkəld]: with your hands chained together like a prisoner • *cobwebbed:* tied by strands of a spider's web **64** *smolder:* burn without flame **68** *purl:* type of knitting stitch **70** *despicable* [dɪ'spɪkəbl]: very unpleasant

My mother did not knit or anything like that. But whenever she would bring things back from the cleaner's, her good blouses, winter coats, she'd save up the safety pins and make them into a chain. Then she'd pin the chain somewhere – her bed, the pillow, a chair-back, the oven mitt in the kitchen – so she wouldn't lose them. Then she'd forget about them. I would come upon them, here and there in the house, the houses; tracks of her presence, remnants of some lost intention, like signs on a road that turns out to lead nowhere. Throwbacks to domesticity.

"Well then," Serena says. She stops winding, leaving me with my hands still garlanded with animal hair, and takes the cigarette end from her mouth to butt it out. "Nothing yet?"

I know what she's talking about. There are not that many subjects that could be spoken about, between us; there's not much common ground, except this one mysterious and chancy thing.

"No," I say. "Nothing."

"Too bad," she says. It's hard to imagine her with a baby. But the Marthas would take care of it mostly. She'd like me pregnant though, over and done with and out of the way, no more humiliating sweaty tangles, no more flesh triangles under her starry canopy of silver flowers. Peace and quiet. I can't imagine she'd want such good luck, for me, for any other reason.

"Your time's running out," she says. Not a question, a matter of fact.

"Yes," I say neutrally.

She's lighting another cigarette, fumbling with the lighter. Definitely her hands are getting worse. But it would be a mistake to offer to do it for her, she'd be offended. A mistake to notice weakness in her.

"Maybe he can't," she says.

I don't know who she means. Does she mean the Commander, or God? If it's God, she should say won't. Either way it's heresy. It's only women who can't, who remain stubbornly closed, damaged, defective.

"No," I say. "Maybe he can't."

I look up at her. She looks down. It's the first time we've looked into each other's eyes in a long time. Since we met.

The moment stretches out between us, bleak and level. She's trying to see whether or not I'm up to reality.

"Maybe," she says, holding the cigarette, which she has failed to light. "Maybe you should try it another way."

Does she mean on all fours? "What other way?" I say. I must keep serious.

"Another man," she says.

"You know I can't," I say, careful not to let my irritation show. "It's against the law. You know the penalty."

"Yes," she says. She's ready for this, she's thought it through. "I know you can't officially. But it's done. Women do it frequently. All the time."

"With doctors, you mean?" I say, remembering the sympathetic brown eyes, the gloveless hand. The last time I went it was a different doctor. Maybe someone caught the other one out, or a woman reported him. Not that they'd take her word, without evidence.

"Some do that," she says, her tone almost affable now, though distanced; it's as if we're considering a choice of nail polish. "That's how Ofwarren did it. The wife knew, of course." She pauses to let this sink in. "I would help you. I would make sure nothing went wrong."

I think about this. "Not with a doctor," I say.

"No," she agrees, and for this moment at least we are cronies, this could be a kitchen table, it could be a date we're discussing, some girlish stratagem of ploys and flirtation.

"Sometimes they blackmail. But it doesn't have to be a doctor. It could be someone we trust."

"Who?" I say.

"I was thinking of Nick," she says, and her voice is almost soft. "He's been with us a long time. He's loyal. I could fix it with him."

So that's who does her little black-market errands for her. Is this what he always gets, in return?

"What about the Commander?" I say.

"Well," she says, with firmness; no, more than that, a clenched look, like a purse snapping shut. "We just won't tell him, will we?"

▷ **9** *throwback:* Rückschritt **38** *bleak:* empty and unpleasant **50** *sympathetic:* showing understanding for another person's situation **54** *affable:* pleasant, friendly **59** *crony* (derog): person who you spend a lot of time with and have a similar attitude to **61** *stratagem* ['strætədʒəm]: plan • *ploy:* trick

This idea hangs between us, almost visible, almost palpable: heavy, formless, dark; collusion of a sort, betrayal of a sort. She does want that baby.

"It's a risk," I say. "More than that." It's my life on the line; but that's where it will be sooner or later, one way or another, whether I do or don't. We both know this.

"You might as well," she says. Which is what I think too.

"All right," I say. "Yes."

She leans forward. "Maybe I could get something for you," she says. Because I have been good. "Something you want," she adds, wheedling almost.

"What's that?" I say. I can't think of anything I truly want that she'd be likely or able to give me.

"A picture," she says, as if offering me some juvenile treat, an ice cream, a trip to the zoo. I look up at her again, puzzled.

"Of her," she says. "Your little girl. But only maybe."

She knows where they've put her then, where they're keeping her. She's known all along. Something chokes in my throat. The bitch, not to tell me, bring me news, any news at all. Not even to let on. She's made of wood, or iron, she can't imagine. But I can't say this, I can't lose sight, even of so small a thing. I can't let go of this hope. I can't speak.

She's actually smiling, coquettishly even; there's a hint of her former small-screen mannequin's allure, flickering over her face like momentary static. "It's too damn hot for this, don't you think?" she says. She lifts the wool from my two hands, where I have been holding it all this time. Then she takes the cigarette she's been fiddling with and, a little awkwardly, presses it into my hand, closing my fingers around it. "Find yourself a match," she says. "They're in the kitchen, you can ask Rita for one. You can tell her I said so. Only the one though," she adds roguishly. "We don't want to ruin your health!"

CHAPTER 32

Rita's sitting at the kitchen table. There's a glass bowl with ice cubes floating in it on the table in front of her. Radishes made into flowers, roses or tulips, bob in it. On the chopping board in front of her she's cutting more, with a paring knife, her large hands deft, indifferent. The rest of her body does not move, nor does her face. It's as if she's doing it in her sleep, this knife trick. On the white enamel surface is a pile of radishes, washed but uncut. Little Aztec hearts.

She hardly bothers to look up as I enter. "You got it all, huh," is what she says, as I take the parcels out for her inspection.

"Could I have a match?" I ask her. Surprising how much like a small, begging child she makes me feel, simply by her scowl, her stolidity; how importunate and whiny.

"Matches?" she says. "What do you want matches for?"

"She said I could have one," I say, not wanting to admit to the cigarette.

"Who said?" She continues with the radishes, her rhythm unbroken. "No call for you to have matches. Burn the house down."

"You can go and ask her if you like," I say. "She's out on the lawn."

Rita rolls her eyes to the ceiling, as if consulting silently some deity there. Then she sighs, rises heavily, and wipes her hands with ostentation on her apron, to show me how much trouble I am. She goes to the cupboard over the sink, taking her time, locates her key-bunch in her pocket, unlocks the cupboard door. "Keep 'em in here, summer," she says as if to herself. "No call for a fire in this weather." I remember from April that it's Cora who lights the fires, in the sitting room and the dining room, in cooler weather.

The matches are wooden ones, in a cardboard sliding-top box, the kind I used to covet in order to make dolls' drawers out of them. She

▷ **2** *collusion:* act of working together secretly to deceive sb. **11** *wheedle:* speak in a way that shows you want to persuade sb. to do sth. **31** *roguishly* ['roʊgɪʃli]: (here) playfully **34** *bob:* float up and down **43** *stolidity:* Sturheit, Stumpfheit • *importunate:* wanting sth. that you do not usually get **50** *deity* ['deɪəti]: god **51–52** *with ostentation:* with deliberate show

opens the box, peers into it, as if deciding which one she'll let me have. "Her own business," she mutters.

"No way you can tell her a thing." She plunges her big hand down, selects a match, hands it over to me. "Now don't you go setting fire to nothing," she says. "Not them curtains in your room. Too hot the way it is."

"I won't," I say. "That's not what it's for."

She does not deign to ask me what it is for. "Don't care if you eat it, or what," she says. "She said you could have one, so I give you one, is all."

She turns away from me and sits again at the table. Then she picks an ice cube out of the bowl and pops it into her mouth. This is an unusual thing for her to do. I've never seen her nibble while working. "You can have one of them too," she says. "A shame, making you wear all them pillowcases on your head, in this weather."

I am surprised: she doesn't usually offer me anything. Maybe she feels that if I've risen in status enough to be given a match, she can afford her own small gesture. Have I become, suddenly, one of those who must be appeased?

"Thank you," I say. I transfer the match carefully to my zippered sleeve where the cigarette is, so it won't get wet, and take an ice cube. "Those radishes are pretty," I say, in return for the gift she's made me, of her own free will.

"I like to do things right, is all," she says, grumpy again. "No sense otherwise."

I go along the passage, up the stairs, hurrying. In the curved hallway mirror I flit past, a red shape at the edge of my own field of vision, a wraith of red smoke. I have smoke on my mind all right, already I can feel it in my mouth, drawn down into the lungs, filling me in a long rich dirty cinnamon sigh, and then the rush as the nicotine hits the bloodstream.

After all this time it could make me sick. I wouldn't be surprised. But even that thought is welcome.

Along the corridor I go, where should I do it? In the bathroom, running the water to clear the air, in the bedroom, wheezy puffs out the open window? Who's to catch me at it? Who knows?

Even as I luxuriate in the future this way, rolling anticipation around in my mouth, I think of something else.

I don't need to smoke this cigarette.

I could shred it up and flush it down the toilet. Or I could eat it and get the high that way, that can work too, a little at a time, save up the rest.

That way I could keep the match. I could make a small hole, in the mattress, slide it carefully in. Such a thin thing would never be noticed. There it would be, at night, under me while I'm in bed. Sleeping on it.

I could burn the house down. Such a fine thought, it makes me shiver.

An escape, quick and narrow.

I lie on my bed, pretending to nap.

The Commander, last night, fingers together, looking at me as I sat rubbing oily lotion into my hands. Odd, I thought about asking him for a cigarette, but decided against it. I know enough not to ask for too much at once. I don't want him to think I'm using him. Also I don't want to interrupt him.

Last night he had a drink, Scotch and water. He's taken to drinking in my presence, to unwind after the day, he says. I'm to gather he is under pressure. He never offers me one, though, and I don't ask: we both know what my body is for. When I kiss him goodnight, as if I mean it, his breath smells of alcohol, and I breathe it in like smoke. I admit I relish it, this lick of dissipation.

Sometimes after a few drinks he becomes silly, and cheats at Scrabble. He encourages me to do it too, and we take extra letters and make words with them that don't exist, words like *smurt* and *crup*, giggling over them. Sometimes he turns on his short-wave radio, displaying before me a minute or two of Radio Free America, to show me he can. Then he turns it off again. Damn Cubans, he says. All that filth about universal daycare.

▷ **1** *peer into sth.:* look carefully at sth. (e.g. a dark place) **8** *deign to do sth.* [deɪn]: sich herablassen, etwas zu tun **19** *appease sb.:* do sb. favors so they will stay friendly **28** *wraith:* ghost **37** *luxuriate in sth.* [lʌg'zjʊərieɪt]: enjoy sth. **57** *unwind* [ˌʌn'waɪnd]: relax • *gather:* understand **61** *relish sth.:* enjoy sth. • *dissipation:* act of behaving immorally **68** *filth:* rubbish; offensive words • *universal daycare:* care for all small children whose parents are working

Sometimes, after the games, he sits on the floor beside my chair, holding my hand. His head is a little below mine, so that when he looks up at me it's at a juvenile angle. It must amuse him, this fake subservience.

He's way up there, says Ofglen. He's at the top, and I mean the very top. At such times it's hard to imagine it.

Occasionally I try to put myself in his position. I do this as a tactic, to guess in advance how he may be moved to behave towards me. It's difficult for me to believe I have power over him, of any sort, but I do; although it's of an equivocal kind. Once in a while I think I can see myself, though blurrily, as he may see me. There are things he wants to prove to me, gifts he wants to bestow, services he wants to render, tendernesses he wants to inspire.

He wants, all right. Especially after a few drinks.

Sometimes he becomes querulous, at other times, philosophical; or he wishes to explain things, justify himself. As last night.

The problem wasn't only with the women, he says. The main problem was with the men. There was nothing for them any more.

Nothing? I say. But they had …

There was nothing for them to do, he says.

They could make money, I say, a little nastily. Right now I'm not afraid of him. It's hard to be afraid of a man who is sitting watching you put on hand lotion. This lack of fear is dangerous.

It's not enough, he says. It's too abstract. I mean there was nothing for them to do with women.

What do you mean? I say. What about all the Pornycorners, it was all over the place, they even had it motorized.

I'm not talking about sex, he says. That was part of it, the sex was too easy. Anyone could just buy it. There was nothing to work for, nothing to fight for. We have the stats from that time. You know what they were complaining about the most? Inability to feel. Men were turning off on sex, even. They were turning off on marriage.

Do they feel now? I say.

Yes, he says, looking at me. They do. He stands up, comes around the desk to the chair where I'm sitting. He puts his hands on my shoulders, from behind. I can't see him.

I like to know what you think, his voice says, from behind me.

I don't think a lot, I say lightly. What he wants is intimacy, but I can't give him that.

There's hardly any point in my thinking, is there? I say. What I think doesn't matter.

Which is the only reason he can tell me things.

Come now, he says, pressing a little with his hands. I'm interested in your opinion. You're intelligent enough, you must have an opinion.

About what? I say.

What we've done, he says. How things have worked out.

I hold myself very still. I try to empty my mind. I think about the sky, at night, when there's no moon. I have no opinion, I say.

He sighs, relaxes his hands, but leaves them on my shoulders. He knows what I think, all right.

You can't make an omelette without breaking eggs, is what he says. We thought we could do better.

Better? I say, in a small voice. How can he think this is better?

Better never means better for everyone, he says. It always means worse, for some.

I lie flat, the damp air above me like a lid. Like earth. I wish it would rain. Better still, a thunderstorm, black clouds, lightning, ear-splitting sound. The electricity might go off. I could go down to the kitchen then, say I'm afraid, sit with Rita and Cora around the kitchen table, they would permit my fear because it's one they share, they'd let me in. There would be candles burning, we would watch each other's faces come and go in the flickering, in the white flashes of jagged light from outside the windows. Oh Lord, Cora would say. Oh Lord save us.

I look up at the ceiling, the round circle of plaster flowers. Draw a circle, step into it, it will protect you. From the center was the chandelier, and from the chandelier a twisted strip of sheet was hanging down. That's where she was swinging, just lightly, like a pendulum; the way you could swing as a child, hanging by your hands from a tree branch. She was safe then, protected altogether, by the time Cora opened the door. Sometimes I think she's still in here, with me.

I feel buried.

▷ **3** *juvenile:* of young people **4** *subservience:* act of showing that you are beneath sb. in rank **10** *equivocal* [ɪ'kwɪvəkl]: ambiguous, not easy to understand **11** *blurry:* not clear **15** *querulous* ['kwerʊləs]: wanting to argue **30** *stats:* statistics

CHAPTER 33

Late afternoon, the sky hazy, the sunlight diffuse but heavy and everywhere, like bronze dust. I glide with Ofglen along the sidewalk; the pair of us, and in front of us another pair, and across the street another. We must look good from a distance: picturesque, like Dutch milkmaids on a wallpaper frieze, like a shelf full of period-costume ceramic salt and pepper shakers, like a flotilla of swans or anything that repeats itself with at least minimum grace and without variation. Soothing to the eye, the eyes, the Eyes, for that's who this show is for. We're off to the Prayvaganza, to demonstrate how obedient and pious we are.

Not a dandelion in sight here, the lawns are picked clean. I long for one, just one, rubbishy and insolently random and hard to get rid of and perennially yellow as the sun. Cheerful and plebian, shining for all alike. Rings, we would make from them, and crowns and necklaces, stains from the bitter milk on our fingers. Or I'd hold one under her chin: *Do you like butter?* Smelling them, she'd get pollen on her nose. (Or was that buttercups?) Or gone to seed: I can see her, running across the lawn, that lawn there just in front of me, at two, three years old, waving one like a sparkler, a small wand of white fire, the air filling with tiny parachutes. *Blow, and you tell the time.* All that time, blowing away in the summer breeze. It was daisies for love though, and we did that too.

We line up to get processed through the checkpoint, standing in our twos and twos and twos, like a private girls' school that went for a walk and stayed out too long. Years and years too long, so that everything has become overgrown, legs, bodies, dresses all together. As if enchanted. A fairy tale, I'd like to believe. Instead we are checked through, in our twos, and continue walking.

After a while we turn right, heading past Lilies and down towards the river. I wish I could go that far, to where the wide banks are, where we used to lie in the sun, where the bridges arch over. If you went down the river long enough, along its sinewy windings, you'd reach the sea; but what could you do there? Gather shells, loll on the oily stones.

We aren't going to the river though, we won't see the little cupolas on the buildings down that way, white with blue and gold trim, such chaste gaiety. We turn in at a more modern building, a huge banner draped above its door – WOMEN'S PRAYVAGANZA TODAY. The banner covers the building's former name, some dead President they shot. Below the red writing there's a line of smaller print, in black, with the outline of a winged eye on either side of it: GOD IS A NATIONAL RESOURCE. On either side of the doorway stand the inevitable Guardians, two pairs, four in all, arms at their sides, eyes front. They're like store mannequins almost, with their neat hair and pressed uniforms and plaster-hard young faces. No pimply ones today. Each has a submachine gun slung ready, for whatever dangerous or subversive acts they think we might commit inside.

The Prayvaganza is to be held in the covered courtyard, where there's an oblong space, a skylight roof. It isn't a citywide Prayvaganza, that would be on the football field; it's only for this district. Ranks of folding wooden chairs have been placed along the right side, for the Wives and daughters of high-ranking officials or officers, there's not that much difference. The galleries above, with their concrete railings, are for the lower-ranking women, the Marthas, the Econowives in their multicolored stripes. Attendance at Prayvaganzas isn't compulsory for them, especially if they're on duty or have young children, but the galleries seem to be filling up anyway. I suppose it's a form of entertainment, like a show or a circus.

A number of the Wives are already seated, in their best embroidered blue. We can feel their eyes on us as we walk in our red dresses two by two across to the side opposite them. We are being looked at, assessed, whispered about; we can feel it, like tiny ants running on our bare skins.

Here there are no chairs. Our area is cordoned off with a silky twisted scarlet rope, like the kind they used to have in movie theaters to restrain the customers. This rope segregates us, marks us off, keeps the others from contamination by us, makes for us a corral or pen; so into it we go, arranging ourselves in rows, which we know very well how to do, kneeling then on the cement floor.

▷ **13** *perennially* [-'---]: always, year after year • *plebian* [plə'bi:ən]: simple, unrefined **19** *sparkler:* Wunderkerze **27** *enchanted:* verzaubert **32** *sinewy* ['sɪnju:i]: sehnig **33** *loll*: sit or lie lazily **37** *chaste:* keusch • *gaiety:* happiness

"Head for the back," Ofglen murmurs at my side. "We can talk better." And when we are kneeling, heads bowed slightly, I can hear from all around us a susurration, like the rustling of insects in tall dry grass: a cloud of whispers. This is one of the places where we can exchange news more freely, pass it from one to the next. It's hard for them to single out any one of us or hear what's being said. And they wouldn't want to interrupt the ceremony, not in front of the television cameras.

Ofglen digs me in the side with her elbow, to call my attention, and I look up, slowly and stealthily. From where we're kneeling we have a good view of the entrance to the courtyard, where people are coming steadily in. It must be Janine she meant me to see, because there she is, paired with a new woman, not the former one; someone I don't recognize. Janine must have been transferred then, to a new household, a new posting. It's early for that, has something gone wrong with her breast milk? That would be the only reason they'd move her, unless there's been a fight over the baby; which happens more than you'd think. Once she had it, she may have resisted giving it up. I can see that. Her body under the red dress looks very thin, skinny almost, and she's lost that pregnant glow. Her face is white and peaked, as if the juice is being sucked out of her.

"It was no good, you know," Ofglen says near the side of my head. "It was a shredder after all."

She means Janine's baby, the baby that passed through Janine on its way to somewhere else. The baby Angela. It was wrong, to name her too soon. I feel an illness, in the pit of my stomach. Not an illness, an emptiness. I don't want to know what was wrong with it. "My God," I say. To go through all that, for nothing. Worse than nothing.

"It's her second," Ofglen says. "Not counting her own, before. She had an eighth-month miscarriage, didn't you know?"

We watch as Janine enters the roped-off enclosure, in her veil of untouchability, of bad luck. She sees me, she must see me, but she looks right through me. No smile of triumph this time. She turns, kneels, and all I can see now is her back and the thin bowed shoulders.

"She thinks it's her fault," Ofglen whispers. "Two in a row. For being sinful. She used a doctor, they say, it wasn't her Commander's at all."

I can't say I do know or Ofglen will wonder how. As far as she's aware, she herself is my only source, for this kind of information; of which she has a surprising amount. How would she have found out about Janine? The Marthas? Janine's shopping partner? Listening at closed doors, to the Wives over their tea and wine, spinning their webs. Will Serena Joy talk about me like that, if I do as she wants? *Agreed to it right away, really she didn't care, anything with two legs and a good youknowwhat was fine with her. They aren't squeamish, they don't have the same feelings we do.* And the rest of them leaning forward in their chairs, *My dear*, all horror and prurience. How could she? Where? When?

As they did no doubt with Janine. "That's terrible," I say. It's like Janine though to take it upon herself, to decide the baby's flaws were due to her alone. But people will do anything rather than admit that their lives have no meaning. No use, that is. No plot.

One morning while we were getting dressed, I noticed that Janine was still in her white cotton nightgown. She was just sitting there on the edge of her bed.

I looked over towards the double doors of the gymnasium, where the Aunt usually stood, to see if she'd noticed, but the Aunt wasn't there. By that time they were more confident about us; sometimes they left us unsupervised in the classroom and even the cafeteria for minutes at a time. Probably she'd ducked out for a smoke or a cup of coffee.

Look, I said to Alma, who had the bed next to mine.

Alma looked at Janine. Then we both walked over to her. Get your clothes on, Janine, Alma said, to Janine's white back. We don't want extra prayers on account of you. But Janine didn't move.

By that time Moira had come over too. It was before she'd broken free, the second time. She was still limping from what they'd done to her feet. She went around the bed so she could see Janine's face.

Come here, she said to Alma and me. The others were beginning to gather too, there was a little crowd. Go on back, Moira said to them. Don't make a thing of it, what if she walks in?

▷ **3** *susurration:* Rascheln **19** *I can see that:* I can imagine that **47** *squeamish:* oversensitive **49** *prurience:* the state of being overinterested in details to do with sex

I was looking at Janine. Her eyes were open, but they didn't see me at all. They were rounded, wide, and her teeth were bared in a fixed smile. Through the smile, through her teeth, she was whispering to herself. I had to lean down close to her.

Hello, she said, but not to me. My name's Janine. I'm your waitperson for this morning. Can I get you some coffee to begin with?

Christ, said Moira, beside me.

Don't swear, said Alma.

Moira took Janine by the shoulders and shook her. Snap out of it, Janine, she said roughly. And don't use that word.

Janine smiled. You have a nice day, now, she said.

Moira slapped her across the face, twice, back and forth. Get back here, she said. Get right back here! You can't stay there, you aren't there any more. That's all gone.

Janine's smile faltered. She put her hand up to her cheek.

What did you hit me for? she said. Wasn't it good? I can bring you another. You didn't have to hit me.

Don't you know what they'll do? Moira said. Her voice was low, but hard, intent. Look at me. My name is Moira and this is the Red Center. Look at me.

Janine's eyes began to focus. Moira? she said. I don't know any Moira.

They won't send you to the Infirmary, so don't even think about it, Moira said. They won't mess around with trying to cure you. They won't even bother to ship you to the Colonies. You go too far away and they just take you up to the Chemistry Lab and shoot you. Then they burn you up with the garbage like an Unwoman. So forget it.

I want to go home, Janine said. She began to cry.

Jesus God, Moira said. That's enough. She'll be here in one minute, I promise you. So put your goddamn clothes on and shut up.

Janine kept whimpering, but she also stood up and started to dress.

She does that again and I'm not here, Moira said to me, you just have to slap her like that. You can't let her go slipping over the edge. That stuff is catching.

She must have already been planning, then, how she was going to get out.

CHAPTER 34

The sitting space in the courtyard is filled now; we rustle and wait. At last the Commander in charge of this service comes in. He's balding and squarely built and looks like an aging football coach. He's dressed in his uniform, sober black with the rows of insignia and decorations. It's hard not to be impressed, but I make an effort: I try to imagine him in bed with his Wife and his Handmaid, fertilizing away like mad, like a rutting salmon, pretending to take no pleasure in it. When the Lord said be fruitful and multiply, did he mean this man?

This Commander ascends the steps to the podium, which is draped with a red cloth embroidered with a large white-winged eye. He gazes over the room, and our soft voices die. He doesn't even have to raise his hands. Then his voice goes into the microphone and out through the speakers, robbed of its lower tones so that it's sharply metallic, as if it's being made not by his mouth, his body, but by the speakers themselves. His voice is metal-colored, horn-shaped.

"Today is a day of thanksgiving," he begins, "a day of praise."

I tune out through the speech about victory and sacrifice. Then there's a long prayer, about unworthy vessels, then a hymn: "There is a Balm in Gilead."

"There is a Bomb in Gilead," was what Moira used to call it.

Now comes the main item. The twenty Angels enter, newly returned from the fronts, newly decorated, accompanied by their honour guard, marching one-two one-two into the central open space. Attention, at ease. And now the twenty veiled daughters, in white, come shyly forward, their mothers holding their elbows. It's mothers, not fathers, who give away daughters these days and help with the arrangement of the marriages. The marriages are of course arranged. These girls haven't been allowed to be alone with a man for years; for however many years we've all been doing this.

Are they old enough to remember anything of the time before, playing baseball, in jeans and sneakers, riding their bicycles?

▷ **44** *rutting:* in a time of sexual activity **56–57** *"There … Gilead":* African-American spiritual song (based on Jeremiah 8:22); in AE *balm* and *bomb* (l. 58) are pronounced bɑːm.

Reading books, all by themselves? Even though some of them are no more than fourteen – *Start them soon* is the policy, *there's not a moment to be lost* – still they'll remember. And the ones after them will, for three or four or five years; but after that they won't. They'll always have been in white, in groups of girls; they'll always have been silent.

We've given them more than we've taken away, said the Commander. Think of the trouble they had before. Don't you remember the singles bars, the indignity of high-school blind dates? The meat market. Don't you remember the terrible gap between the ones who could get a man easily and the ones who couldn't? Some of them were desperate, they starved themselves thin or pumped their breasts full of silicone, had their noses cut off. Think of the human misery.

He waved a hand at his stacks of old magazines. They were always complaining. Problems this, problems that. Remember the ads in the Personal columns, *Bright attractive woman, thirty-five* ... This way they all get a man, nobody's left out. And then if they did marry, they could be left with a kid, two kids, the husband might just get fed up and take off, disappear, they'd have to go on welfare. Or else he'd stay around and beat them up. Or if they had a job, the children in daycare or left with some brutal ignorant woman, and they'd have to pay for that themselves, out of their wretched little paycheques. Money was the only measure of worth, for everyone, they got no respect as mothers. No wonder they were giving up on the whole business. This way they're protected, they can fulfil their biological destinies in peace. With full support and encouragement. Now, tell me. You're an intelligent person, I like to hear what you think. What did we overlook?

Love, I said.

Love? said the Commander. What kind of love?

Falling in love, I said.

The Commander looked at me with his candid boy's eyes.

Oh yes, he said. I've read the magazines, that's what they were pushing, wasn't it? But look at the stats, my dear. Was it really worth it, falling in love? Arranged marriages have always worked out just as well, if not better.

*

Love, said Aunt Lydia with distaste. Don't let me catch you at it. No mooning and June-ing around here, girls. Wagging her finger at us. *Love* is not the point.

Those years were just an anomaly, historically speaking, the Commander said, just a fluke. All we've done is return things to Nature's norm.

Women's Prayvaganzas are for group weddings like this, usually. The men's are for military victories. These are the things we are supposed to rejoice in the most, respectively. Sometimes though, for the women, they're for a nun who recants. Most of that happened earlier, when they were rounding them up, but they still unearth a few these days, dredge them up from underground, where they've been hiding, like moles. They have that look about them too: weak-eyed, stunned by too much light. The old ones they send off to the Colonies right away, but the young fertile ones they try to convert, and when they succeed we all come here to watch them go through the ceremony, renounce their celibacy, sacrifice it to the common good. They kneel and the Commander prays and then they take the red veil, as the rest of us have done. They aren't allowed to become Wives though; they're considered, still, too dangerous for positions of such power. There's an odor of witch about them, something mysterious and exotic; it remains despite the scrubbing and the welts on their feet and the time they've spent in Solitary. They always have those welts, they've always done that time, so rumor goes: they don't let go easily. Many of them choose the Colonies instead. None of us likes to draw one for a shopping partner. They are more broken than the rest of us; it's hard to feel comfortable with them.

The mothers have stood the white-veiled girls in place and have returned to their chairs. There's a little crying going on among them, some mutual patting and hand-holding, the ostentatious use of handkerchiefs. The Commander continues with the service:

▷ **38** *mooning and June-ing:* (here) having strong feelings connected with love (*moon:* nachträumen; *June:* used as a rhyme with "moon") **41** *fluke:* thing that happens by accident **46** *recant:* give up a belief you held before **49** *mole:* Maulwurf **58** *welt:* mark on the skin after being beaten with a stick or a belt

"I will that women adorn themselves in modest apparel," he says, "with shamefacedness and sobriety; not with braided hair, or gold, or pearls, or costly array;

"But (which becometh women professing godliness) with good works.

"Let the woman learn in silence with *all* subjection." Here he looks us over. "All," he repeats.

"But I suffer not a woman to teach, nor to usurp authority over the man, but to be in silence.

"For Adam was first formed, then Eve.

"And Adam was not deceived, but the woman being deceived was in the transgression.

"Notwithstanding she shall be saved by childbearing, if they continue in faith and charity and holiness with sobriety."

Saved by childbearing, I think. What did we suppose would save us, in the time before?

"He should tell that to the Wives," Ofglen murmurs, "when they're into the sherry." She means the part about sobriety. It's safe to talk again, the Commander has finished the main ritual and they're doing the rings, lifting the veils. Boo, I think in my head. Take a good look, because it's too late now. The Angels will qualify for Handmaids, later, especially if their new Wives can't produce. But you girls are stuck. What you see is what you get, zits and all. But you aren't expected to love him. You'll find that out soon enough. Just do your duty in silence. When in doubt, when flat on your back, you can look at the ceiling. Who knows what you may see, up there? Funeral wreaths and angels, constellations of dust, stellar or otherwise, the puzzles left by spiders. There's always something to occupy the inquiring mind.

Is anything wrong, dear? the old joke went.

No, why?

You moved.

Just don't move.

What we're aiming for, says Aunt Lydia, is a spirit of camaraderie among women. We must all pull together.

Camaraderie, shit, says Moira through the hole in the toilet cubicle. Right fucking on, Aunt Lydia, as they used to say. How much you want to bet she's got Janine down on her knees? What you think they get up to in that office of hers? I bet she's got her working away on that dried-up hairy old withered –

Moira! I say.

Moira what? she whispers. You know you've thought it.

It doesn't do any good to talk like that, I say, feeling nevertheless the impulse to giggle. But I still pretended to myself, then, that we should try to preserve something resembling dignity.

You were always such a wimp, Moira says, but with affection. It does so do good. It does.

And she's right, I know that now as I kneel on this undeniably hard floor, listening to the ceremony drone on. There is something powerful in the whispering of obscenities, about those in power. There's something delightful about it, something naughty, secretive, forbidden, thrilling. It's like a spell, of sorts. It deflates them, reduces them to the common denominator where they can be dealt with. In the paint of the washrooom cubicle someone unknown had scratched: *Aunt Lydia sucks*. It was like a flag waved from a hilltop in rebellion. The mere idea of Aunt Lydia doing such a thing was in itself heartening.

So now I imagine, among these Angels and their drained white brides, momentous grunts and sweating, damp furry encounters; or, better, ignominious failures, cocks like three-week-old carrots, anguished fumblings upon flesh cold and unresponding as uncooked fish.

When it's over at last and we are walking out, Ofglen says to me in her light, penetrating whisper: "We know you're seeing him alone."

"Who?" I say, resisting the urge to look at her. I know who.

"Your Commander," she says. "We know you have been."

I ask her how.

"We just know," she says. "What does he want? Kinky sex?"

▷ **1–14** *I will that women adorn … sobriety:* reference to I Timothy 2:9–15 **1** *adorn yourself in sth.:* wear sth. • *modest apparel:* simple clothing **2** *sobriety* [soʊ'braɪəti]: quality of being modest, well-behaved and serious **3** *array:* clothes **4** *becometh sb.* (old use) = *becomes sb.:* jdm. gut steht **8** *suffer not:* (here) not allow • *usurp sth.* [ju'sɜːp]: have/take sth. (e.g. power) illegally **23** *zit:* Pickel **46** *wimp* (infml): weak person **68** *kinky:* unconventional

It would be hard to explain to her what he does want, because I still have no name for it. How can I describe what really goes on between us? She would laugh, for one thing. It's easier for me to say, "In a way." That at least has the dignity of coercion.

She thinks about this. "You'd be surprised," she says, "how many of them do."

"I can't help it," I say. "I can't say I won't go." She ought to know that.

We're on the sidewalk now and it's not safe to talk, we're too close to the others and the protective whispering of the crowd is gone. We walk in silence, lagging behind, until finally she judges she can say, "Of course you can't. But find out and tell us."

"Find out what?" I say.

I feel rather than see the slight turning of her head. "Anything you can."

CHAPTER 35

Now there's a space to be filled, in the too-warm air of my room, and a time also; a space-time, between here and now and there and then, punctuated by dinner. The arrival of the tray, carried up the stairs as if for an invalid. An invalid, one who has been invalidated. No valid passport. No exit.

That was what happened, the day we tried to cross at the border, with our fresh passports that said we were not who we were: that Luke, for instance, had never been divorced, that we were therefore lawful, under the new law.

The man went inside with our passports, after we'd explained about the picnic and he'd glanced into the car and seen our daughter asleep, in her zoo of mangy animals. Luke patted my arm and got out of the car as if to stretch his legs and watched the man through the window of the immigration building. I stayed in the car. I lit a cigarette, to steady myself, and drew the smoke in, a long breath of counterfeit relaxation.

I was watching two soldiers in the unfamiliar uniforms that were beginning, by then, to be familiar; they were standing idly beside the yellow-and-black-striped lift-up barrier. They weren't doing much. One of them was watching a flock of birds, gulls, lifting and eddying and landing on the bridge railing beyond. Watching him, I watched them too. Everything was the color it usually is, only brighter.

It's going to be all right, I said, prayed in my head. Oh let it. Let us cross, let us across. Just this once and I'll do anything. What I thought I could do for whoever was listening that would be of the least use or even interest I'll never know.

Then Luke got back into the car, too fast, and turned the key and reversed. He was picking up the phone, he said. And then he began to drive very quickly, and after that there was the dirt road and the woods and we jumped out of the car and began to run. A cottage, to hide in, a boat, I don't know what we thought. He said the passports

▷ **4** *coercion:* action of forcing sb. to do what they do not want to **31** *counterfeit* ['kaʊtərfɪt]: false

were foolproof, and we had so little time to plan. Maybe he had a plan, a map of some kind in his head. As for me, I was only running: away, away.

I don't want to be telling this story.

I don't have to tell it. I don't have to tell anything, to myself or to anyone else. I could just sit here, peacefully. I could withdraw.

It's possible to go so far in, so far down and back, they could never get you out.

Nolite te bastardes carborundorum. Fat lot of good it did her.

Why fight?

That will never do.

Love? said the Commander.

That's better. That's something I know about. We can talk about that.

Falling in love, I said. Falling into it, we all did then, one way or another. How could he have made such light of it? Sneered even. As if it was trivial for us, a frill, a whim. It was, on the contrary, heavy going. It was the central thing; it was the way you understood yourself; if it never happened to you, not ever, you would be like a mutant, a creature from outer space. Everyone knew that.

Falling in love, we said; *I fell for him*. We were falling women. We believed in it, this downward motion: so lovely, like flying, and yet at the same time so dire, so extreme, so unlikely. *God is love*, they said once, but we reversed that, and love, like Heaven, was always just around the corner. The more difficult it was to love the particular man beside us, the more we believed in Love, abstract and total. We were waiting, always, for the incarnation. That word, made flesh.

And sometimes it happened, for a time. That kind of love comes and goes and is hard to remember afterwards, like pain. You would look at the man one day and you would think, *I loved you*, and the tense would be past, and you would be filled with a sense of wonder, because it was such an amazing and precarious and dumb thing to have done; and you would know too why your friends had been evasive about it, at the time.

There is a good deal of comfort, now, in remembering this.

Or sometimes, even when you were still loving, still falling, you'd wake up in the middle of the night, when the moonlight was coming through the window onto his sleeping face, making the shadows in the sockets of his eyes darker and more cavernous than in daytime, and you'd think, Who knows what they do, on their own or with other men? Who knows what they say or where they are likely to go? Who can tell what they really are? Under their daily-ness.

Likely you would think at those times: What if he doesn't love me?

Or you'd remember stories you'd read, in the newspapers, about women who had been found – often women but sometimes they would be men, or children, that was the worst – in ditches or forests or refrigerators in abandoned rented rooms, with their clothes on or off, sexually abused or not; at any rate killed. There were places you didn't want to walk, precautions you took that had to do with locks on windows and doors, drawing the curtains, leaving on lights. These things you did were like prayers; you did them and you hoped they would save you. And for the most part they did. Or something did; you could tell by the fact that you were still alive.

But all of that was pertinent only in the night, and had nothing to do with the man you loved, at least in daylight. With that man you wanted it to work, to work out. Working out was also something you did to keep your body in shape, for the man. If you worked out enough, maybe the man would too. Maybe you would be able to work it out together, as if the two of you were a puzzle that could be solved; otherwise, one of you, most likely the man, would go wandering off on a trajectory of his own, taking his addictive body with him and leaving you with bad withdrawal, which you could counteract by exercise. If you didn't work it out it was because one of you had the wrong attitude. Everything that went on in your life was thought to be due to some positive or negative power emanating from inside your head.

If you don't like it, change it, we said, to each other and to ourselves. And so we would change the man, for another one. Change,

▷ **9** *fat lot of good it did her* (infml): it did not do her anything good or useful **23** *dire:* serious, terrible **27** *incarnation:* act of God coming to earth in human form as Jesus • *the word made flesh:* reference to Luke 1:14 **32** *precarious:* dangerous **49** *take precautions:* Vorsichtsmaßnahmen ergreifen **54** *pertinent:* of importance **61** *trajectory:* Flugbahn

we were sure, was for the better always. We were revisionists; what we revised was ourselves.

It's strange to remember how we used to think, as if everything were available to us, as if there were no contingencies, no boundaries; as if we were free to shape and reshape forever the ever-expanding perimeters of our lives. I was like that too, I did that too. Luke was not the first man for me, and he might not have been the last. If he hadn't been frozen that way. Stopped dead in time, in mid-air, among the trees back there, in the act of falling.

In former times they would send you a little package, of the belongings: what he had with him when he died. That's what they would do, in wartime, my mother said. How long were you supposed to mourn, and what did they say? Make your life a tribute to the loved one. And he was, the loved. One.

Is, I say. *Is, is,* only two letters, you stupid shit, can't you manage to remember it, even a short word like that?

I wipe my sleeve across my face. Once I wouldn't have done that, for fear of smearing, but now nothing comes off. Whatever expression is there, unseen by me, is real.

You'll have to forgive me. I'm a refugee from the past, and like other refugees I go over the customs and habits of being I've left or been forced to leave behind me, and it all seems just as quaint, from here, and I am just as obsessive about it. Like a White Russian drinking tea in Paris, marooned in the twentieth century, I wander back, try to regain those distant pathways; I become too maudlin, lose myself. Weep. Weeping is what it is, not crying. I sit in this chair and ooze like a sponge.

So. More waiting. Lady in waiting: that's what they used to call those stores where you could buy maternity clothes. Woman in waiting sounds more like someone in a train station. Waiting is also a place: it is wherever you wait. For me it's this room. I am a blank, here, between parentheses. Between other people.

The knock comes at my door. Cora, with the tray.

But it isn't Cora. "I've brought it for you," says Serena Joy.

And then I look up and around, and get out of my chair and come towards her. She's holding it, a Polaroid print, square and glossy. So they still make them, cameras like that. And there will be family albums, too, with all the children in them; no Handmaids though. From the point of view of future history, this kind, we'll be invisible. But the children will be in them all right, something for the Wives to look at, downstairs, nibbling at the buffet and waiting for the birth.

"You can only have it for a minute," Serena Joy says, her voice low and conspiratorial. "I have to return it, before they know it's missing."

It must have been a Martha who got it for her. There's a network of the Marthas, then, with something in it for them. That's nice to know.

I take it from her, turn it around so I can see it right-side-up. Is this her, is this what she's like? My treasure.

So tall and changed. Smiling a little now, so soon, and in her white dress as if for an olden-days First Communion.

Time has not stood still. It has washed over me, washed me away, as if I'm nothing more than a woman of sand, left by a careless child too near the water. I have been obliterated for her. I am only a shadow now, far back behind the glib shiny surface of this photograph. A shadow of a shadow, as dead mothers become. You can see it in her eyes: I am not there.

But she exists, in her white dress. She grows and lives. Isn't that a good thing? A blessing?

Still, I can't bear it, to have been erased like that. Better she'd brought me nothing.

I sit at the little table, eating creamed corn with a fork. I have a fork and a spoon, but never a knife. When there's meat they cut it up for me ahead of time, as if I'm lacking manual skills or teeth. I have both, however. That's why I'm not allowed a knife.

▷ **4** *contingency:* Ungewissheit, Eventualität **22** *quaint:* pleasantly old-fashioned **23** *White Russian:* Russian (often aristocratic) who fled the Russian Revolution in 1917 **24** *marooned:* ausgesetzt **25** *maudlin:* foolishly emotional **53** *glib:* (here) deceptive

CHAPTER 36

I knock on his door, hear his voice, adjust my face, go in. He's standing by the fireplace; in his hand he's got an almost-empty drink. He usually waits till I get here to start on the hard liquor, though I know they have wine with dinner. His face is a little flushed. I try to estimate how many he's had.

"Greetings," he says. "How is the fair little one this evening?"

A few, I can tell by the elaborateness of the smile he composes and aims. He's in the courtly phase.

"I'm fine," I say.

"Up for a little excitement?"

"Pardon?" I say. Behind this act of his I sense embarrassment, an uncertainty about how far he can go with me, and in what direction.

"Tonight I have a little surprise for you," he says. He laughs; it's more like a snigger. I notice that everything this evening is *little*. He wishes to diminish things, myself included. "Something you'll like."

"What's that?" I say. "Chinese chequers?" I can take these liberties; he appears to enjoy them, especially after a couple of drinks. He prefers me frivolous.

"Something better," he says, attempting to be tantalizing.

"I can hardly wait."

"Good," he says. He goes to his desk, fumbles with a drawer. Then he comes towards me, one hand behind his back.

"Guess," he says.

"Animal, vegetable, or mineral?" I say.

"Oh, animal," he says with mock gravity. "Definitely animal, I'd say." He brings his hand out from behind his back. He's holding a handful, it seems, of feathers, mauve and pink. Now he shakes this out. It's a garment, apparently, and for a woman: there are the cups for the breasts, covered in purple sequins. The sequins are tiny stars. The feathers are around the thigh holes, and along the top. So I wasn't that wrong about the girdle, after all.

I wonder where he found it. All such clothing was supposed to have been destroyed. I remember seeing that on television, in news clips filmed in one city after another. In New York it was called the Manhattan Cleanup. There were bonfires in Times Square, crowds chanting around them, women throwing their arms up thankfully into the air when they felt the cameras on them, clean-cut stony-faced young men tossing things onto the flames, armfuls of silk and nylon and fake fur, lime-green, red, violet; black satin, gold lamé, glittering silver; bikini underpants, see-through brassieres with pink satin hearts sewn on to cover the nipples. And the manufacturers and importers and salesmen down on their knees, repenting in public, conical paper hats like dunce hats on their heads, SHAME printed on them in red.

But some items must have survived the burning, they couldn't possibly have got it all. He must have come by this in the same way he came by the magazines, not honestly: it reeks of black market. And it's not new, it's been worn before, the cloth under the arms is crumpled and slightly stained, with some other woman's sweat.

"I had to guess the size," he says. "I hope it fits."

"You expect me to put that on?" I say. I know my voice sounds prudish, disapproving. Still there is something attractive in the idea. I've never worn anything remotely like this, so glittering and theatrical, and that's what it must be, an old theater costume, or something from a vanished nightclub act; the closest I ever came were bathing suits, and a camisole set, peach lace, that Luke bought for me once. Yet there's an enticement in this thing, it carries with it the childish allure of dressing up. And it would be so flaunting, such a sneer at the Aunts, so sinful, so free. Freedom, like everything else, is relative.

"Well," I say, not wishing to seem too eager. I want him to feel I'm doing him a favor. Now we may come to it, his deep-down real desire. Does he have a pony whip, hidden behind the door? Will he produce boots, bend himself or me over the desk?

"It's a disguise," he says. "You'll need to paint your face too; I've got the stuff for it. You'll never get in without it."

"In where?" I ask.

"Tonight I'm taking you out."

▷ **14** *snigger:* laugh in an unpleasant way **15** *diminish sth.* [-'--]: make sth. smaller **16** *Chinese chequers:* (Brettspiel) Halma **19** *tantalizing:* making sb. feel as if they cannot have sth. **29** *sequin* ['si:kwɪn]: Paillette **43** *dunce hat:* conical hat formerly placed on the head of a bad learner in the classroom **56** *camisole:* Mieder **57** *enticement:* temptation **58** *allure:* attraction • *flaunting:* showing off in an immodest way

"Out?" It's an archaic phrase. Surely there is nowhere, any more, where a man can take a woman, out.

"Out of here," he says.

I know without being told that what he's proposing is risky, for him but especially for me; but I want to go anyway. I want anything that breaks the monotony, subverts the perceived respectable order of things.

I tell him I don't want him to watch me while I put this thing on; I'm still shy in front of him, about my body. He says he will turn his back, and does so, and I take off my shoes and stockings and my cotton underpants and slide the feathers on, under the tent of my dress. Then I take off the dress itself and slip the thin sequined straps over my shoulders. There are shoes, too, mauve ones with absurdly high heels. Nothing quite fits; the shoes are a little too big, the waist on the costume is too tight, but it will do.

"There," I say, and he turns around. I feel stupid; I want to see myself in a mirror.

"Charming," he says. "Now for the face."

All he has is a lipstick, old and runny and smelling of artificial grapes, and some eyeliner and mascara. No eye shadow, no blusher. For a moment I think I won't remember how to do any of this, and my first try with the eyeliner leaves me with a smudged black lid, as if I've been in a fight; but I wipe it off with the vegetable-oil hand lotion and try again. I rub some of the lipstick along my cheekbones, blending it in. While I do all this, he holds a large silver-backed hand-mirror for me. I recognize it as Serena Joy's. He must have borrowed it from her room.

Nothing can be done about my hair.

"Terrific," he says. By this time he is quite excited; it's as if we're dressing for a party.

He goes to the cupboard and gets out a cloak, with a hood. It's light blue, the color for Wives. This too must be Serena's.

"Pull the hood down over your face," he says. Try not to smear the makeup. It's for getting through the checkpoints."

"But what about my pass?" I say.

"Don't worry about that," he says. "I've got one for you."

And so we set out.

*

We glide together through the darkening streets. The Commander has hold of my right hand, as if we're teenagers at the movies. I clutch the sky-blue cape tightly about me, as a good Wife should. Through the tunnel made by the hood I can see the back of Nick's head. His hat is on straight, he's sitting up straight, his neck is straight, he is all very straight. His posture disapproves of me, or am I imagining it? Does he know what I've got on under this cloak, did he procure it? And if so, does this make him angry or lustful or envious or anything at all? We do have something in common: both of us are supposed to be invisible, both of us are functionaries. I wonder if he knows this. When he opened the door of the car for the Commander, and, by extension, for me, I tried to catch his eye, make him look at me, but he acted as if he didn't see me. Why not? It's a soft job for him, running little errands, doing little favors, and there's no way he'd want to jeopardize it.

The checkpoints are no problem, everything goes as smoothly as the Commander said it would, despite the heavy pounding, the pressure of blood in my head. Chickenshit, Moira would say.

Past the second checkpoint, Nick says, "Here, Sir?" and the Commander says "Yes."

The car pulls over and the Commander says, "Now I'll have to ask you to get down onto the floor of the car."

"Down?" I say.

"We have to go through the gateway," he says, as if this means something to me. I tried to ask him where we were going, but he said he wanted to surprise me. "Wives aren't allowed."

So I flatten myself and the car starts again, and for the next few minutes I see nothing. Under the cloak it's stifling hot. It's a winter cloak, not a cotton summer one, and it smells of mothballs. He must have borrowed it from storage, knowing she wouldn't notice. He has considerately moved his feet to give me room. Nevertheless my forehead is against his shoes. I have never been this close to his shoes before. They feel hard, unwinking, like the shells of beetles: black, polished, inscrutable. They seem to have nothing to do with feet.

▷ **31** *cloak:* long wide kind of coat without sleeves • *hood:* Kapuze **44** *procure sth.* (fml): get sth. that is difficult to find **52** *jeopardize sth.* ['dʒepərdaɪz]: put sth. at risk **67** *storage:* place where things that are not needed are kept for later use

We pass through another checkpoint. I hear the voices, impersonal, deferential, and the window rolling electrically down and up for the passes to be shown. This time he won't show mine, the one that's supposed to be mine, as I'm no longer in official existence, for now.

Then the car starts and then it stops again, and the Commander is helping me up.

"We'll have to be fast," he says. "This is a back entrance. You should leave the cloak with Nick. On the hour, as usual," he says to Nick. So this too is something he's done before.

He helps me out of the cloak; the car door is opened. I feel air on my almost bare skin, and realize I've been sweating. As I turn to shut the car door behind me I can see Nick looking at me through the glass. He sees me now. Is it contempt I read, or indifference, is this merely what he expected of me?

We're in an alleyway behind a building, red brick and fairly modern. A bank of trash cans is set out beside the door, and there's a smell of fried chicken, going bad. The Commander has a key to the door, which is plain and gray and flush with the wall and, I think, made of steel. Inside it there's a concrete-block corridor lit with fluorescent overhead lights; some kind of functional tunnel.

"Here," the Commander says. He slips around my wrist a tag, purple, on an elastic band, like the tags for airport luggage.

"If anyone asks you, say you're an evening rental," he says. He takes me by the bare upper arm and steers me forward. What I want is a mirror, to see if my lipstick is all right,whether the feathers are too ridiculous, too frowzy. In this light I must look lurid. Though it's too late now.

Idiot, says Moira.

CHAPTER 37

We go along the corridor and through another flat gray door and along another corridor, softly lit and carpeted this time, in a mushroom color, browny-pink. Doors open off it, with numbers on them: a hundred and one, a hundred and two, the way you count during a thunderstorm, to see how close you are to being struck. It's a hotel then. From behind one of the doors comes laughter, a man's and also a woman's. It's a long time since I've heard that.

We emerge into a central courtyard. It's wide and also high: it goes up several storeys to a skylight at the top. There's a fountain in the middle of it, a round fountain spraying water in the shape of a dandelion gone to seed. Potted plants and trees sprout here and there, vines hang down from the balconies. Oval-sided glass elevators slide up and down the walls like giant molluscs.

I know where I am. I've been here before: with Luke, in the afternoons, a long time ago. It was a hotel, then. Now it's full of women.

I stand still and stare at them. I can stare, here, look around me, there are no white wings to keep me from it. My head, shorn of them, feels curiously light; as if a weight has been removed from it, or substance.

The women are sitting, lounging, strolling, leaning against one another. There are men mingled with them, a lot of men, but in their dark uniforms or suits, so similar to one another, they form only a kind of background. The women on the other hand are tropical, they are dressed in all kinds of bright festive gear. Some of them have on outfits like mine, feathers and glister, cut high up the thighs, low over the breasts. Some are in olden-days lingerie, shortie nightgowns, baby-doll pyjamas, the occasional see-through negligée. Some are in bathing suits, one piece or bikini; one, I see, is wearing a crocheted affair, with big scallop shells covering the tits. Some are in jogging shorts and sun halters, some in exercise costumes like the ones they

▷ **2** *deferential:* showing respect **19** *flush with sth.:* on the same level as sth. **27** *frowzy* (AE infml): untidy, shabby **46** *shorn of sth.:* (here) without sth. that is usually there **54** *glister* (old use): glitter **57** *crocheted* [kroʊˈʃeɪd]: gehäkelt **58** *affair:* (here) costume

used to show on television, body-tight, with knitted pastel leg warmers. There are even a few in cheerleaders' outfits, little pleated skirts, outsized letters across the chest. I guess they've had to fall back on a mélange, whatever they could scrounge or salvage. All wear makeup, and I realize how unaccustomed I've become to seeing it, on women, because their eyes look too big to me, too dark and shimmering, their mouths too red, too wet, blood-dipped and glistening; or, on the other hand, too clownish.

At first glance there's a cheerfulness to this scene. It's like a masquerade party; they are like oversized children, dressed up in togs they've rummaged from trunks. Is there joy in this? There could be, but have they chosen it? You can't tell by looking.

There are a great many buttocks in this room. I am no longer used to them.

"It's like walking into the past," says the Commander. His voice sounds pleased, delighted even. "Don't you think?"

I try to remember if the past was exactly like this. I'm not sure, now. I know it contained these things, but somehow the mix is different. A movie about the past is not the same as the past.

"Yes," I say. What I feel is not one simple thing. Certainly I am not dismayed by these women, not shocked by them. I recognize them as truants. The official creed denies them, denies their very existence, yet here they are. That is at least something.

"Don't gawk," says the Commander. "You'll give yourself away. Just act natural." Again he leads me forward. Another man has spotted him, has greeted him and set himself in motion towards us. The Commander's grip tightens on my upper arm. "Steady," he whispers. "Don't lose your nerve."

All you have to do, I tell myself, is keep your mouth shut and look stupid. It shouldn't be that hard.

The Commander does the talking for me, to this man and to the others who follow him. He doesn't say much about me, he doesn't need to. He says I'm new, and they look at me and dismiss me and confer together about other things. My disguise performs its function.

He retains hold of my arm, and as he talks his spine straightens imperceptibly, his chest expands, his voice assumes more and more the sprightliness and jocularity of youth. It occurs to me he is showing off. He is showing me off, to them, and they understand that, they are decorous enough, they keep their hands to themselves, but they review my breasts, my legs, as if there's no reason why they shouldn't. But also he is showing off to me. He is demonstrating, to me, his mastery of the world. He's breaking the rules, under their noses, thumbing his nose at them, getting away with it. Perhaps he's reached that state of intoxication which power is said to inspire, the state in which you believe you are indispensable and can therefore do anything, absolutely anything you feel like, anything at all. Twice, when he thinks no one is looking, he winks at me.

It's a juvenile display, the whole act, and pathetic; but it's something I understand.

When he's done enough of this he leads me away again, to a puffy flowered sofa of the kind they once had in hotel lobbies; in this lobby, in fact, it's a floral design I remember, dark blue background, pink art nouveau flowers. "I thought your feet might be getting tired," he says, "in those shoes." He's right about that, and I'm grateful. He sits me down, and sits himself down beside me. He puts an arm around my shoulders. The fabric of his sleeve is raspy against my skin, so unaccustomed lately to being touched.

"Well?" he says. "What do you think of our little club?"

I look around me again. The men are not homogeneous, as I first thought. Over by the fountain there's a group of Japanese, in lightish-gray suits, and in the far corner there's a splash of white: Arabs, in those long bathrobes they wear, the headgear, the striped sweatbands.

"It's a club?" I say.

"Well, that's what we call it, among ourselves. The club."

"I thought this sort of thing was strictly forbidden," I say.

▷ **2** *pleated skirt:* Faltenrock **4** *scrounge sth.:* get sth. with difficulty from sb. else **10** *togs:* clothes **11** *rummage sth.:* (here) find sth. by searching through lots of things **13** *buttocks:* the part of the body you sit on **22** *truant:* (usu.) schoolchild who does not go to school on a schoolday; (here) woman who is not where she should be • *deny sb./sth.:* (here) claim sb./sth. does not exist **24** *gawk:* stare • *give yourself away:* show sth. that you do not want to show **37** *sprightliness:* liveliness • *jocularity:* quality of being fun-loving **39** *decorous* ['dekərəs]: modest, polite **43** *thumb your nose at sb.:* make a gesture that shows you do not care about other people's attitudes **44** *intoxication:* drunkenness **45** *indispensable:* necessary for the functioning of sth. **47** *wink at sb.:* jdm. zuzwinkern **48** *pathetic:* sad, silly **56** *fabric:* cloth • *raspy:* rough, scratchy

"Well, officially," he says. "But everyone's human, after all."

I wait for him to elaborate on this, but he doesn't, so I say, "What does that mean?"

"It means you can't cheat Nature," he says. "Nature demands variety, for men. It stands to reason, it's part of the procreational strategy. It's Nature's plan." I don't say anything, so he goes on. "Women know that instinctively. Why did they buy so many different clothes, in the old days? To trick the men into thinking they were several different women. A new one each day."

He says this as if he believes it, but he says many things that way. Maybe he believes it, maybe he doesn't, or maybe he does both at the same time. Impossible to tell what he believes.

"So now that we don't have different clothes," I say, "you merely have different women." This is irony, but he doesn't acknowledge it.

"It solves a lot of problems," he says, without a twitch.

I don't reply to this. I am getting fed up with him. I feel like freezing on him, passing the rest of the evening in sulky wordlessness. But I can't afford that and I know it. Whatever this is, it's still an evening out.

What I'd really like to do is talk with the women, but I see scant chance of that.

"Who are these people?" I ask him.

"It's only for officers," he says. "From all branches; and senior officials. And trade delegations, of course. It stimulates trade. It's a good place to meet people. You can hardly do business without it. We try to provide at least as good as they can get elsewhere. You can overhear things too; information. A man will sometimes tell a woman things he wouldn't tell another man."

"No," I say, "I mean the women."

"Oh," he says. "Well, some of them are real pros. Working girls" – he laughs – "from the time before. They couldn't be assimilated; anyway, most of them prefer it here."

"And the others?"

"The others?" he says. "Well, we have quite a collection. That one there, the one in green, she's a sociologist. Or was. That one was a lawyer, that one was in business, an executive position; some sort of fast-food chain or maybe it was hotels. I'm told you can have quite a good conversation with her if all you feel like is talking. They prefer it here, too."

"Prefer it to what?" I say.

"To the alternatives," he says. "You might even prefer it yourself, to what you've got." He says this coyly, he's fishing, he wants to be complimented, and I know that the serious part of the conversation has come to an end.

"I don't know," I say, as if considering it. "It might be hard work."

"You'd have to watch your weight, that's for sure," he says. "They're strict about that. Gain ten pounds and they put you in Solitary." Is he joking? Most likely, but I don't want to know.

"Now," he says, "to get you into the spirit of the place, how about a little drink?"

"I'm not supposed to," I say. "As you know."

"Once won't hurt," he says. "Anyway, it wouldn't look right if you didn't. No nicotine-and-alcohol taboos here! You see, they do have some advantages here."

"All right," I say. Secretly I like the idea, I haven't had a drink for years.

"What'll it be, then?" he says. "They've got everything here. Imported."

"A gin and tonic," I say. "But weak, please. I wouldn't want to disgrace you."

"You won't do that," he says, grinning. He stands up; then, surprisingly, takes my hand and kisses it, on the palm. Then he moves off, heading for the bar. He could have called over a waitress, there are some of these, in identical black miniskirts with pompons on their breasts, but they seem busy and hard to flag down.

Then I see her. Moira. She's standing with two other women, over near the fountain. I have to look hard, again, to make sure it's her; I do this in pulses, quick flickers of the eyes, so no one will notice.

She's dressed absurdly, in a black outfit of once-shiny satin that looks the worse for wear. It's strapless, wired from the inside, pushing up the breasts, but it doesn't quite fit Moira, it's too large, so that one breast is plumped out and the other one isn't. She's tugging absent-

▷ **2** *elaborate on sth.* [ɪ'læbəreɪt] (v): explain sth. in more detail **5** *procreational:* Fortpflanzungs- **20** *scant:* very little **30** *pros:* professionals **36** *executive* [ɪg'zekjətɪv]: management **42–43** *be fishing (for compliments):* try to get compliments from others **72** *plumped out:* (here) made to look big

mindedly at the top, pulling it up. There's a wad of cotton attached to the back, I can see it as she half-turns; it looks like a sanitary pad that's been popped like a piece of popcorn. I realize that it's supposed to be a tail. Attached to her head are two ears, of a rabbit or deer, it's not easy to tell; one of the ears has lost its starch or wiring and is flopping halfway down. She has a black bow tie around her neck and is wearing black net stockings and black high heels. She always hated high heels.

The whole costume, antique and bizarre, reminds me of something from the past, but I can't think what. A stage play, a musical comedy? Girls dressed for Easter, in rabbit suits. What is the significance of it here, why are rabbits supposed to be sexually attractive to men? How can this bedraggled costume appeal?

Moria is smoking a cigarette. She takes a drag, passes it to the woman on her left, who's in red spangles with a long pointed tail attached, and silver horns; a devil outfit. Now she has her arms folded across her front, under her wired-up breasts. She stands on one foot, then the other, her feet must hurt; her spine sags slightly. She gazes without interest or speculation around the room. This must be familiar scenery.

I will her to look at me, to see me, but her eyes slide over me as if I'm just another palm tree, another chair. Surely she must turn, I'm willing so hard, she must look at me, before one of the men comes over to her, before she disappears. Already the other woman with her, the blonde in the short pink bedjacket with the tatty fur trim, has been appropriated, has entered the glass elevator, has ascended out of sight. Moira swivels her head around again, checking perhaps for prospects. It must be hard to stand there unclaimed, as if she's at a high-school dance, being looked over. This time her eyes snag on me. She sees me. She knows enough not to react.

We stare at one another, keeping our faces blank, apathetic. Then she makes a small motion of her head, a slight jerk to the right. She takes the cigarette back from the woman in red, holds it to her mouth, lets her hand rest in the air a moment, all five fingers outspread. Then she turns her back on me.

Our old signal. I have five minutes to get to the women's washroom, which must be somewhere to her right. I look around: no sign of it. Nor can I risk getting up and walking anywhere, without the

Commander. I don't know enough, I don't know the ropes, I might be challenged.

A minute, two. Moira begins to saunter off, not glancing around. She can only hope I've understood her and will follow.

The Commander comes back, with two drinks. He smiles down at me, places the drinks on the long black coffee table in front of the sofa, sits. "Enjoying yourself?" he says. He wants me to. This after all is a treat.

I smile at him. "Is there a washroom?" I say.

"Of course," he says. He sips at his drink. He does not volunteer directions.

"I need to go to it." I am counting in my head now, seconds, not minutes.

"It's over there." He nods.

"What if someone stops me?"

"Just show them your tag," he says. "It'll be all right. They'll know you're taken."

I get up, wobble across the room. I lurch a little, near the fountain, almost fall. It's the heels. Without the Commander's arm to steady me I'm off balance. Several of the men look at me, with surprise I think rather than lust. I feel like a fool. I hold my left arm conspicuously in front of me, bent at the elbow, with the tag turned outwards. Nobody says anything.

▷ **13** *bedraggled* [bɪ'dræɡəld]: untidy **14** *drag* (infml): Zug **15** *spangles:* shiny ornaments like sequins **18** *sag:* lean downwards **21** *will sb. to do sth.:* use the power of your mind to try and make sb. do sth. **26** *appropriate sb./sth.:* take possession of sb./sth. **27** *swivel* ['swɪvəl]: turn around **28** *prospects:* (here) possible clients **29** *snag on sb./sth.:* get caught on sb./sth. **31** *apathetic:* without feeling **39** *know the ropes:* know the rules of behavior, know what is expected **56** *wobble:* walk unsteadily • *lurch:* almost fall forward **59** *conspicuous:* that can be easily seen

CHAPTER 38

I find the entrance to the women's washroom. It still says *Ladies*, in scrolly gold script. There's a corridor leading in to the door, and a woman seated at a table beside it, supervising the entrances and exits. She's an older woman, wearing a purple caftan and gold eyeshadow, but I can tell she is nevertheless an Aunt. The cattle prod's on the table, its thong around her wrist. No nonsense here.

"Fifteen minutes," she says to me. She gives me an oblong of purple cardboard from a stack of them on the table. It's like a fitting room, in the department stores of the time before. To the woman behind me I hear her say, "You were just here."

"I need to go again," the woman says.

"Rest break once an hour," says the Aunt. "You know the rules."

The woman begins to protest, in a whiny desperate voice. I push open the door.

I remember this. There's a rest area, gently lit in pinkish tones, with several easy chairs and a sofa, in lime-green bamboo-shoot print, with a wall clock above it in a gold filigree frame. Here they haven't removed the mirror, there's a long one opposite the sofa. You need to know, here, what you look like. Through an archway beyond there's the row of toilet cubicles, also pink, and wash basins and more mirrors.

Several women are sitting in the chairs and on the sofa, with their shoes off, smoking. They stare at me as I come in. There's perfume in the air and stale smoke, and the scent of working flesh.

"You new?" one of them says.

"Yes," I say, looking around for Moira, who is nowhere in sight.

The women don't smile. They return to their smoking as if it's serious business. In the room beyond, a woman in a cat suit with a tail made of orange fake fur is re-doing her makeup. This is like backstage: greasepaint, smoke, the materials of illusion.

I stand hesitant, not knowing what to do. I don't want to ask about Moira, I don't know whether it's safe. Then a toilet flushes and Moira comes out of a pink cubicle. She teeters towards me; I wait for a sign.

"It's all right," she says, to me and to the other women. "I know her." The others smile now, and Moira hugs me. My arms go around her, the wires propping up her breasts dig into my chest. We kiss each other, on one cheek, then the other.

Then we stand back.

"Godawful," she says. She grins at me. "You look like the Whore of Babylon."

"Isn't that what I'm supposed to look like?" I say. "You look like something the cat dragged in."

"Yes," she says, pulling up her front, "not my style and this thing is about to fall to shreds. I wish they'd dredge up someone who still knows how to make them. Then I could get something halfway decent."

"You pick that out?" I say. I wonder if maybe she's chosen it, out of the others, because it was less garish. At least it's only black and white.

"Hell no," she says. "Government issue. I guess they thought it was me."

I still can't believe it's her. I touch her arm again. Then I begin to cry.

"Don't do that," she says. "Your eyes'll run. Anyway there isn't time. Shove over." This she says to the two women on the sofa, her usual peremptory rough-cut slapdash manner, and as usual she gets away with it.

"My break's up anyway," says one woman, who's wearing a baby-blue laced-up Merry Widow and white stockings. She stands up, shakes my hand. "Welcome," she says.

The other woman obligingly moves over, and Moira and I sit down. The first thing we do is take off our shoes.

"What the hell are you doing here?" Moira says then. "Not that it isn't great to see you. But it's not so great for you. What'd you do wrong? Laugh at his dick?"

I look up at the ceiling. "Is it bugged?" I say. I wipe around my eyes, gingerly, with my fingertips. Black comes off.

"Probably," says Moira. "You want a cig?"

"I'd love one," I say.

"Here," she says to the woman next to her. "Lend me one, will you?"

▷ **2** *scrolly:* having rounded ornaments **33** *teeter:* walk unsteadily **39–40** *the Whore of Babylon:* immoral woman (cf. Revelation 17:3–6) **44** *dredge up sb./sth.:* (here) find sb./sth. (esp. that is difficult to find) **47** *garish* ['gerɪʃ]: brightly ugly **48–49** *it is me:* it suits me **52** *shove over* [ʃʌv]: move over **53** *peremptory* [pə'remptərɪ]: expecting to be obeyed **53–54** *get away with sth.:* be able to do sth. other people do not like without being punished for it **62** *dick* (sl): penis

The woman hands over, ungrudging. Moira is still a skilful borrower. I smile at that.

"On the other hand, it might not be," says Moira. "I can't imagine they'd care about anything we have to say. They've already heard most of it, and anyway nobody gets out of here except in a black van. But you must know that, if you're here."

I pull her head over so I can whisper in her ear. "I'm temporary," I tell her. "It's just tonight. I'm not supposed to be here at all. He smuggled me in."

"Who?" she whispers back. "That shit you're with? I've had him, he's the pits."

"He's my Commander," I say.

She nods. "Some of them do that, they get a kick out of it. It's like screwing on the altar or something: your gang are supposed to be such chaste vessels. They like to see you all painted up. Just another crummy power trip."

This interpretation hasn't occurred to me. I apply it to the Commander, but it seems too simple for him, too crude. Surely his motivations are more delicate than that. But it may only be vanity that prompts me to think so.

"We don't have much time left," I say. "Tell me everything."

Moira shrugs. "What's the point?" she says. But she knows there is a point, so she does.

This is what she says, whispers, more or less. I can't remember exactly, because I had no way of writing it down. I've filled it out for her as much as I can: we didn't have much time so she just gave the outlines. Also she told me this in two sessions, we managed a second break together. I've tried to make it sound as much like her as I can. It's a way of keeping her alive.

"I left that old hag Aunt Elizabeth tied up like a Christmas turkey behind the furnace. I wanted to kill her, I really felt like it, but now I'm just as glad I didn't or things would be a lot worse for me. I couldn't believe how easy it was to get out of the Center. In that brown outfit I just walked right through. I kept on going as if I knew where I was heading, till I was out of sight. I didn't have any great plan; it wasn't an organized thing, like they thought, though when they were trying to get it out of me I made up a lot of stuff. You do that, when they use the electrodes and the other things. You don't care what you say.

"I kept my shoulders back and chin up and marched along, trying to think of what to do next. When they busted the press they'd picked up a lot of the women I knew, and I thought they'd most likely have the rest by now. I was sure they had a list. We were dumb to think we could keep it going the way we did, even underground, even when we'd moved everything out of the office and into people's cellars and back rooms. So I knew better than to try any of those houses.

"I had some sort of an idea of where I was in relation to the city, though I was walking along a street I couldn't remember having seen before. But I figured out from the sun where north was. Girl Scouts was some use after all. I thought I might as well head that way, see if I could find the Yard or the Square or anything around it. Then I would know for sure where I was. Also I thought it would look better for me to be going in towards the center of things, rather than away. It would look more plausible.

"They'd set up more checkpoints while we were inside the Center, they were all over the place. The first one scared the shit out of me. I came on it suddenly around the corner. I knew it wouldn't look right if I turned around in full view and went back, so I bluffed it through, the same as I had at the gate, putting on that frown and keeping myself stiff and pursing my lips and looking right through them, as if they were festering sores. You know the way the Aunts look when they say the word man. It worked like a charm, and it did at the other checkpoints, too.

"But the insides of my head were going around like crazy. I only had so much time, before they found the old bat and sent out the alarm. Soon enough they'd be looking for me: one fake Aunt, on foot. I tried to think of someone, I ran over and over the people I knew. At last I tried to remember what I could about our mailing list. We'd destroyed it, of course, early on; or we didn't destroy it, we divided it up among us and each one of us memorized a section, and then we destroyed it. We were still using the mails then, but we didn't put our logo on the envelopes any more. It was getting far too risky.

▷ **1** *ungrudging:* giving sth. to sb. without bad feelings **11** *the pits* (sl): the lowest possible quality **14** *screw* (sl): have sex **15** *chaste:* keusch **16** *crummy* (sl): stupid, bad **30** *hag* (derog sl): (ugly) woman **40** *bust sth.:* raid sth. and destroy it **50** *the Yard, the Square:* places in Cambridge, Massachusetts **60** *festering sore:* eiternde Wunde **64** *bat* (derog sl): woman

"So I tried to recall my section of the list. I won't tell you the name I chose, because I don't want them to get in trouble, if they haven't already. It could be I've spilled all this stuff, it's hard to remember what you say when they're doing it. You'll say anything.

"I chose them because they were a married couple, and those were safer than anyone single and especially anyone gay. Also I remembered the designation beside their name. Q, it said, which meant Quaker. We had the religious denominations marked where there were any, for marches. That way you could tell who might turn out to what. It was no good calling on the C's to do abortion stuff, for instance; not that we'd done much of that lately. I remembered their address, too. We'd grilled each other on those addresses, it was important to remember them exactly, zip code and all.

"By this time I'd hit Mass Ave. and I knew where I was. And I knew where they were too. Now I was worrying about something else: when these people saw an Aunt coming up the walk, wouldn't they just lock the door and pretend not to be home? But I had to try it anyway, it was my only chance. I figured they weren't likely to shoot me. It was about five o'clock by this time. I was tired of walking, especially that Aunt's way like a goddamn soldier, poker up the ass, and I hadn't had anything to eat since breakfast.

"What I didn't know of course was that in those early days the Aunts and even the Center were hardly common knowledge. It was all secret at first, behind barbed wire. There might have been objections to what they were doing, even then. So although people had seen the odd Aunt around, they weren't really aware of what they were for. They must have thought they were some kind of army nurse. Already they'd stopped asking questions, unless they had to.

"So these people let me in right away. It was the woman who came to the door. I told her I was doing a questionnaire. I did that so she wouldn't look surprised, in case anyone was watching. But as soon as I was inside the door, I took off the headgear and told them who I was. They could have phoned the police or whatever, I know I was taking a chance, but like I say there wasn't any choice. Anyway they didn't. They gave me some clothes, a dress of hers, and burned the Aunt's outfit and the pass in their furnace; they knew that had to be done right away. They didn't like having me there, that much was clear, it made them very nervous. They had two little kids, both under seven. I could see their point.

"I went to the can, what a relief that was. Bathtub full of plastic fish and so on. Then I sat upstairs in the kids' room and played with them and their plastic blocks while their parents stayed downstairs and decided what to do about me. I didn't feel scared by then, in fact I felt quite good. Fatalistic, you could say. Then the woman made me a sandwich and a cup of coffee and the man said he'd take me to another house. They hadn't risked phoning.

"The other house was Quakers too, and they were paydirt, because they were a station on the Underground Femaleroad. After the first man left, they said they'd try to get me out of the country. I won't tell you how, because some of the stations may still be operating. Each one of them was in contact with only one other one, always the next one along. There were advantages to that – it was better if you were caught – but disadvantages too, because if one station got busted the entire chain backed up until they could make contact with one of their couriers, who could set up an alternate route. They were better organized than you'd think, though. They'd infiltrated a couple of useful places; one of them was the post office. They had a driver there with one of those handy little trucks. I made it over the bridge and into the city proper in a mail sack. I can tell you that now because they got him, soon after that. He ended up on the Wall. You hear about these things; you hear a lot in here, you'd be surprised. The Commanders tell us themselves, I guess they figure why not, there's no one we can pass it on to, except each other, and that doesn't count.

"I'm making this sound easy but it wasn't. I nearly shat bricks the whole time. One of the hardest things was knowing that these other people were risking their lives for you when they didn't have to. But they said they were doing it for religious reasons and I shouldn't take it personally. That helped some. They had silent prayers every evening. I found that hard to get used to at first, because it reminded me too much of that shit at the Center. It made me feel sick to my stomach, to tell you the truth. I had to make an effort, tell myself that this was a whole other thing. I hated it at first. But I figure it was what

▷ **3** *spill sth.* (infml): tell sth. (that you do not really want to tell) **12** *grill sb. on sth.* (infml): test sb. to make sure they know sth. **13** *zip code:* Postleitzahl **20** *poker:* Schürhaken **26** *the odd:* the occasional **40** *can* (AE sl): toilet **47** *paydirt:* a lucky choice **48** *Underground Femaleroad:* allusion to the Underground Railroad that helped runaway slaves get to Canada in the 19th century **59** *the city proper:* the actual city (here: Boston) **64** *shit bricks (shat – shat):* be very frightened

kept them going. They knew more or less what would happen to them if they got caught. Not in detail, but they knew. By that time they'd started putting some of it on the TV, the trials and so forth.

"It was before the sectarian roundups began in earnest. As long as you said you were some sort of a Christian and you were married, for the first time that is, they were still leaving you pretty much alone. They were concentrating first on the others. They got them more or less under control before they started in on everybody else.

"I was underground it must have been eight or nine months. I was taken from one safe house to another, there were more of those then. They weren't all Quakers, some of them weren't even religious. They were just people who didn't like the way things were going.

"I almost made it out. They got me up as far as Salem, then in a truck full of chickens into Maine. I almost puked from the smell; you ever thought what it would be like to be shat on by a truckload of chickens, all of them carsick? They were planning to get me across the border there; not by car or truck, that was already too difficult, but by boat, up the coast. I didn't know that until the actual night, they never told you the next step until right before it was happening. They were careful that way.

"So I don't know what happened. Maybe somebody got cold feet about it, or somebody outside got suspicious. Or maybe it was the boat, maybe they thought the guy was out in his boat at night too much. By that time it must have been crawling with Eyes up there, and everywhere else close to the border. Whatever it was, they picked us up just as we were coming out the back door to go down to the dock. Me and the guy, and his wife too. They were an older couple, in their fifties. He'd been in the lobster business, back before all that happened to the shore fishing there. I don't know what became of them after that, because they took me in a separate van.

"I thought it might be the end, for me. Or back to the Center and the attentions of Aunt Lydia and her steel cable. She enjoyed that, you know. She pretended to do all that love-the-sinner, hate-the-sin stuff, but she enjoyed it. I did consider offing myself, and maybe I would have if there'd been any way. But they had two of them in the back of the van with me, watching me like a hawk; didn't say a hell of a lot, just sat and watched me in that wall-eyed way they have. So it was no go.

"We didn't end up at the Center though, we went somewhere else. I won't go into what happened after that. I'd rather not talk about it. All I can say is they didn't leave any marks.

"When that was over they showed me a movie. Know what it was about? It was about life in the Colonies. In the Colonies, they spend their time cleaning up. They're very clean-minded these days. Sometimes it's just bodies, after a battle. The ones in city ghettoes are the worst, they're left around longer, they get rottener. This bunch doesn't like dead bodies lying around, they're afraid of a plague or something. So the women in the Colonies there do the burning. The other Colonies are worse, though, the toxic dumps and the radiation spills. They figure you've got three years maximum, at those, before your nose falls off and your skin pulls away like rubber gloves. They don't bother to feed you much, or give you protective clothing or anything, it's cheaper not to. Anyway they're mostly people they want to get rid of. They say there's other Colonies, not so bad, where they do agriculture: cotton and tomatoes and all that. But those weren't the ones they showed me the movie about.

"It's old women, I bet you've been wondering why you haven't seen too many of those around any more, and Handmaids who've screwed up their three chances, and incorrigibles like me. Discards, all of us. They're sterile, of course. If they aren't that way to begin with, they are after they've been there for a while. When they're unsure, they do a little operation on you, so there won't be any mistakes. I'd say it's about a quarter men in the Colonies, too. Not all of those Gender Traitors end up on the Wall.

"All of them wear long dresses, like the ones at the Center, only gray. Women and the men too, judging from the group shots. I guess it's supposed to demoralize the men, having to wear a dress. Shit, it would demoralize me enough. How do you stand it? Everything considered, I like this outfit better.

"So after that, they said I was too dangerous to be allowed the privilege of returning to the Red Center. They said I would be a corrupting influence. I had my choice, they said, this or the Colonies.

▷ **14** *puke* (infml): vomit **24** *crawl with sth.*: be full of sth. **34** *offing yourself* (sl): killing yourself **37** *wall-eyed:* (here) having no expression in the eyes **46** *this bunch* (sl): this group of people (here: the leaders of Gilead) **59** *screw up* (infml): fail to give the desired results • *discard* (n): sth./sb. that is no longer needed

Well, shit, nobody but a nun would pick the Colonies. I mean, I'm not a martyr. I'd already had my tubes tied, years ago, so I didn't even need the operation. Nobody in here with viable ovaries either, you can see what kind of problems it would cause.

"So here I am. They even give you face cream. You should figure out some way of getting in here. You'd have three or four good years before your snatch wears out and they send you to the boneyard. The food's not bad and there's drink and drugs, if you want it, and we only work nights."

"Moira," I say. "You don't mean that." She is frightening me now, because what I hear in her voice is indifference, a lack of volition. Have they really done it to her then, taken away something – what? – that used to be so central to her? But how can I expect her to go on, with my idea of her courage, live it through, act it out, when I myself do not?

I don't want her to be like me. Give in, go along, save her skin. That is what it comes down to. I want gallantry from her, swashbuckling, heroism, single-handed combat. Something I lack.

"Don't worry about me," she says. She must know some of what I'm thinking. "I'm still here, you can see it's me. Anyway, look at it this way: it's not so bad, there's lots of women around. Butch paradise, you might call it."

Now she's teasing, showing some energy, and I feel better.

"Do they let you?" I say.

"Let, hell, they encourage it. Know what they call this place, among themselves? Jezebel's. The Aunts figure we're all damned anyway, they've given up on us, so it doesn't matter what sort of vice we get up to, and the Commanders don't give a piss what we do in our off time. Anyway, women on women sort of turns them on."

"What about the others?" I say.

"Put it this way," she says, "they're not too fond of men."

She shrugs again. It might be resignation.

Here is what I'd like to tell. I'd like to tell a story about how Moira escaped, for good this time. Or if I couldn't tell that, I'd like to say she blew up Jezebel's, with fifty Commanders inside it. I'd like her to end with something daring and spectacular, some outrage, something that would befit her. But as far as I know that didn't happen. I don't know how she ended, or even if she did, because I never saw her again.

CHAPTER 39

The Commander has a room key. He got it from the front desk, while I waited on the flowered sofa. He shows it to me, slyly. I am to understand.

We ascend in the glass half-egg of the elevator, past the vinedraped balconies. I am to understand also that I am on display.

He unlocks the door of the room. Everything is the same, the very same as it was, once upon a time. The drapes are the same, the heavy flowered ones that match the bedspread, orange poppies on royal blue, and the thin white ones to draw against the sun; the bureau and bedside tables, square-cornered, impersonal; the lamps; the pictures on the walls: fruit in a bowl, stylized apples, flowers in a vase, buttercups and Devil's paintbrushes keyed to the drapes. All is the same.

I tell the Commander just a minute, and go into the bathroom. My ears are ringing from the smoke, the gin has filled me with lassitude. I wet a washcloth and press it to my forehead. After a while I look to see if there are any little bars of soap in individual wrappers. There are. The kind with the gypsy on them, from Spain.

I breathe in the soap smell, the disinfectant smell, and stand in the white bathroom, listening to the distant sounds of water running, toilets being flushed. In a strange way I feel comforted, at home. There is something reassuring about the toilets. Bodily functions at least remain democratic. Everybody shits, as Moira would say.

I sit on the edge of the bathtub, gazing at the blank towels.

Once they would have excited me. They would have meant the aftermath, of love.

*

▷ **2** *have your tubes tied* (infml): have an operation to make you unable to have babies **7** *snatch* (sl): vagina • *boneyard* (sl): graveyard **11** *volition:* will to succeed or survive **17** *swashbuckling:* (kind of pirate-like) adventure **21** *butch:* (masculine) lesbian **26** *Jezebel's:* immoral woman (reference to I Kings 18:4–13 and II Kings 9:29–37) **34** *for good:* forever **40** *slyly* (here): not openly **46** *poppy:* Mohnblume **49–50** *buttercup:* Butterblume **50** *Devil's paintbrush:* Teufelskralle • *keyed to sth.:* matching sth. (in color) **52** *lassitude:* state of not caring **63** *aftermath:* time immediately after an important happening

I saw your mother, Moira said.

Where? I said. I felt jolted, thrown off. I realized I'd been thinking of her as dead.

Not in person, it was in that film they showed us, about the Colonies. There was a close-up, it was her all right. She was wrapped up in one of those gray things but I know it was her.

Thank God, I said.

Why, thank God? said Moira.

I thought she was dead.

She might as well be, said Moira. You should wish it for her.

I can't remember the last time I saw her. It blends in with all the others; it was some trivial occasion. She must have dropped by; she did that, she breezed in and out of my house as if I were the mother and she were the child. She still had that jauntiness. Sometimes, when she was between apartments, just moving in to one or just moving out, she'd use my washer-dryer for her laundry. Maybe she'd come over to borrow something, from me: a pot, a hair-dryer. That too was a habit of hers.

I didn't know it would be the last time or else I would have remembered it better. I can't even remember what we said.

A week later, two weeks, three weeks, when things had become suddenly so much worse, I tried to call her. But there was no answer, and no answer when I tried again.

She hadn't told me she was going anywhere, but then maybe she wouldn't have; she didn't always. She had her own car and she wasn't too old to drive.

Finally I got the apartment superintendent on the phone. He said he hadn't seen her lately.

I was worried. I thought maybe she'd had a heart attack or a stroke, it wasn't out of the question, though she hadn't been sick that I knew of. She was always so healthy. She still worked out at Nautilus and went swimming every two weeks. I used to tell my friends she was healthier than I was and maybe it was true.

Luke and I drove across into the city and Luke bullied the superintendent into opening up the apartment. She could be dead, on the floor, Luke said. The longer you leave it the worse it'll be. You thought of the smell? The superintendent said something about needing a permit, but Luke could be persuasive. He made it clear we weren't going to wait or go away. I started to cry. Maybe that was what finally did it.

When the man got the door open what we found was chaos. There was furniture overturned, the mattress was ripped open, bureau drawers upside-down on the floor, their contents strewn and mounded. But my mother wasn't there.

I'm going to call the police, I said. I'd stopped crying; I felt cold from head to foot, my teeth were chattering.

Don't, said Luke.

Why not? I said. I was glaring at him, I was angry now. He stood there in the wreck of the living room, just looking at me. He put his hands into his pockets, one of those aimless gestures people make when they don't know what else to do.

Just don't, is what he said.

Your mother's neat, Moira would say, when we were at college. Later: she's got pizzazz. Later still: she's cute.

She's not cute, I would say. She's my mother.

Jeez, said Moira, you ought to see mine.

I think of my mother, sweeping up deadly toxins; the way they used to use up old women, in Russia, sweeping dirt. Only this dirt will kill her. I can't quite believe it. Surely her cockiness, her optimism and energy, her pizzazz, will get her out of this. She will think of something.

But I know this isn't true. It is just passing the buck, as children do, to mothers.

I've mourned for her already. But I will do it again, and again.

I bring myself back, to the here, to the hotel. This is where I need to be. Now, in this ample mirror under the white light, I take a look at myself.

It's a good look, slow and level. I'm a wreck. The mascara has smudged again, despite Moira's repairs, the purplish lipstick has bled,

▷ **2** *jolted:* disturbed by an unexpected strong movement **14** *jauntiness:* liveliness **27** *apartment superintendent:* Hausmeister **43** *strewn:* scattered around **44** *mounded:* piled up **48** *glare at sb.:* look at sb. with anger **54** *pizzazz* (infml): lively style **62** *pass the buck* (sl): pass on the responsibility to sb. else

hair trails aimlessly. The moulting pink feathers are tawdry as carnival dolls and some of the starry sequins have come off. Probably they were off to begin with and I didn't notice. I am a travesty, in bad makeup and someone else's clothes, used glitz.

I wish I had a toothbrush.

I could stand here and think about it, but time is passing.

I must be back at the house before midnight; otherwise I'll turn into a pumpkin, or was that the coach? Tomorrow's the Ceremony, according to the calendar, so tonight Serena wants me serviced, and if I'm not there she'll find out why, and then what?

And the Commander, for a change, is waiting; I can hear him pacing in the main room. Now he pauses outside the bathroom door, clears his throat, a stagy *ahem*. I turn on the hot water tap, to signify readiness or something approaching it. I should get this over with. I wash my hands. I must beware of inertia.

When I come out he's lying down on the king-sized bed, with, I note, his shoes off. I lie down beside him, I don't have to be told. I would rather not; but it's good to lie down, I am so tired.

Alone at last, I think. The fact is that I don't want to be alone with him, not on a bed. I'd rather have Serena there too. I'd rather play Scrabble.

But my silence does not deter him. "Tomorrow, isn't it?" he says softly. "I thought we could jump the gun." He turns towards me.

"Why did you bring me here?" I say coldly.

He's stroking my body now, from stem as they say to stern, cat stroke along the left flank, down the left leg. He stops at the foot, his fingers encircling the ankle, briefly, like a bracelet, where the tattoo is, a Braille he can read, a cattle brand. It means ownership.

I remind myself that he is not an unkind man; that, under other circumstances, I even like him.

His hand pauses. "I thought you might enjoy it for a change." He knows that isn't enough. "I guess it was a sort of experiment." That isn't enough either. "You said you wanted to know."

He sits up, begins to unbutton. Will this be worse, to have him denuded, of all his cloth power? He's down to the shirt; then, under it, sadly, a little belly. Wisps of hair.

He pulls down one of my straps, slides his other hand in among the feathers, but it's no good, I lie there like a dead bird. He is not a monster, I think. I can't afford pride or aversion, there are all kinds of things that have to be discarded, under the circumstances.

"Maybe I should turn the lights out," says the Commander, dismayed and no doubt disappointed. I see him for a moment before he does this. Without his uniform he looks smaller, older, like something being dried. The trouble is that I can't be, with him, any different from the way I usually am with him. Usually I'm inert. Surely there must be something here for us, other than this futility and bathos.

Fake it, I scream at myself inside my head. You must remember how. Let's get this over with or you'll be here all night. Bestir yourself. Move your flesh around, breathe audibly. It's the least you can do.

▷ **1** *moult:* (usu. of animal hair) come off, fall out **3** *travesty:* Zerrbild, schlechte Karikatur **7–8** *turn into a pumpkin:* allusion to the fairy tale "Cinderella", in which the coach turned (back) into a pumpkin after midnight **9** *serviced:* (hier) begattet **13** *stagy:* not natural, theatrical **15** *inertia* [ɪ'nɜːrʃə]: lack of energy or enthusiasm **23** *jump the gun* (infml): do sth. before the appointed time **25** *from stem to stern:* all the way from the front of a ship to the back **35** *denuded:* made bare; naked **46** *futility:* senselessness • *bathos* ['beɪθɑːs]: (here) banality, lack of emotion **48** *bestir yourself* (fml): start doing sth.

XIII

Night

CHAPTER 40

The heat at night is worse than the heat in daytime. Even with the fan on, nothing moves, and the walls store up warmth, give it out like a used oven. Surely it will rain soon. Why do I want it? It will only mean more dampness. There's lightning far away but no thunder. Looking out the window I can see it, a glimmer, like the phosphorescence you get in stirred seawater, behind the sky, which is overcast and too low and a dull gray infrared. The searchlights are off, which is not usual. A power failure. Or else Serena Joy has arranged it.

I sit in the darkness; no point in having the light on, to advertise the fact that I'm still awake. I'm fully dressed in my red habit again, having shed the spangles, scraped off the lipstick with toilet paper. I hope nothing shows, I hope I don't smell of it, or of him either.

She's here at midnight, as she said she'd be. I can hear her, a faint tapping, a faint shuffling on the muffling rug of the corridor, before her light knock comes. I don't say anything, but follow her back along the hall and down the stairs. She can walk faster, she's stronger than I thought. Her left hand clamps the banister, in pain maybe but holding on, steadying her. I think: she's biting her lip, she's suffering. She wants it all right, that baby. I see the two of us, a blue shape, a red shape, in the brief glass eye of the mirror as we descend. Myself, my obverse.

We go out through the kitchen. It's empty, a dim nightlight's left on; it has the calm of empty kitchens at night. The bowls on the counter, the canisters and stoneware jars loom round and heavy through the shadowy light. The knives are put away into their wooden rack.

"I won't go outside with you," she whispers. Odd, to hear her whispering, as if she is one of us. Usually Wives do not lower their voices. "You go out through the door and turn right. There's another door, it's open. Go up the stairs and knock, he's expecting you. No one will see you. I'll sit here." She'll wait for me then, in case there's trouble; in case Cora and Rita wake up, no one knows why, come in from their room at the back of the kitchen. What will she say to them?

▷ **11** *shed sth.:* get rid of sth., take sth. off **14** *shuffle:* Schlurfen • *muffle:* stop sound from spreading **20** *obverse* (fml): opposite; the other side of a coin

That she couldn't sleep. That she wanted some hot milk. She'll be adroit enough to lie well, I can see that.

"The Commander's in his bedroom upstairs, " she says. "He won't come down this late, he never does." That's what she thinks.

I open the kitchen door, step out, wait a moment for vision. It's so long since I've been outside, alone, at night. Now there's thunder, the storm's moving closer. What has she done about the Guardians? I could be shot for a prowler. Paid them off somehow, I hope: cigarettes, whiskey, or maybe they know all about it, her stud farm, maybe if this doesn't work she'll try them next.

The door to the garage is only steps away. I cross, feet noiseless on the grass, and open it quickly, slip inside. The stairway is dark, darker than I can see. I feel my way up, stair by stair: carpet here, I think of it as mushroom-colored. This must have been an apartment once, for a student, a young single person with a job. A lot of the big houses around here had them. A bachelor, a studio, those were the names for that kind of apartment. It pleases me to be able to remember this. *Separate entrance*, it would say in the ads, and that meant you could have sex, unobserved.

I reach the top of the stairs, knock on the door there. He opens it himself, who else was I expecting? There's a lamp on, only one but enough light to make me blink. I look past him, not wanting to meet his eyes. It's a single room, with a fold-out bed, made up, and a kitchenette counter at the far end, and another door that must lead to the bathroom. This room is stripped down, military, minimal. No pictures on the walls, no plants. He's camping out. The blanket on the bed is gray and says U.S.

He steps back and aside to let me past. He's in his shirt sleeves and is holding a cigarette, lit. I smell the smoke on him, in the warm air of the room, all over. I'd like to take off my clothes, bathe in it, rub it over my skin.

No preliminaries; he knows why I'm here. He doesn't even say anything, why fool around, it's an assignment. He moves away from me, turns off the lamp. Outside, like punctuation, there's a flash of lightning; almost no pause and then the thunder. He's undoing my dress, a man made of darkness, I can't see his face, and I can hardly breathe, hardly stand, and I'm not standing. His mouth is on me, his hands, I can't wait and he's moving, already, love, it's been so long,

I'm alive in my skin, again, arms around him, falling and water softly everywhere, never-ending. I knew it might only be once.

I made that up. It didn't happen that way. Here is what happened.

I reach the top of the stairs, knock on the door. He opens it himself. There's a lamp on; I blink. I look past his eyes, it's a single room, the bed's made up, stripped down, military. No pictures but the blanket says U.S. He's in his shirt sleeves, he's holding a cigarette.

"Here," he says to me, "have a drag." No preliminaries, he knows why I'm here. To get knocked up, to get in trouble, up the pole, those were all names for it once. I take the cigarette from him, draw deeply in, hand it back. Our fingers hardly touch. Even that much smoke makes me dizzy.

He says nothing, just looks at me, unsmiling. It would be better, more friendly, if he would touch me. I feel stupid and ugly, although I know I am not either. Still, what does he think, why doesn't he say something? Maybe he thinks I've been slutting around, at Jezebel's, with the Commander or more. It annoys me that I'm even worrying about what he thinks. Let's be practical.

"I don't have much time," I say. This is awkward and clumsy, it isn't what I mean.

"I could just squirt it into a bottle and you could pour it in," he says. He doesn't smile.

"There's no need to be brutal," I say. Possibly he feels used. Possibly he wants something from me, some emotion, some acknowledgement that he too is human, is more than just a seedpod. "I know it's hard for you," I try.

He shrugs. "I get paid," he says, punk surliness. But still makes no move.

I get paid, you get laid, I rhyme in my head. So that's how we're going to do it. He didn't like the make-up, the spangles. We're going to be tough.

"You come here often?"

▷ **2** *adroit* [ə'drɔɪt]: clever, skilful **8** *prowler:* person who moves around secretly in a place where he or she should not be **9** *stud farm:* place where horses are kept for breeding **47** *get knocked up, etc.* (infml): be made pregnant **54** *slut around* (infml): have sex with different people

"And what's a nice girl like me doing in a spot like this," I reply. We both smile: this is better. This is an acknowledgement that we are acting, for what else can we do in such a setup?

"Abstinence makes the heart grow fonder." We're quoting from late movies, from the time before. And the movies then were from a time before that: this sort of talk dates back to an era well before our own. Not even my mother talked like that, not when I knew her. Possibly nobody ever talked like that in real life, it was all a fabrication from the beginning. Still, it's amazing how easily it comes back to mind, this corny and falsely gay sexual banter. I can see now what it's for, what it was always for: to keep the core of yourself out of reach, enclosed, protected.

I'm sad now, the way we're talking is infinitely sad: faded music, faded paper flowers, worn satin, an echo of an echo. All gone away, no longer possible. Without warning I begin to cry.

At last he moves forward, puts his arms around me, strokes my back, holds me that way, for comfort.

"Come on," he says. "We haven't got much time." With his arm around my shoulders he leads me over to the fold-out bed, lies me down. He even turns down the blanket first. He begins to unbutton, then to stroke, kisses beside my ear. "No romance," he says. "Okay?"

That would have meant something else, once. Once it would have meant: *no strings*. Now it means: *no heroics*. It means: don't risk yourself for me, if it should come to that.

And so it goes. And so.

I knew it might only be once. Goodbye, I thought, even at the time, goodbye.

There wasn't any thunder though, I added that in. To cover up the sounds, which I am ashamed of making.

It didn't happen that way either. I'm not sure how it happened; not exactly. All I can hope for is a reconstruction: the way love feels is always only approximate.

Partway through, I thought about Serena Joy, sitting down there in the kitchen. Thinking: cheap. They'll spread their legs for anyone. All you need to give them is a cigarette.

And I thought afterwards: this is a betrayal. Not the thing itself but my own response. If I knew for certain he was dead, would that make a difference?

I would like to be without shame. I would like to be shameless. I would like to be ignorant. Then I would not know how ignorant I was.

▷ **4** *"Abstinence makes the heart grow fonder":* saying which has been altered from the original proverb "Absence makes the heart grow fonder" • *fond:* loving
10 *corny* (infml): silly • *gay:* (here) light-hearted, happy • *banter:* light-hearted talk
11 *core:* central part

XIV

Salvaging

CHAPTER 41

I wish this story were different. I wish it were more civilized. I wish it showed me in a better light, if not happier, then at least more active, less hesitant, less distracted by trivia. I wish it had more shape. I wish it were about love, or about sudden realizations important to one's life, or even about sunsets, birds, rainstorms, or snow.

Maybe it is about those things, in a sense; but in the meantime there is so much else getting in the way, so much whispering, so much speculation about others, so much gossip that cannot be verified, so many unsaid words, so much creeping about and secrecy. And there is so much time to be endured, time heavy as fried food or thick fog; and then all at once these red events, like explosions, on streets otherwise decorous and matronly and somnambulent.

I'm sorry there is so much pain in this story. I'm sorry it's in fragments, like a body caught in crossfire or pulled apart by force. But there is nothing I can do to change it.

I've tried to put some of the good things in as well. Flowers, for instance, because where would we be without them?

Nevertheless it hurts me to tell it over, over again. Once was enough: wasn't once enough for me at the time? But I keep on going with this sad and hungry and sordid, this limping and mutilated story, because after all I want you to hear it, as I will hear yours too if I ever get the chance, if I meet you or if you escape, in the future or in Heaven or in prison or underground, some other place. What they have in common is that they're not here. By telling you anything at all I'm at least believing in you, I believe you're there, I believe you into being. Because I'm telling you this story I will your existence. I tell, therefore you are.

So I will go on. So I will myself to go on. I am coming to a part you will not like at all, because in it I did not behave well, but I will try nonetheless to leave nothing out. After all you've been through, you deserve whatever I have left, which is not much but includes the truth.

*

▷ **12** *decorous* ['dekərəs]: (here) pleasant and quiet • *somnambulent:* (here) sleepy
20 *sordid:* very unpleasant, nasty

This is the story, then.

I went back to Nick. Time after time, on my own, without Serena knowing. It wasn't called for, there was no excuse. I did not do it for him, but for myself entirely. I didn't even think of it as giving myself to him, because what did I have to give? I did not feel munificent, but thankful, each time he would let me in. He didn't have to.

In order to do this I became reckless, I took stupid chances. After being with the Commander I would go upstairs in the usual way, but then I would go along the hall and down the Marthas' stairs at the back and through the kitchen. Each time I would hear the kitchen door click shut behind me and I would almost turn back, it sounded so metallic, like a mousetrap or a weapon, but I would not turn back. I would hurry across the few feet of illuminated lawn, the searchlights were back on again, expecting at any moment to feel the bullets rip through me even in advance of their sound. I would make my way by touch up the dark staircase and come to rest against the door, the thud of blood in my ears. Fear is a powerful stimulant. Then I would knock softly, a beggar's knock. Each time I would expect him to be gone; or worse, I would expect him to say I could not come in. He might say he wasn't going to break any more rules, put his neck in the noose, for my sake. Or even worse, tell me he was no longer interested. His failure to do any of these things I experienced as the most incredible benevolence and luck.

I told you it was bad.

Here is how it goes.

He opens the door. He's in his shirt sleeves, his shirt untucked, hanging loose; he's holding a toothbrush, or a cigarette or a glass with something in it. He has his own little stash up here, black-market stuff I suppose. He's always got something in his hand, as if he's been going about his life as usual, not expecting me, not waiting. Maybe he doesn't expect me, or wait. Maybe he has no notion of the future, or does not bother or dare to imagine it.

"Is it too late?" I say.

He shakes his head for no. It is understood between us by now that it is never too late, but I go through the ritual politeness of asking. It makes me feel more in control, as if there is a choice, a decision that could be made one way or the other. He steps aside and I move past him and he closes the door. Then he crosses the room and closes the window. After that he turns out the light. There is not much talking between us any more, not at this stage. Already I am half out of my clothes. We save the talking for later.

With the Commander I close my eyes, even when I am only kissing him goodnight. I do not want to see him up close. But now, here, each time, I keep my eyes open. I would like a light on somewhere, a candle perhaps, stuck into a bottle, some echo of college, but anything like that would be too great a risk; so I have to make do with the search-light, the glow of it from the grounds below, filtered through his white curtains which are the same as mine. I want to see what can be seen, of him, take him in, memorize him, save him up so I can live on the image, later: the lines of his body, the texture of his flesh, the glisten of sweat on his pelt, his long sardonic unrevealing face. I ought to have done that with Luke, paid more attention, to the details, the moles and scars, the singular creases; I didn't and he's fading. Day by day, night by night he recedes, and I become more faithless.

For this one I'd wear pink feathers, purple stars, if that were what he wanted; or anything else, even the tail of a rabbit. But he does not require such trimmings. We make love each time as if we know beyond a shadow of a doubt that there will never be any more, for either of us, with anyone, ever. And then when there is, that too is always a surprise, extra, a gift.

Being here with him is safety; it's a cave, where we huddle together while the storm goes on outside. This is a delusion, of course. This room is one of the most dangerous places I could be. If I were caught there would be no quarter, but I'm beyond caring. And how have I come to trust him like this, which is foolhardy in itself? How can I assume I know him, or the least thing about him and what he really does?

I dismiss these uneasy whispers. I talk too much. I tell him things I shouldn't. I tell him about Moira, about Ofglen; not about Luke though. I want to tell him about the woman in my room, the one who was there before me, but I don't. I'm jealous of her. If she's been here before me too, in this bed, I don't want to hear about it.

▷ **5** *munificent* [mju'nɪfɪsent]: giving sth. generously **21** *noose:* Schlinge **28** *stash:* secret store of sth. **51** *pelt:* skin • *sardonic:* spöttisch **64** *no quarter:* no mercy **65** *foolhardy:* foolish, unwise

I tell him my real name, and feel that therefore I am known. I act like a dunce. I should know better. I make of him an idol, a cardboard cutout.

He on the other hand talks little: no more hedging or jokes. He barely asks questions. He seems indifferent to most of what I have to say, alive only to the possibilities of my body, though he watches me while I'm speaking. He watches my face.

Impossible to think that anyone for whom I feel such gratitude could betray me.

Neither of us says the word *love*, not once. It would be tempting fate; it would be romance, bad luck.

Today there are different flowers, drier, more defined, the flowers of high summer: daisies, black-eyed Susans, starting us on the long downward slope to fall. I see them in the gardens, as I walk with Ofglen, to and fro. I hardly listen to her, I no longer credit her. The things she whispers seem to me unreal. What use are they, for me, now?

You could go into his room at night, she says. Look through his desk. There must be papers, notations.

The door is locked, I murmur.

We could get you a key, she says. Don't you want to know who he is, what he does?

But the Commander is no longer of immediate interest to me. I have to make an effort to keep my indifference towards him from showing.

Keep on doing everything exactly the way you were before, Nick says. Don't change anything. Otherwise they'll know. He kisses me, watching me all the time. Promise? Don't slip up.

I put his hand on my belly. It's happened, I say. I feel it has. A couple of weeks and I'll be certain.

This I know is wishful thinking.

He'll love you to death, he says. So will she.

But it's yours, I say. It will be yours, really. I want it to be.

We don't pursue this, however.

I can't, I say to Ofglen. I'm too afraid. Anyway I'd be no good at that, I'd get caught.

I scarcely take the trouble to sound regretful, so lazy have I become.

We could get you out, she says. We can get people out if we really have to, if they're in danger. Immediate danger.

The fact is that I no longer want to leave, escape, cross the border to freedom. I want to be here, with Nick, where I can get at him.

Telling this, I'm ashamed of myself. But there's more to it than that. Even now, I can recognize this admission as a kind of boasting. There's pride in it, because it demonstrates how extreme and therefore justified it was, for me. How well worth it. It's like stories of illness and near-death, from which you have recovered; like stories of war. They demonstrate seriousness.

Such seriousness, about a man, then, had not seemed possible to me before.

Some days I was more rational. I did not put it, to myself, in terms of love. I said, I have made a life for myself, here, of a sort. That must have been what the settlers' wives thought, and women who survived wars, if they still had a man. Humanity is so adaptable, my mother would say. Truly amazing, what people can get used to, as long as there are a few compensations.

It won't be long now, says Cora, doling out my monthly stack of sanitary napkins. Not long now, smiling at me shyly but also knowingly. Does she know? Do she and Rita know what I'm up to, creeping down their stairs at night? Do I give myself away, day-dreaming, smiling at nothing, touching my face lightly when I think they aren't watching?

Ofglen is giving up on me. She whispers less, talks more about the weather. I do not feel regret about this. I feel relief.

▷ **4** *hedging:* avoiding the real subject by talking about different things **57** *dole sth. out:* hand sth. out **58** *sanitary napkin:* Damenbinde

CHAPTER 42

The bell is tolling; we can hear it from a long way off. It's morning, and today we've had no breakfast. When we reach the main gate we file through it, two by two. There's a heavy contingent of guards, special detail Angels, with riot gear – the helmets with the bulging dark plexiglass visors that make them look like beetles, the long clubs, the gas-canister guns – in cordon around the outside of the Wall. That's in case of hysteria. The hooks on the Wall are empty.

This is a district Salvaging, for women only. Salvagings are always segregated. It was announced yesterday. They tell you only the day before. It's not enough time, to get used to it.

To the tolling of the bell we walk along the paths once used by students, past buildings that were once lecture halls and dormitories. It's very strange to be in here again. From the outside you can't tell that anything's changed, except that the blinds on most of the windows are drawn down. These buildings belong to the Eyes now.

We file onto the wide lawn in front of what used to be the library. The white steps going up are still the same, the main entrance is unaltered. There's a wooden stage erected on the lawn, something like the one they used every spring, for Commencement, in the time before. I think of hats, pastel hats worn by some of the mothers, and of the black gowns the students would put on, and the red ones. But this stage is not the same after all, because of the three wooden posts that stand on it, with the loops of rope.

At the front of the stage there is a microphone; the television camera is discreetly off to the side.

I've only been to one of these before, two years ago. Women's Salvagings are not frequent. There is less need for them. These days we are so well behaved.

I don't want to be telling this story.

We take our places in the standard order: Wives and daughters on the folding wooden chairs placed towards the back, Econowives and Marthas around the edges and on the library steps, and Handmaids at the front, where everyone can keep an eye on us. We don't sit on chairs, but kneel, and this time we have cushions, small red velvet ones with nothing written on them, not even *Faith*.

Luckily the weather is all right: not too hot, cloudy-bright.

It would be miserable kneeling here in the rain. Maybe that's why they leave it so late to tell us: so they'll know what the weather will be like. That's as good a reason as any.

I kneel on my red velvet cushion. I try to think about tonight, about making love, in the dark, in the light reflected off the white walls. I remember being held.

There's a long piece of rope which winds like a snake in front of the first row of cushions, along the second, and back through the lines of chairs, bending like a very old, very slow river viewed from the air, down to the back. The rope is thick and brown and smells of tar. The front end of the rope runs up onto the stage. It's like a fuse, or the string of a balloon.

On stage, to the left, are those who are to be salvaged: two Handmaids, one Wife. Wives are unusual, and despite myself I look at this one with interest. I want to know what she has done.

They have been placed here before the gates were opened. All of them sit on folding wooden chairs, like graduating students who are about to be given prizes. Their hands rest in their laps, looking as if they are folded sedately. They sway a little, they've probably been given injections or pills, so they won't make a fuss. It's better if things go smoothly. Are they attached to their chairs? Impossible to say, under all that drapery.

Now the official procession is approaching the stage, mounting the steps at the right: three women, one Aunt in front, two Salvagers in their black hoods and cloaks a pace behind her. Behind them are the other Aunts. The whisperings among us hush. The three arrange themselves, turn towards us, the Aunt flanked by the two black-robed Salvagers.

It's Aunt Lydia. How many years since I've seen her? I'd begun to think she existed only in my head, but here she is, a little older. I have a good view, I can see the deepening furrows to either side of her nose, the engraved frown. Her eyes blink, she smiles nervously, peering to left and right, checking out the audience, and lifts a hand to fidget

▷ **4** *special detail:* (hier) Sondereinheit **19** *Commencement* (AE): the ceremony at which students receive their diplomas at the end of an academic year

with her headdress. An odd strangling sound comes over the P.A. system: she is clearing her throat.

I've begun to shiver. Hatred fills my mouth like spit.

The sun comes out, and the stage and its occupants light up like a Christmas crèche. I can see the wrinkles under Aunt Lydia's eyes, the pallor of the seated women, the hairs on the rope in front of me on the grass, the blades of grass. There is a dandelion, right in front of me, the color of egg yolk. I feel hungry. The bell stops tolling.

Aunt Lydia stands up, smooths down her skirt with both hands, and steps forward to the mike. "Good afternoon, ladies," she says, and there is an instant and ear-splitting feedback whine from the P.A. system. From among us, incredibly, there is laughter. It's hard not to laugh, it's the tension, and the look of irritation on Aunt Lydia's face as she adjusts the sound. This is supposed to be dignified.

"Good afternoon, ladies," she says again, her voice now tinny and flattened. It's *ladies* instead of *girls* because of the Wives. "I'm sure we are all aware of the unfortunate circumstances that bring us all here together on this beautiful morning, when I am certain we would all rather be doing something else, at least I speak for myself, but duty is a hard taskmaster, or may I say on this occasion taskmistress, and it is in the name of duty that we are here today."

She goes on like this for some minutes, but I don't listen. I've heard this speech, or one like it, often enough before: the same platitudes, the same slogans, the same phrases: the torch of the future, the cradle of the race, the task before us. It's hard to believe there will not be polite clapping after this speech, and tea and cookies served on the lawn.

That was the prologue, I think. Now she'll get down to it.

Aunt Lydia rummages in her pocket, produces a crumpled piece of paper. This she takes an undue length of time to unfold and scan. She's rubbing our noses in it, letting us know exactly who she is, making us watch her as she silently reads, flaunting her prerogative. Obscene, I think. Let's get this over with.

"In the past," says Aunt Lydia, "it has been the custom to precede the actual Salvagings with a detailed account of the crimes of which the prisoners stand convicted. However, we have found that such a public account, especially when televised, is invariably followed by a rash, if I may call it that, an outbreak I should say, of exactly similar crimes. So we have decided in the best interests of all to discontinue this practice. The Salvagings will proceed without further ado."

A collective murmur goes up from us. The crimes of others are a secret language among us. Through them we show ourselves what we might be capable of, after all. This is not a popular announcement. But you would never know it from Aunt Lydia, who smiles and blinks as if washed in applause. Now we are left to our own devices, our own speculations. The first one, the one they're now raising from her chair, black-gloved hands on her upper arms: reading? No, that's only a hand cut off, on the third conviction. Unchastity, or an attempt on the life of her Commander? Or the Commander's Wife, more likely. That's what we're thinking. As for the Wife, there's mostly just one thing they get salvaged for. They can do almost anything to us, but they aren't allowed to kill us, not legally. Not with knitting needles or garden shears, or knives purloined from the kitchen, and especially not when we are pregnant. It could be adultery, of course. It could always be that.

Or attempted escape.

"Ofcharles," Aunt Lydia announces. No one I know. The woman is brought forward; she walks as if she's really concentrating on it, one foot, the other foot, she's definitely drugged. There's a groggy off-center smile on her mouth. One side of her face contracts, an uncoordinated wink, aimed at the camera. They'll never show it, of course, this isn't live. The two Salvagers tie her hands, behind her back.

From behind me there's a sound of retching.

That's why we don't get breakfast.

"Janine, most likely," Ofglen whispers. I've seen it before, the white bag placed over the head, the woman helped up onto the high stool as if she's being helped up the steps of a bus, steadied there, the noose adjusted delicately around the neck, like a vestment, the stool kicked away. I've heard the long sigh go up, from around me, the sigh like air coming out of an air mattress, I've seen Aunt Lydia place her

▷ **1–2** *P.A. system:* Public Address system **5** *Christmas crèche:* scene of the Nativity of Christ using figures or statues **15** *tinny:* having a high thin sound **20** *taskmaster:* person who gives other people work to do **32** *flaunt sth.:* show off sth. in an obvioius way • *prerogative* [prɪ'rɑːgətɪv]: privilege **38** *rash* (n): series of things that happen within a short period of time **40** *without further ado* [ə'duː]: without further delay, immediately **63** *retch:* vomit **68** *vestment:* piece of ritual clothing (used in church services, etc.)

hand over the mike, to stifle the other sounds coming from behind her, I've leaned forward to touch the rope in front of me, in time with the others, both hands on it, the rope hairy, sticky with tar in the hot sun, then placed my hand on my heart to show my unity with the Salvagers and my consent, and my complicity in the death of this woman. I have seen the kicking feet and the two in black who now seize hold of them and drag downwards with all their weight. I don't want to see it any more. I look at the grass instead. I describe the rope.

CHAPTER 43

The three bodies hang there, even with the white sacks over their heads looking curiously stretched, like chickens strung up by the necks in a meatshop window; like birds with their wings clipped, like flightless birds, wrecked angels. It's hard to take your eyes off them. Beneath the hems of the dresses the feet dangle, two pairs of red shoes, one pair of blue. If it weren't for the ropes and the sacks it could be a kind of dance, a ballet, caught by flash-camera: mid-air. They look arranged. They look like showbiz. It must have been Aunt Lydia who put the blue one in the middle.

"Today's Salvaging is now concluded," Aunt Lydia announces into the mike. "But ..."

We turn to her, listen to her, watch her. She has always known how to space her pauses. A ripple runs over us, a stir. Something else, perhaps, is going to happen.

"But you may stand up, and form a circle." She smiles down upon us, generous, munificent. She is about to give us something. *Bestow.* "Orderly, now."

She is talking to us, to the Handmaids. Some of the Wives are leaving now, some of the daughters. Most of them stay, but they stay behind, out of the way, they watch merely. They are not part of the circle.

Two Guardians have moved forward and are coiling up the thick rope, getting it out of the way. Others move the cushions. We are milling around now, on the grass space in front of the stage, some jockeying for position at the front, next to the center, many pushing just as hard to work their way to the middle where they will be shielded. It's a mistake to hang back too obviously in any group like this; it stamps you as lukewarm, lacking in zeal. There's an energy building here, a murmur, a tremor of readiness and anger. The bodies tense, the eyes are brighter, as if aiming.

I don't want to be at the front, or at the back either. I'm not sure what's coming, though I sense it won't be anything I want to see up

▷ **36** *lukewarm:* lau, halbherzig • *zeal:* enthusiasm for a cause

close. But Ofglen has hold of my arm, she tugs me with her, and now we're in the second line, with only a thin hedge of bodies in front of us. I don't want to see, yet I don't pull back either. I've heard rumors, which I only half believed. Despite everything I already know, I say to myself: they wouldn't go that far.

"You know the rules for a Particicution," Aunt Lydia says. "You will wait until I blow the whistle. After that, what you do is up to you, until I blow the whistle again. Understood?"

A noise comes from among us, a formless assent.

"Well then," says Aunt Lydia. She nods. Two Guardians, not the same ones that have taken away the rope, come forward now from behind the stage. Between them they half carry, half drag a third man. He too is in a Guardian's uniform, but he has no hat on and the uniform is dirty and torn. His face is cut and bruised, deep reddish-brown bruises; the flesh is swollen and knobby, stubbled with unshaven beard. This doesn't look like a face but like an unknown vegetable, a mangled bulb or tuber, something that's grown wrong. Even from where I'm standing I can smell him: he smells of shit and vomit. His hair is blond and falls over his face, spiky with what? Dried sweat?

I stare at him with revulsion. He looks drunk. He looks like a drunk that's been in a fight. Why have they brought a drunk in here?

"This man," says Aunt Lydia, "has been convicted of rape." Her voice trembles with rage, and a kind of triumph. "He was once a Guardian. He has disgraced his uniform. He has abused his position of trust. His partner in viciousness has already been shot. The penalty for rape, as you know, is death. Deuteronomy 22:23–29. I might add that this crime involved two of you and took place at gunpoint. It was also brutal. I will not offend your ears with any details, except to say that one woman was pregnant and the baby died."

A sigh goes up from us; despite myself I feel my hands clench. It is too much, this violation. The baby too, after what we go through. It's true, there is a bloodlust; I want to tear, gouge, rend.

We jostle forward, our heads turn from side to side, our nostrils flare, sniffing death, we look at one another, seeing the hatred. Shooting was too good. The man's head swivels groggily around: has he even heard her?

Aunt Lydia waits a moment; then she gives a little smile and raises her whistle to her lips. We hear it, shrill and silver, an echo from a volleyball game of long ago.

The two Guardians let go of the third man's arms and step back. He staggers – is he drugged? – and falls to his knees. His eyes are shrivelled up inside the puffy flesh of his face, as if the light is too bright for him. They've kept him in darkness. He raises one hand to his cheek, as though to feel if he is still there. All of this happens quickly, but it seems to be slowly.

Nobody moves forward. The women are looking at him with horror; as if he's a half-dead rat dragging itself across a kitchen floor. He's squinting around at us, the circle of red women. One corner of his mouth moves up, incredible – a smile?

I try to look inside him, inside the trashed face, see what he must really look like. I think he's about thirty. It isn't Luke.

But it could have been, I know that. It could be Nick. I know that whatever he's done I can't touch him.

He says something. It comes out thick, as if his throat is bruised, his tongue huge in his mouth, but I hear it anyway. He says, "I didn't ..."

There's a surge forward, like a crowd at a rock concert in the former time, when the doors opened, that urgency coming like a wave through us. The air is bright with adrenalin, we are permitted anything and this is freedom, in my body also, I'm reeling, red spreads everywhere, but before that tide of cloth and bodies hits him Ofglen is shoving through the women in front of us, propelling herself with her elbows, left, right, and running towards him. She pushes him down, sideways, then kicks his head viciously, one, two, three times, sharp painful jabs with the foot, well-aimed. Now there are sounds, gasps, a low noise like growling, yells, and the red bodies tumble forward and I can no longer see, he's obscured by arms, fists, feet. A high scream comes from somewhere, like a horse in terror.

I keep back, try to stay on my feet. Something hits me from behind. I stagger. When I regain my balance and look around, I see the Wives and daughters leaning forward in their chairs, the Aunts on the

▷ **17** *mangled:* verstümmelt • *tuber:* Knolle **27** *Deuteronomy 22:23–29* [ˌduːtəˈrɑːnəmi] **33** *gouge sth.:* make a hole in sth. with a sharp object • *rend sth.:* tear sth. in two **43** *shrivel up:* become small and dried up

platform gazing down with interest. They must have a better view from up there.

He has become an *it*.

Ofglen is back beside me. Her face is tight, expressionless.

"I saw what you did," I say to her. Now I'm beginning to feel again: shock, outrage, nausea. Barbarism. "Why did you do that? You! I thought you ..."

"Don't look at me," she says. "They're watching."

"I don't care," I say. My voice is rising, I can't help it.

"Get control of yourself," she says. She pretends to brush me off, my arm and shoulder, bringing her face close to my ear. "Don't be stupid. He wasn't a rapist at all, he was a political. He was one of ours. I knocked him out. Put him out of his misery. Don't you know what they're doing to him?"

One of ours, I think. A Guardian. It seems impossible.

Aunt Lydia blows her whistle again, but they don't stop at once. The two Guardians move in, pulling them off, from what's left. Some lie on the grass where they've been hit or kicked by accident. Some have fainted. They straggle away, in twos and threes or by themselves. They seem dazed.

"You will find your partners and re-form your line," Aunt Lydia says into the mike. Few pay attention to her. A woman comes towards us, walking as if she's feeling her way with her feet, in the dark: Janine. There's a smear of blood across her cheek, and more of it on the white of her headdress.

She's smiling, a bright diminutive smile. Her eyes have come loose.

"Hi there," she says. "How are you doing?" She's holding something, tightly, in her right hand. It's a clump of blond hair. She gives a small giggle.

"Janine," I say. But she's let go, totally now, she's in free fall, she's in withdrawal.

"You have a nice day," she says, and walks on past us, towards the gate.

I look after her. Easy out, is what I think. I don't even feel sorry for her, although I should. I feel angry. I'm not proud of myself for this, or for any of it. But then, that's the point.

My hands smell of warm tar. I want to go back to the house and up to the bathroom and scrub and scrub, with the harsh soap and the pumice, to get every trace of this smell off my skin. The smell makes me feel sick.

But also I'm hungry. This is monstrous, but nevertheless it's true. Death makes me hungry. Maybe it's because I've been emptied; or maybe it's the body's way of seeing to it that I remain alive, continue to repeat its bedrock prayer: *I am, I am*. I am, still.

I want to go to bed, make love, right now.

I think of the word *relish*.

I could eat a horse.

▷ **44** *bedrock:* firm, solid

CHAPTER 44

Things are back to normal.

How can I call this normal? But compared with this morning, it is normal.

For lunch there was a cheese sandwich, on brown bread, a glass of milk, celery sticks, canned pears. A schoolchild's lunch. I ate everything up, not quickly, but revelling in the taste, the flavors lush on my tongue. Now I am going shopping, the same as usual. I even look forward to it. There's a certain consolation to be taken from routine.

I go out the back door, along the path. Nick is washing the car, his hat on sideways. He doesn't look at me. We avoid looking at each other, these days. Surely we'd give something away by it, even out here in the open, with no one to see.

I wait at the corner for Ofglen. She's late. At last I see her coming, a red and white shape of cloth, like a kite, walking at the steady pace we've all learned to keep. I see her and notice nothing at first. Then, as she comes nearer, I think that there must be something wrong with her. She looks wrong. She is altered in some indefinable way; she's not injured, she's not limping. It's as if she has shrunk.

Then when she's nearer still I see what it is. She isn't Ofglen. She's the same height, but thinner, and her face is beige, not pink. She comes up to me, stops.

"Blessed be the fruit," she says. Straight-faced, straight-laced.

"May the Lord open," I reply. I try not to show surprise.

"You must be Offred," she says. I say yes, and we begin our walk.

Now what, I think. My head is churning, this is not good news, what has become of her, how do I find out without showing too much concern? We aren't supposed to form friendships, loyalties, among one another. I try to remember how much time Ofglen has to go at her present posting.

"We've been sent good weather," I say.

"Which I receive with joy." The voice placid, flat, unrevealing. We pass the first checkpoint without saying anything further. She's taciturn, but so am I. Is she waiting for me to start something, reveal myself, or is she a believer, engrossed in inner meditation?

"Has Ofglen been transferred, so soon?" I ask, but I know she hasn't. I saw her only this morning. She would have said.

"I am Ofglen," the woman says. Word perfect. And of course she is, the new one, and Ofglen, wherever she is, is no longer Ofglen. I never did know her real name. That is how you can get lost, in a sea of names. It wouldn't be easy to find her, now.

We go to Milk and Honey, and to All Flesh, where I buy chicken and the new Ofglen gets three pounds of hamburger. There are the usual lines. I see several women I recognize, exchange with them the infinitesimal nods with which we show each other we are known, at least to someone, we still exist. Outside All Flesh I say to the new Ofglen, "We should go to the Wall." I don't know what I expect from this; some way of testing her reaction, perhaps. I need to know whether or not she is one of us. If she is, if I can establish that, perhaps she'll be able to tell me what has really happened to Ofglen.

"As you like," she says. Is that indifference, or caution?

On the Wall hang the three women from this morning, still in their dresses, still in their shoes, still with the white bags over their heads. Their arms have been untied and are stiff and proper at their sides. The blue one is in the middle, the two red ones on either side, though the colors are no longer as bright; they seem to have faded, grown dingy, like dead butter-flies or tropical fish drying on land. The gloss is off them. We stand and look at them in silence.

"Let that be a reminder to us," says the new Ofglen finally.

I say nothing at first, because I am trying to make out what she means. She could mean that this is a reminder to us of the unjustness and brutality of the regime. In that case I ought to say yes. Or she could mean the opposite, that we should remember to do what we are told and not get into trouble, because if we do we will be rightfully punished. If she means that, I should say praise be. Her voice was bland, toneless, no clues there.

I take a chance. "Yes," I say.

▷ **6** *revel in sth.:* enjoy sth. very much • *lush:* making you feel pleasure **22** *straight-faced:* without smiling • *straight-laced:* strict, with old-fashioned views **25** *churn:* turn violently **33** *taciturn* ['tæsɪtɜːn]: not speaking, silent **34** *engrossed in sth.:* busily concentrating on sth.

To this she does not respond, although I sense a flicker of white at the edge of my vision, as if she's looked quickly at me.

After a moment we turn away and begin the long walk back, matching our steps in the approved way, so that we seem to be in unison.

I think maybe I should wait before attempting anything further. It's too soon to push, to probe. I should give it a week, two weeks, maybe longer, watch her carefully, listen for tones in her voice, unguarded words, the way Ofglen listened to me. Now that Ofglen is gone I am alert again, my sluggishness has fallen away, my body is no longer for pleasure only but senses its jeopardy. I should not be rash, I should not take unnecessary risks. But I need to know. I hold back until we're past the final checkpoint and there are only blocks to go, but then I can no longer control myself.

"I didn't know Ofglen very well," I say. "I mean the former one."

"Oh?" she says. The fact that she's said anything, however guarded, encourages me.

"I've only known her since May," I say. I can feel my skin growing hot, my heart speeding up. This is tricky. For one thing, it's a lie. And how do I get from there to the next vital word? "Around the first of May I think it was. What they used to call May Day."

"Did they?" she says, light, indifferent, menacing. "That isn't a term I remember. I'm surprised you do. You ought to make an effort ..." She pauses. "To clear your mind of such ..." She pauses again. "Echoes."

Now I feel cold, seeping over my skin like water. What she is doing is warning me.

She isn't one of us. But she knows.

I walk the last blocks in terror. I've been stupid, again. More than stupid. It hasn't occurred to me before, but now I see: if Ofglen's been caught, Ofglen may talk, about me among others. She will talk. She won't be able to help it.

But I haven't done anything, I tell myself, not really. All I did was know. All I did was not tell.

They know where my child is. What if they bring her, threaten something to her, in front of me? Or do it. I can't bear to think what they might do. Or Luke, what if they have Luke. Or my mother or Moira or almost anyone. Dear God, don't make me choose. I would not be able to stand it, I know that; Moira was right about me. I'll say anything they like, I'll incriminate anyone. It's true, the first scream, whimper even, and I'll turn to jelly, I'll confess to any crime, I'll end up hanging from a hook on the Wall. Keep your head down, I used to tell myself, and see it through. It's no use.

This is the way I talk to myself, on the way home.

At the corner we turn to one another in the usual way.

"Under His Eye," says the new, treacherous Ofglen.

"Under His Eye," I say, trying to sound fervent. As if such play-acting could help, now that we've come this far.

Then she does an odd thing. She leans forward, so that the stiff white blinkers on our heads are almost touching, so that I can see her pale beige eyes up close, the delicate web of lines across her cheeks, and whispers, very quickly, her voice faint as dry leaves. "She hanged herself," she says. "After the Salvaging. She saw the van coming for her. It was better."

Then she's walking away from me down the street.

▷ **11** *jeopardy* ['dʒepərdi]: danger, risk • *rash* (adj): voreilig

CHAPTER 45

I stand a moment, emptied of air, as if I've been kicked.

So she's dead, and I am safe, after all. She did it before they came. I feel great relief. I feel thankful to her. She has died that I may live. I will mourn later.

Unless this woman is lying. There's always that.

I breathe in, deeply, breathe out, giving myself oxygen. The space in front of me blackens, then clears. I can see my way.

I turn, open the gate, keeping my hand on it a moment to steady myself, walk in. Nick is there, still washing the car, whistling a little. He seems very far away.

Dear God, I think, I will do anything you like. Now that you've let me off, I'll obliterate myself, if that's what you really want; I'll empty myself, truly, become a chalice. I'll give up Nick, I'll forget about the others, I'll stop complaining. I'll accept my lot. I'll sacrifice. I'll repent. I'll abdicate. I'll renounce.

I know this can't be right but I think it anyway. Everything they taught at the Red Center, everything I've resisted, comes flooding in. I don't want pain. I don't want to be a dancer, my feet in the air, my head a faceless oblong of white cloth. I don't want to be a doll hung up on the Wall, I don't want to be a wingless angel. I want to keep on living, in any form. I resign my body freely, to the uses of others. They can do what they like with me. I am abject.

I feel, for the first time, their true power.

I go along past the flower beds, the willow tree, aiming for the back door. I will go in, I will be safe. I will fall on my knees, in my room, gratefully breathe in lungfuls of the stale air, smelling of furniture polish.

Serena Joy has come out of the front door; she's standing on the steps. She calls to me. What is it she wants? Does she want me to go in to the sitting room and help her wind gray wool? I won't be able to hold my hands steady, she'll notice something. But I walk over to her anyway, since I have no choice.

On the top step she towers above me. Her eyes flare, hot blue against the shrivelled white of her skin. I look away from her face, down at the ground; at her feet, the tip of her cane.

"I trusted you," she says. "I tried to help you."

Still I don't look up at her. Guilt pervades me, I've been found out, but for what? For which of my many sins am I accused? The only way to find out is to keep silent. To start excusing myself now, for this or that, would be a blunder. I could give away something she hasn't even guessed.

It might be nothing. It might be the match hidden in my bed. I hang my head.

"Well?" she asks. "Nothing to say for yourself?"

I look up at her. "About what?" I manage to stammer. As soon as it's out it sounds impudent.

"Look," she says. She brings her free hand from behind her back. It's her cloak she's holding, the winter one. "There was lipstick on it," she says. "How could you be so vulgar? I told him ..." She drops the cloak, she's holding something else, her hand all bone. She throws that down as well. The purple sequins fall, slithering down over the step like snakeskin, glittering in the sunlight. "Behind my back," she says. "You could have left me something." Does she love him, after all? She raises her cane. I think she is going to hit me, but she doesn't. "Pick up that disgusting thing and get to your room. Just like the other one. A slut. You'll end up the same."

I stoop, gather. Behind my back Nick has stopped whistling.

I want to turn, run to him, throw my arms around him.

This would be foolish. There is nothing he can do to help. He too would drown.

I walk to the back door, into the kitchen, set down my basket, go upstairs. I am orderly and calm.

▷ **22** *abject:* without self-respect **46** *impudent* ['ɪmpjədənt]: rude

XV

Night

CHAPTER 46

I sit in my room, at the window, waiting. In my lap is a handful of crumpled stars.

This could be the last time I have to wait. But I don't know what I'm waiting for. What are you waiting for? they used to say. That meant *Hurry up*. No answer was expected. For what are you waiting is a different question, and I have no answer for that one either.

Yet it isn't waiting, exactly. It's more like a form of suspension. Without suspense. At last there is no time.

I am in disgrace, which is the opposite of grace. I ought to feel worse about it.

But I feel serene, at peace, pervaded with indifference. Don't let the bastards grind you down. I repeat this to myself but it conveys nothing. You might as well say, Don't let there be air; or, Don't be.

I suppose you could say that.

There's nobody in the garden.

I wonder if it will rain.

Outside, the light is fading. It's reddish already. Soon it will be dark. Right now it's darker. That didn't take long.

There are a number of things I could do. I could set fire to the house, for instance. I could bundle up some of my clothes, and the sheets, and strike my one hidden match. If it didn't catch, that would be that. But if it did, there would at least be an event, a signal of some kind to mark my exit. A few flames, easily put out. In the meantime I could let loose clouds of smoke and die by suffocation.

I could tear my bedsheet into strips and twist it into a rope of sorts and tie one end to the leg of my bed and try to break the window. Which is shatterproof.

I could go to the Commander, fall on the floor, my hair dishevelled, as they say, grab him around the knees, confess, weep, implore.

▷ **7** *suspension:* Schwebezustand **24** *suffocation:* lack of air **28** *dishevelled:* untidy

Nolite te bastardes carborundorum, I could say. Not a prayer. I visualize his shoes, black, well shined, impenetrable, keeping their own counsel.

Instead I could noose the bedsheet round my neck, hook myself up in the closet, throw my weight forward, choke myself off.

I could hide behind the door, wait until she comes, hobbles along the hall, bearing whatever sentence, penance, punishment, jump out at her, knock her down, kick her sharply and accurately in the head. To put her out of her misery, and myself as well. To put her out of our misery.

It would save time.

I could walk at a steady pace down the stairs and out the front door and along the street, trying to look as if I knew where I was going, and see how far I could get. Red is so visible.

I could go to Nick's room, over the garage, as we have done before. I could wonder whether or not he would let me in, give me shelter. Now that the need is real.

I consider these things idly. Each one of them seems the same size as all the others. Not one seems preferable. Fatigue is here, in my body, in my legs and eyes. That is what gets you in the end. Faith is only a word, embroidered.

I look out at the dusk and think about its being winter. The snow falling, gently, effortlessly, covering everything in soft crystal, the mist of moonlight before a rain, blurring the outlines, obliterating color. Freezing to death is painless, they say, after the first chill. You lie back in the snow like an angel made by children and go to sleep.

Behind me I feel her presence, my ancestress, my double, turning in mid-air under the chandelier, in her costume of stars and feathers, a bird stopped in flight, a woman made into an angel, waiting to be found. By me this time. How could I have believed I was alone in here? There were always two of us. Get it over, she says. I'm tired of this melodrama, I'm tired of keeping silent. There's no one you can protect, your life has value to no one. I want it finished.

As I'm standing up I hear the black van. I hear it before I see it; blended with the twilight, it appears out of its own sound like a solidification, a clotting of the night. It turns into the driveway, stops. I can just make out the white eye, the two wings. The paint must be phosphorescent. Two men detach themselves from the shape of it, come up the front steps, ring the bell. I hear the bell toll, ding-dong, like the ghost of a cosmetics woman, down in the hall.

Worse is coming, then.

I've been wasting my time. I should have taken things into my own hands while I had the chance. I should have stolen a knife from the kitchen, found some way to the sewing scissors. There were the garden shears, the knitting needles; the world is full of weapons if you're looking for them. I should have paid attention.

But it's too late to think about that now, already their feet are on the dusty-rose carpeting of the stairs; a heavy muted tread, pulse in the forehead. My back's to the window.

I expect a stranger, but it's Nick who pushes open the door, flicks on the light. I can't place that, unless he's one of them. There was always that possibility. Nick, the private Eye. Dirty work is done by dirty people.

You shit, I think. I open my mouth to say it, but he comes over, close to me, whispers. "It's all right. It's Mayday. Go with them." He calls me by my real name. Why should this mean anything?

"Them?" I say. I see the two men standing behind him, the overhead light in the hallway making skulls of their heads.

"You must be crazy." My suspicion hovers in the air above him, a dark angel warning me away. I can almost see it. Why shouldn't he know about Mayday? All the Eyes must know about it; they'll have squeezed it, crushed it, twisted it out of enough bodies, enough mouths by now.

"Trust me," he says; which in itself has never been a talisman, carries no guarantee.

But I snatch at it, this offer. It's all I'm left with.

One in front, one behind, they escort me down the stairs. The pace is leisurely, the lights are on. Despite the fear, how ordinary it is. From here I can see the clock. It's no time in particular.

Nick is no longer with us. He may have gone down the back stairs, not wishing to be seen.

▷ **2–3** *keep your own counsel:* mind your own business **36** *clot sth.:* cause sth. (esp. cream) to become thick **66** *snatch at sth.:* catch hold of sth. quickly

Serena Joy stands in the hallway, under the mirror, looking up, incredulous. The Commander is behind her, the sitting room door is open. His hair is very gray. He looks worried and helpless, but already withdrawing from me, distancing himself.

Whatever else I am to him, I am also at this point a disaster. No doubt they've been having a fight, about me; no doubt she's been giving him hell. I still have it in me to feel sorry for him. Moira is right, I am a wimp.

"What has she done?" says Serena Joy. She wasn't the one who called them, then. Whatever she had in store for me, it was more private.

"We can't say, Ma'am," says the one in front of me.

"Sorry."

"I need to see your authorization," says the Commander. "You have a warrant?"

I could scream now, cling to the banister, relinquish dignity. I could stop them, at least for a moment. If they're real they'll stay, if not they'll run away. Leaving me here. "Not that we need one, Sir, but all is in order," says the first one again. "Violation of state secrets."

The Commander puts his hand to his head. What have I been saying, and to whom, and which one of his enemies has found out? Possibly he will be a security risk, now. I am above him, looking down; he is shrinking. There have already been purges among them, there will be more. Serena Joy goes white.

"Bitch," she says. "After all he did for you." Cora and Rita press through from the kitchen. Cora has begun to cry. I was her hope, I've failed her. Now she will always be childless.

The van waits in the driveway, its double doors stand open. The two of them, one on either side now, take me by the elbows to help me in. Whether this is my end or a new beginning I have no way of knowing: I have given myself over into the hands of strangers, because it can't be helped.

And so I step up, into the darkness within; or else the light.

▷ **15** *warrant:* piece of paper showing that sb. is to be arrested **16** *relinquish sth.:* let go of sth. **23** *purge:* Säuberung

Historical Notes

HISTORICAL NOTES ON THE HANDMAID'S TALE

Being a partial transcript of the proceedings of the Twelfth Symposium on Gileadean Studies, held as part of the International Historical Association Convention, which took place at the University of Denay, Nunavit, on June 25, 2195.

Chair: *Professor Maryann Crescent Moon, Department of Caucasian Anthropology, University of Denay, Nunavit.*

Keynote Speaker: *Professor James Darcy Pieixoto, Director, Twentieth and Twenty-First Century Archives, Cambridge University, England.*

CRESCENT MOON: I am delighted to welcome you all here this morning, and I'm pleased to see that so many of you have turned out for Professor Pieixoto's, I am sure, fascinating and worthwhile talk. We of the Gileadean Research Association believe that this period well repays further study, responsible as it ultimately was for redrawing the map of the world, especially in this hemisphere.

But before we proceed, a few announcements. The fishing expedition will go forward tomorrow as planned, and for those of you who have not brought suitable rain gear and insect repellent, these are available for a nominal charge at the Registration Desk. The Nature Walk and Outdoor Period-Costume Sing-Song have been rescheduled for the day after tomorrow, as we are assured by our own infallible Professor Johnny Running Dog of a break in the weather at that time.

Let me remind you of the other events sponsored by the Gileadean Research Association that are available to you at this convention, as part of our Twelfth Symposium. Tomorrow afternoon, Professor Gopal Chatterjee, of the Department of Western Philosophy, Univer-

▷ **1** *proceedings:* course of discussions and lectures at a conference, etc. **5** *Chair:* Vorsitz **7** *Keynote Speaker:* particularly important speaker introducing the subject at a conference, etc. **18** *insect repellent:* spray or cream used to keep insects away **22** *infallible:* unfehlbar

sity of Baroda, India, will speak on "Krishna and Kali Elements in the State Religion of the Early Gilead Period," and there is a morning presentation on Thursday by Professor Sieglinda Van Buren from the Department of Military History at the University of San Antonio, Republic of Texas. Professor Van Buren will give what I am sure will be a fascinating illustrated lecture on "The Warsaw Tactic: Policies of Urban Core Encirclement in the Gileadean Civil Wars." I am sure all of us will wish to attend these.

I must also remind our keynote speaker – although I am sure it is not necessary – to keep within his time period, as we wish to leave space for questions, and I expect none of us wants to miss lunch, as happened yesterday. *(Laughter.)*

Professor Pieixoto scarcely needs any introduction, as he is well known to all of us, if not personally, then through his extensive publications. These include "Sumptuary Laws Through the Ages: An Analysis of Documents," and the well-known study, "Iran and Gilead: Two Late-Twentieth-Century Monotheocracies, as Seen Through Diaries." As you all know, he is the co-editor, with Professor Knotly Wade, also of Cambridge, of the manuscript under consideration today, and was instrumental in its transcription, annotation, and publication. The title of his talk is "Problems of Authentication in Reference to *The Handmaid's Tale*."

Professor Pieixoto.

Applause.

PIEIXOTO: Thank you. I am sure we all enjoyed our charming Arctic Char last night at dinner, and now we are enjoying an equally charming Arctic Chair. I use the word "enjoy" in two distinct senses, precluding, of course, the obsolete third. *(Laughter.)*

But let me be serious. I wish, as the title of my little chat implies, to consider some of the problems associated with the soi-disant manuscript which is well known to all of you by now, and which goes by the title of *The Handmaid's Tale*. I say soi-disant because what we have before us is not the item in its original form. Strictly speaking, it was not a manuscript at all when first discovered, and bore no title. The superscription "The Handmaid's Tale" was appended to it by Professor Wade, partly in homage to the great Geoffrey Chaucer; but those of you who know Professor Wade informally, as I do, will understand when I say that I am sure all puns were intentional, particularly that having to do with the archaic vulgar signification of the word tail; that being, to some extent, the bone, as it were, of contention, in that phase of Gileadean society of which our saga treats. *(Laughter, applause.)*

This item – I hesitate to use the word *document* – was unearthed on the site of what was once the city of Bangor, in what, at the time prior to the inception of the Gileadean regime, would have been the State of Maine. We know that this city was a prominent way-station on what our author refers to as "The Underground Femaleroad," since dubbed by some of our historical wags "The Underground Frailroad." *(Laughter, groans.)* For this reason, our Association has taken a particular interest in it.

The item in its pristine state consisted of a metal footlocker, U.S. Army issue, circa perhaps 1955. This fact of itself need have no significance, as it is known that such footlockers were frequently sold as "army surplus" and must therefore have been widespread. Within this footlocker, which was sealed with tape of the kind once used on packages to be sent by post, were approximately thirty tape cassettes, of the type that became obsolete sometime in the eighties or nineties with the advent of the compact disc.

I remind you that this was not the first such discovery. You are doubtless familiar, for instance, with the item known as "The A.B. Memoirs," located in a garage in a suburb of Seattle, and with "The Diary of P.," excavated by accident during the erection of a new meeting house in the vicinity of what was once Syracuse, New York.

Professor Wade and I were very excited by this new discovery. Luckily we had, several years before, with the aid of our excellent resident antiquarian technician, reconstructed a machine capable of

▷ **15** *sumptuary:* Sparsamkeits- **17** *Monotheocracy:* (here) country governed as a religious state by believers in one god (from "monotheism" and "theocracy") **25–26** *Arctic Char:* type of salmon **26** *enjoy:* get pleasure from sth.; experience sth.; (old use) have sex with sb. **28** *obsolete:* no longer in use **30** *soi-disant* (French): so-called **36** *in homage to sb.* ['hɑːmɪdʒ]: in honour of sb. • *Geoffrey Chaucer* (ca. 1342–1400): English poet and author of *The Canterbury Tales* which contained individual stories with names such as "The Lawyer's Tale" or "The Wife of Bath's Tale" **40–41** *bone of contention:* subject causing disagreement ("bone" is slang for "erect penis") **45** *prior to* (fml): before • *inception* (fml): beginnings **48** *since:* since then • *dub sth.:* give sth a (humorous) name • *wag* (old-fashioned): person who makes jokes **49** *frail:* weak, not robust **51** *footlocker* (AE): small metal box for personal belongings kept at the foot of a soldier's bed **58** *advent:* appearance, arrival **62** *excavate sth.:* dig sth. up

playing such tapes, and we immediately set about the painstaking work of transcription.

There were some thirty tapes in the collection altogether, with varying proportions of music to spoken word. In general, each tape begins with two or three songs, as camouflage no doubt: then the music is broken off and the speaking voice takes over. The voice is a woman's and, according to our voice-print experts, the same one throughout. The labels on the cassettes were authentic period labels, dating, of course, from some time before the inception of the Early Gilead era, as all such secular music was banned under the regime. There were, for instance, four tapes entitled "Elvis Presley's Golden Years," three of "Folk Songs of Lithuania," three of "Boy George Takes It Off," and two of "Mantovani's Mellow Strings," as well as some titles that sported a mere single tape each: "Twisted Sister at Carnegie Hall" is one of which I am particularly fond.

Although the labels were authentic, they were not always appended to the tape with the corresponding songs. In addition, the tapes were arranged in no particular order, being loose at the bottom of the box; nor were they numbered. Thus it was up to Professor Wade and myself to arrange the blocks of speech in the order in which they appeared to go; but, as I have said elsewhere, all such arrangements are based on some guesswork and are to be regarded as approximate, pending further research.

Once we had the transcription in hand – and we had to go over it several times, owing to the difficulties posed by accent, obscure referents, and archaisms – we had to make some decision as to the nature of the material we had thus so laboriously acquired. Several possibilities confronted us. First, the tapes might be a forgery. As you know, there have been several instances of such forgeries, for which publishers have paid large sums, wishing to trade no doubt on the sensationalism of such stories. It appears that certain periods of history quickly become, both for other societies and for those that follow them, the stuff of not especially edifying legend and the occasion for a good deal of hypocritical self-congratulation. If I may be permitted an editorial aside, allow me to say that in my opinion we must be cautious about passing moral judgement upon the Gileadeans. Surely we have learned by now that such judgements are of necessity culture-specific. Also, Gileadean society was under a good deal of pressure, demographic and otherwise, and was subject to factors from which we ourselves are happily more free. Our job is not to censure but to understand. *(Applause.)*

To return from my digression: tape like this, however, is very difficult to fake convincingly, and we were assured by the experts who examined them that the physical objects themselves are genuine. Certainly the recording itself, that is, the superimposition of voice upon music tape, could not have been done within the past hundred and fifty years.

Supposing, then, the tapes to be genuine, what of the nature of the account itself? Obviously, it could not have been recorded during the period of time it recounts, since, if the author is telling the truth, no machine or tapes would have been available to her, nor would she have had a place of concealment for them. Also, there is a certain reflective quality about the narrative that would to my mind rule out synchronicity. It has a whiff of emotion recollected, if not in tranquillity, at least *post facto*.

If we could establish an identity for the narrator, we felt, we might be well on the way to an explanation of how this document – let me call it that for the sake of brevity – came into being. To do this, we tried two lines of investigation.

First, we attempted, through old town plans of Bangor and other remaining documentation, to identify the inhabitants of the house that must have occupied the site of the discovery at about that time. Possibly, we reasoned, this house may have been a "safe house" on the Underground Femaleroad during our period, and our author may have been kept hidden in, for instance, the attic or cellar there for some weeks or months, during which she would have had the oppor-

▷ **1** *painstaking:* requiring a lot of effort **10** *secular:* worldly **14** *sport sth.:* have sth., contain sth. **23** *pending:* awaiting **26** *referent:* thing that is referred to **27** *laborious:* taking a lot of time and great effort **28** *forgery* ['fɔːrdʒəri]: thing which is false but which looks authentic **30** *trade on sth.:* take financial advantage of sth. **33** *edifying* (adj): erbaulich **34** *hypocritical:* heuchlerisch **35** *an editorial aside:* (here) a remark on the side, which is not part of the topic under discussion **44** *genuine* ['dʒenjuɪn]: authentic **45** *superimposition* (fml): act of putting one thing on another **52** *concealment:* hiding **54** *synchronicity* [sɪnkrə'nɪsəti]: (here) act of recording experiences while they are taking place • *whiff:* slight flavor **54–55** *emotion recollected in tranquillity:* reference to the English poet William Wordsworth's (1770–1850) definition of good poetry (i.e. the excitement of the moment should have passed before it is turned into a poem) **55** *post facto* (Latin): after the fact **58** *brevity:* shortness

tunity to make the recordings. Of course, there was nothing to rule out the possibility that the tapes had been moved to the site in question after they had been made. We hoped to be able to trace and locate the descendants of the hypothetical occupants, whom we hoped might lead us to other material: diaries, perhaps, or even family anecdotes passed down through the generations.

Unfortunately, this trail led nowhere. Possibly these people, if they had indeed been a link in the underground chain, had been discovered and arrested, in which case any documentation referring to them would have been destroyed. So we pursued a second line of attack. We searched records of the period, trying to correlate known historical personages with the individuals who appear in our author's account. The surviving records of the time are spotty, as the Gileadean regime was in the habit of wiping its own computers and destroying printouts after various purges and internal upheavals, but some printouts remain. Some indeed were smuggled to England, for propaganda use by the various Save-the-Women societies, of which there were many in the British Isles at that time.

We held out no hope of tracing the narrator herself directly. It was clear from internal evidence that she was among the first wave of women recruited for reproductive purposes and allotted to those who both required such services and could lay claim to them through their position in the elite. The regime created an instant pool of such women by the simple tactic of declaring all second marriages and non-marital liaisons adulterous, arresting the female partners, and, on the grounds that they were morally unfit, confiscating the children they already had, who were adopted by childless couples of the upper echelons who were eager for progeny by any means. (In the middle period, this policy was extended to cover all marriages not contracted within the state church.)

Men highly placed in the regime were thus able to pick and choose among women who had demonstrated their reproductive fitness by having produced one or more healthy children, a desirable characteristic in an age of plummeting Caucasian birth rates, a phenomenon observable not only in Gilead but in most northern Caucasian societies of the time.

The reasons for this decline are not altogether clear to us. Some of the failure to reproduce can undoubtedly be traced to the widespread availability of birth control of various kinds, including abortion, in the immediate pre-Gilead period. Some infertility, then, was willed, which may account for the differing statistics among Caucasians and non-Caucasians; but the rest was not. Need I remind you that this was the age of the R-strain syphilis and also the infamous AIDS epidemic, which, once they spread to the population at large, eliminated many young sexually active people from the reproductive pool? Still-births, miscarriages, and genetic deformities were widespread and on the increase, and this trend has been linked to the various nuclear-plant accidents, shutdowns, and incidents of sabotage that characterized the period, as well as to leakages from chemical and biological-warfare stockpiles and toxic-waste disposal sites, of which there were many thousands, both legal and illegal – in some instances these materials were simply dumped into the sewage system – and to the uncontrolled use of chemical insecticides, herbicides, and other sprays.

But whatever the causes, the effects were noticeable, and the Gilead regime was not the only one to react to them at the time. Romania, for instance, had anticipated Gilead in the eighties by banning all forms of birth control, imposing compulsory pregnancy tests on the female population, and linking promotion and wage increases to fertility.

The need for what I may call birth services was already recognized in the pre-Gilead period, where it was being inadequately met by "artificial insemination," "fertility clinics," and the use of "surrogate mothers," who were hired for the purpose. Gilead outlawed the first two as irreligious, but legitimized and enforced the third, which was considered to have biblical precedents; they thus replaced the serial polygamy common in the pre-Gilead period with the older form of

▷ **1–2** *rule out the possibility that ...:* say that ... was impossible **11** *correlate sth. with sth. else:* match sth. to sth. else **13** *spotty* (AE): not complete **14** *wipe sth.:* remove information, etc. from sth. **15** *upheaval:* major social or political change **21** *allot sb./sth. to sb.:* allow sb. to have sb./sth. **22** *lay claim to sth.:* say that you have a right to sth. **23** *pool:* supply of things (here, women) **28** *echelon* ['eʃəlɑːn]: rank or position of authority • *progeny* ['prɑːdʒəni]: Nachkommen **34** *plummet:* fall suddenly • *Caucasian:* white person **43** *R-strain syphilis:* a sexually transmitted disease • *infamous* ['ɪnfəməs] (fml): berüchtigt **45** *still-birth:* birth of a baby which is already dead **49** *leakage:* Austritt, Ausströmen **50** *stockpile:* supply of sth. that may be used in the future **59** *promotion:* Beförderung **66–67** *serial polygamy:* state of having different partners one after the other

simultaneous polygamy practised both in early Old Testament times and in the former State of Utah in the nineteenth century. As we know from the study of history, no new system can impose itself upon a previous one without incorporating many of the elements to be found in the latter, as witness the pagan elements in mediaeval Christianity and the evolution of the Russian "K.G.B." from the Czarist secret service that preceded it; and Gilead was no exception to this rule. Its racist policies, for instance, were firmly rooted in the pre-Gilead period, and racist fears provided some of the emotional fuel that allowed the Gilead takeover to succeed as well as it did.

Our author, then, was one of many, and must be seen within the broad outlines of the moment in history of which she was a part. But what else do we know about her, apart from her age, some physical characteristics that could be anyone's, and her place of residence? Not very much. She appears to have been an educated woman, insofar as a graduate of any North American college of the time may be said to have been educated. *(Laughter, some groans.)* But the woods, as you say, were full of these, so that is no help. She does not see fit to supply us with her original name, and indeed all official records of it would have been destroyed upon her entry into the Rachel and Leah Re-education Center. "Offred" gives no clue, since, like "Ofglen" and "Ofwarren," it was a patronymic, composed of the possessive preposition and the first name of the gentleman in question. Such names were taken by these women upon their entry into a connection with the household of a specific Commander, and relinquished by them upon leaving it.

The other names in the document are equally useless for the purposes of identification and authentication. "Luke" and "Nick" drew blanks, as did "Moira" and "Janine." There is a high probability that these were, in any case, pseudonyms, adopted to protect these individuals should the tapes be discovered. If so, this would substantiate our view that the tapes were made inside the borders of Gilead, rather than outside, to be smuggled back for use by the Mayday underground.

Elimination of the above possibilities left us with one remaining. If we could identify the elusive "Commander," we felt, at least some progress would have been made. We argued that such a highly placed individual had probably been a participant in the first of the top-secret Sons of Jacob Think Tanks, at which the philosophy and social structure of Gilead were hammered out. These were organized shortly after the recognition of the superpower arms stalemate and the signing of the classified Spheres of Influence Accord, which left the superpowers free to deal, unhampered by interference, with the growing number of rebellions within their own empires. The official records of the Sons of Jacob meetings were destroyed after the middle-period Great Purge, which discredited and liquidated a number of the original architects of Gilead; but we have access to some information through the diary kept in cipher by Wilfred Limpkin, one of the sociobiologists present. (As we know, the sociobiological theory of natural polygamy was used as a scientific justification for some of the odder practices of the regime, just as Darwinism was used by earlier ideologies.)

From the Limpkin material we know that there are two possible candidates, that is, two whose names incorporate the element "Fred": Frederick R. Waterford and B. Frederick Judd. No photographs survive of either, although Limpkin describes the latter as a stuffed shirt, and, I quote, "somebody for whom foreplay is what you do on a golf course." *(Laughter.)* Limpkin himself did not long survive the inception of Gilead, and we have his diary only because he foresaw his own end and placed it with his sister-in-law in Calgary.

Waterford and Judd both have characteristics that recommend them to us. Waterford possessed a background in market research, and was, according to Limpkin, responsible for the design of the female costumes and for the suggestion that the Handmaids wear red, which he seems to have borrowed from the uniforms of German prisoners of war in Canadian "P.O.W." camps of the Second World

▷ **2** *Utah:* reference to the religious sect of Mormons (the Church of Jesus Christ of Latter-day Saints), founded by Joseph Smith in 1830, which is based in Utah and which originally allowed a man to have several wives **5** *as witness:* as can be seen from • *pagan:* heidnisch **18–19** *see fit to do sth.:* consider it necessary to do sth. **22** *patronymic:* of a name that refers to the father (here: man) **29** *draw a blank:* eine Niete ziehen **31–32** *substantiate sth.:* support sth. **36** *elusive:* (here) mysterious, unknown **39** *Sons of Jacob:* Jacob was the father of the new nation, Israel (cf. also p. 204, l. 24) **41** *stalemate:* Pattsituation **42** *classified:* secret **43** *unhampered:* not prevented from doing sth. **48** *cipher* ['saɪfə]: secret code **51** *Darwinism:* (here) belief in natural selection and survival of the fittest **57** *stuffed shirt* (infml): old-fashioned, serious person **60** *Calgary:* city in the west of Canada

War era. He seems to have been the originator of the term "Particicution," which he lifted from an exercise programme popular sometime in the last third of the century; the collective rope ceremony, however, was suggested by an English village custom of the seventeenth century. *Salvaging* may have been his too, although by the time of Gilead's inception it had spread from its origin in the Philippines to become a general term for the elimination of one's political enemies. As I have said elsewhere, there was little that was truly original with or indigenous to Gilead: its genius was synthesis.

Judd, on the other hand, seems to have been less interested in packaging and more concerned with tactics. It was he who suggested the use of an obscure "C.I.A." pamphlet on the destabilization of foreign governments as a strategic handbook for the Sons of Jacob, and he, too, who drew up the early hit lists of prominent "Americans" of the time. He also is suspected of having orchestrated the President's Day Massacre, which must have required maximum infiltration of the security system surrounding Congress, and without which the Constitution could never have been suspended. The National Homelands and the Jewish boat-person plan were both his, as was the idea of privatizing the Jewish repatriation scheme, with the result that more than one boatload of Jews was simply dumped into the Atlantic, to maximize profits. From what we know of Judd, this would not have bothered him much. He was a hard-liner, and is credited by Limpkin with the remark, "Our big mistake was teaching them to read. We won't do that again."

It is Judd who is credited with devising the form, as opposed to the name, of the Particicution ceremony, arguing that it was not only a particularly horrifying and effective way of ridding yourself of subversive elements, but that it would also act as a steam valve for the female elements in Gilead. Scapegoats have been notoriously useful throughout history, and it must have been most gratifying for these Handmaids, so rigidly controlled at other times, to be able to tear a man apart with their bare hands every once in a while. So popular and effective did this practice become that it was regularized in the middle period, when it took place four times a year, on solstices and equinoxes. There are echoes here of the fertility rites of early Earth-goddess cults. As we heard at the panel discussion yesterday afternoon, Gilead was, although undoubtedly patriarchial in form, occasionally matriarchal in content, like some sectors of the social fabric that gave rise to it. As the architects of Gilead knew, to institute an effective totalitarian system or indeed any system at all you must offer some benefits and freedoms, at least to a privileged few, in return for those you remove.

In this connection a few comments upon the crack female control agency known as the "Aunts" is perhaps in order. Judd – according to the Limpkin material – was of the opinion from the outset that the best and most cost-effective way to control women for reproductive and other purposes was through women themselves. For this there were many historical precedents; in fact, no empire imposed by force or otherwise has ever been without this feature: control of the indigenous by members of their own group. In the case of Gilead, there were many women willing to serve as Aunts, either because of a genuine belief in what they called "traditional values," or for the benefits they might thereby acquire. When power is scarce, a little of it is tempting. There was, too, a negative inducement: childless or infertile or older women who were not married could take service in the Aunts and thereby escape redundancy, and consequent shipment to the infamous Colonies, which were composed of portable populations used mainly as expendable toxic cleanup squads, though if lucky you could be assigned to less hazardous tasks, such as cotton picking and fruit harvesting.

The idea, then, was Judd's, but the implementation has the mark of Waterford upon it. Who else among the Sons of Jacob Think-Tankers would have come up with the notion that the Aunts should take names derived from commercial products available to women in the immediate pre-Gilead period, and thus familiar and reassuring to

▷ **2** *lift sth.* (infml): use sth. (esp. an idea) from a source without crediting it **11** *packaging:* Verpackung **15** *orchestrate sth.:* plan the details of sth. **18–19** *National Homelands:* reference to the re-settlement of black people (a similar term was used during apartheid South Africa) **29** *steam valve:* (here) outlet for strong emotions **30** *scapegoat:* Sündenbock **35** *solstice:* Sonnenwende **36** *equinox* ['ekwɪnɑ:ks]: Tagundnachtgleiche **39–40** *social fabric:* the basic structure of a society **44** *crack* (adj; infml): expert and highly trained **51** *indigenous* [ɪn'dɪdʒənəs] (n): local people **54** *scarce:* rare **55** *inducement:* reason to make you do sth. **57** *redundancy:* Überflüssigsein **59** *expendable:* entbehrlich **62** *implementation:* act of putting sth. into practice **64** *notion:* idea

them – the names of cosmetic lines, cake mixes, frozen desserts, and even medicinal remedies? It was a brilliant stroke, and confirms us in our opinion that Waterford was, in his prime, a man of considerable ingenuity. So, in his own way, was Judd.

Both of these gentlemen were known to have been childless, and thus eligible for a succession of Handmaids. Professor Wade and I have speculated in our joint paper, "The Notion of 'Seed' in Early Gilead", that both – like many of the Commanders – had come in contact with a sterility-causing virus that was developed by secret pre-Gilead gene-splicing experiments with mumps, and which was intended for insertion into the supply of caviar used by top officials in Moscow. (The experiment was abandoned after the Spheres of Influence Accord, because the virus was considered too uncontrollable and therefore too dangerous by many, although some wished to sprinkle it over India.)

However, neither Judd nor Waterford was married to a woman who was or ever had been known either as "Pam" or as "Serena Joy." This latter appears to have been a somewhat malicious invention by our author. Judd's wife's name was Bambi Mae, and Waterford's was Thelma. The latter had, however, once worked as a television personality of the type described. We know this from Limpkin, who makes several snide remarks about it. The regime itself took pains to cover up such former lapses from orthodoxy by the spouses of its elite.

The evidence on the whole favors Waterford. We know, for instance, that he met his end, probably soon after the events our author describes, in one of the earliest purges; he was accused of liberal tendencies, of being in possession of a substantial and unauthorized collection of heretical pictorial and literary materials, and of harboring a subversive. This was before the regime began holding its trials in secret and was still televising them, so the events were recorded in England via satellite and are on videotape deposit in our Archives. The shots of Waterford are not good, but they are clear enough to establish that his hair was indeed gray.

As for the subversive Waterford was accused of harboring, this could have been " Offred" herself, as her flight would have placed her in this category. More likely it was "Nick," who, by the evidence of the very existence of the tapes, must have helped "Offred" to escape. The way in which he was able to do this marks him as a member of the shadowy Mayday underground, which was not identical with the Underground Femaleroad but had connections with it. The latter was purely a rescue operation, the former quasi-military. A number of Mayday operatives are known to have infiltrated the Gileadean power structure at the highest levels, and the placement of one of their members as chauffeur to Waterford would certainly have been a coup; a double coup, as "Nick" must have been at the same time a member of the Eyes, as such chauffeurs and personal servants often were. Waterford would, of course, have been aware of this, but as all high-level Commanders were automatically directors of the Eyes, he would not have paid a great deal of attention to it and would not have let it interfere with his infraction of what he considered to be minor rules. Like most early Gilead Commanders who were later purged, he considered his position to be above attack. The style of Middle Gilead was more cautious.

This is our guesswork. Supposing it to be correct – supposing, that is, that Waterford was indeed the "Commander" – many gaps remain. Some of them could have been filled by our anonymous author, had she had a different turn of mind. She could have told us much about the workings of the Gileadean empire, had she had the instincts of a reporter or a spy. What would we not give, now, for even twenty pages or so of printout from Waterford's private computer! However, we must be grateful for any crumbs the Goddess of History has deigned to vouchsafe us.

As for the ultimate fate of our narrator, it remains obscure. Was she smuggled over the border of Gilead, into what was then Canada, and did she make her way thence to England? This would have been wise, as the Canada of that time did not wish to antagonize its powerful neighbor, and there were roundups and extraditions of such refugees. If so, why did she not take her taped narrative with her? Perhaps her

▷ **3** *in his prime:* at the best time of his life **4** *ingenuity:* cleverness **6** *a succession of sth.:* several instances of sth. in a row **10** *gene-splicing:* act of dividing genes into separate parts **18** *malicious:* deliberately nasty **22** *snide:* unpleasantly critical **23** *lapse:* Ausrutscher • *spouse:* person sb. is married to **30** *harbor sb.:* keep and protect sb. in your home **46** *coup* [kuː]: a wonderful but difficult achievement **51** *infraction:* act of disobeying or breaking (a rule) **58** *turn of mind:* way of thinking **63** *vouchsafe sb. sth.* (fml): give sth. to sb. as a privilege **66** *thence* (fml): from there **67** *antagonize sb.:* make sb. angry **68** *extradition:* Auslieferung

journey was sudden; perhaps she feared interception. On the other hand, she may have been recaptured. If she did indeed reach England, why did she not make her story public, as so many did upon reaching the outside world? She may have feared retaliation against "Luke," supposing him to have been still alive (which is an improbability), or even against her daughter; for the Gileadean regime was not above such measures, and used them to discourage adverse publicity in foreign countries. More than one incautious refugee was known to receive a hand, ear, or foot, vacuum-packed express, hidden in, for instance, a tin of coffee. Or perhaps she was among those escaped Handmaids who had difficulty adjusting to life in the outside world, once they got there, after the protected existence they had led. She may have become, like them, a recluse. We do not know.

We can only deduce, also, the motivations for "Nick's" engineering of her escape. We can assume that once her companion Ofglen's association with Mayday had been discovered, he himself was in some jeopardy, for as he well knew, as a member of the Eyes, Offred herself was certain to be interrogated. The penalties for unauthorized sexual activity with a Handmaid were severe, nor would his status as an Eye necessarily protect him. Gilead society was Byzantine in the extreme, and any transgression might be used against one by one's undeclared enemies within the regime. He could, of course, have assassinated her himself, which might have been the wiser course, but the human heart remains a factor, and, as we know, both of them thought she might be pregnant by him. What male of the Gilead period could resist the possibility of fatherhood, so redolent of status, so highly prized? Instead, he called in a rescue team of Eyes, who may or may not have been authentic but in any case were under his orders. In doing so he may well have brought about his own downfall. This too we shall never know.

Did our narrator reach the outside world safely and build a new life for herself? Or was she discovered in her attic hiding place, arrested, sent to the Colonies or to Jezebel's, or even executed? Our document, though in its own way eloquent, is on these subjects mute. We may call Eurydice forth from the world of the dead, but we cannot make her answer; and when we turn to look at her we glimpse her only for a moment, before she slips from our grasp and flees. As all historians know, the past is a great darkness, and filled with echoes. Voices may reach us from it; but what they say to us is imbued with the obscurity of the matrix out of which they come; and, try as we may, we cannot always decipher them precisely in the clearer light of our own day.

Applause.

Are there any questions?

▷ **1** *interception:* act of being stopped and searched **4** *retaliation:* Vergeltungsschlag **7** *adverse:* opposing, critical **13** *recluse:* person who lives alone and avoids contact with others **14–15** *engineer sth.:* plan sth. and carry out the plan **20** *Byzantine* ['bɪzəntaɪn]: (here) complicated and secret **21** *trangression:* breaking of the law **26** *redolent of sth.* ['redələnt]: making you think of sth. **35** *Eurydice* [ju'rɪdɪsi]: reference to a Greek myth in which Orpheus manages to get his beloved Eurydice back from the world of the dead, but is not allowed to speak to her or look at her on the journey out of the underworld. When he does look back, she disappears back to the underworld. **39** *imbued with sth.:* full of sth. **40** *matrix:* social structure from which a person comes

MAP OF NEW ENGLAND

THE AUTHOR

© Ullstein – Lambert

Born in Ottawa in 1939, Margaret Atwood is one of Canada's leading writers, but she is equally well known in the USA and Europe as she is in her home country.

She has written both fiction and non-fiction about the Canadian experience, for which she was particularly well prepared by being the daughter of an entomologist specializing in forest insects, who interested his daughter in the bush country of northern Ontario and Quebec. Nevertheless, she has by no means limited herself to writing about Canada.

To date her writing includes over a dozen volumes of poetry, five volumes of short stories, eleven novels (including *Surfacing*, 1972, *Cat's Eye*, 1989, *The Blind Assassin*, 2000, and *Oryx and Crake*, 2003), several children's books as well as a large amount of non-fiction, especially literary criticism. She has won many literary prizes for her work, and she has taught English in a number of Canadian universities.

From the beginning, her novels have dealt with women who are forced to reassess their lives after some kind of upheaval either within themselves or in society – as is the case with the protagonist and narrator of *The Handmaid's Tale*.

Margaret Atwood lives on a farm in the Province of Ontario, Canada, with writer Graeme Gibson and their daughter.